VIKING CANADA

THE ENLIGHTENED EATER'S™ WHOLE FOODS GUIDE

Rosie Schwartz, author of the bestselling book *The Enlightened Eater™*, is a Toronto-based consulting dietitian and nutritionist, and a licensed member of the College of Dietitians of Ontario. She has spent her career—in her counselling practice and in the media—translating the science of nutrition into healthy and delicious fare.

Rosie is a contributing editor and award-winning columnist for *Homemaker's* and *CARP News 50Plus*. Her writing has also appeared in magazines such as *Chatelaine, Today's Parent, Family Circle* and *Arthritis News* and in newspapers including *The Globe and Mail*, the *Ottawa Citizen* and the *Gazette* (Montreal). She is now a columnist at *Diabetes Dialogue*. A contributor to television and radio, she has appeared on *Canada AM, Marketplace, Venture* and the *Heart and Stroke Health Show*, in addition to local talk shows across the country. A much-sought-after nutrition commentator for national news programs, for three years Rosie was also the weekly nutrition commentator on *CBC Morning*.

A spokesperson for the Heart and Stroke Foundation, Rosie conducts workshops on nutrition—on land and on board cruise ships sailing in the Mediterranean.

ALSO BY ROSIE SCHWARTZ

The Enlightened Eater™

rosie schwartz

THE ENLIGHTENED EATER'S™

whole foods guide

harvest the power of phyto foods

VIKING
CANADA

VIKING CANADA
Published by the Penguin Group
Penguin Books, a division of Pearson Canada, 10 Alcorn Avenue, Toronto, Ontario,
Canada M4V 3B2
Penguin Books Ltd, 80 Strand, London WC2R 0RL, England
Penguin Putnam Inc., 375 Hudson Street, New York, New York 10014, U.S.A.
Penguin Books Australia Ltd, 250 Camberwell Road, Camberwell, Victoria 3124, Australia
Penguin Books India (P) Ltd, 11, Community Centre, Panchsheel Park, New Delhi – 110 017, India
Penguin Books (NZ) Ltd, cnr Rosedale and Airborne Roads, Albany, Auckland 1310, New Zealand
Penguin Books (South Africa) (Pty) Ltd, 24 Sturdee Avenue, Rosebank 2196, South Africa

Penguin Books Ltd, Registered Offices: 80 Strand, London WC2R 0RL, England

First published 2003

10 9 8 7 6 5 4 3 2 1

Manufactured in Canada.

National Library of Canada Cataloguing in Publication

Schwartz, Rosie
   The enlightened eater's whole foods guide : harvest the power of phyto foods/Rosie Schwartz.

Includes bibliographical references and index.

ISBN 0-670-04363-X

   1. Functional foods. 2. Nutrition. 3. Phytochemicals. I. Title.

RA784.S387 2003   613.2   C2003-901500-9

Visit Penguin Books' website at **www.penguin.ca**

To my father, the late Julius Fuss,
for sharing his passion and respect for good food

contents

acknowledgements

I want to thank the following people:

My family, whom I've tried all my healthy-eating theories on and who still love me and who have ended up being enlightened eaters, and in particular,

My husband, Earl, for being my partner in life, always encouraging and supportive and always full of a zest for life,

My daughter Alyssa, for her fabulous skills both as an editor and in testing recipes and for being there when I needed calming down and direction,

My daughter Farrah, for her endless encouragement and offers of help,

My mother, Elsa Fuss, for a lifetime of nurturing and encouragement,

Nicole de Montbrun, editor extraordinaire, without whom this book might not be,

Dun Gifford and Sara Baer-Sinnott of Oldways Preservation and Exchange Trust of Boston, whose insights and incredible efforts provided the inspiration for this book,

Lucy Waverman, food expert, writer, cookbook author and friend, for always being there when I've sought advice,

Tracey Syvret, for her help in recipe testing.

foreword

This commanding book is a fine example of what can happen when a first-rate communicator ties that skill with an intimate knowledge of a densely detailed subject such as healthy foods. The result here is Rosie Schwartz's common sense guide to enlightened eating, a prize addition to the library for all those wanting to enjoy their food and drink, and be comfortable in the knowledge that they are also helping to extend their own lives.

Rosie's longtime popularity as a TV and print communicator is based on telling it straight and making the devilish details interesting. For example, she has long been a courageous critic of non-nutritious "techno-foods" such as Olestra, the notorious fake fat recently withdrawn from the market. And she consistently warns consumers against unscientific "fad diets" that are doomed to fail over the long haul, based, as they are, on questionable science.

In *The Enlightened Eater's™ Whole Foods Guide,* she cautions against heavy reliance on "functional foods," which are processed food products "fortified" with a variety of compounds claimed to prevent disease and promote good health. In her straightforward way she asks this troublesome question: If highly processed foods are healthy, why do they need to be fortified?

Her reporting about the beta carotene craze is an example of Rosie's strength as a street fighter for healthier eating. When a handful of scientific studies indicated a few years ago that the beta carotene in yellow foods like squash and carrots might protect against lung cancer, chemical companies flooded stores with supplement capsules and functional foods "packed with cancer-fighting beta carotene." Waves of consumers responded, bringing smiles to the faces of supplement manufacturers. But further scientific research revealed that the "true hero," as Rosie reports, was not beta carotene at all, but its cousin, alpha carotene.

The tour de force of *Enlightened Eater's* is its explanation of the intricacies of what she calls "phyto foods." Nutrition scientists have long known that phytonutrients and antioxidants (often called PAX for short) occurring naturally in whole foods play a central role in the health and operating efficiency of the billions of cells in our bodies. PAX not only protect against cell damage and mutation caused by radiation, aging and carcinogenic industrial chemicals, but can also repair cell damage when it occurs. (Cell damage is the root cause of the major chronic diseases that afflict modern societies, including cancers, heart diseases and diabetes.)

Rosie is quite clear about the sad irony of the stealthy creep of techno-foods onto our plates. Just as we have begun to unravel the scientific mysteries of how and why whole, natural foods promote our bodies' health (as they did the bodies of our ancestors), we eat less and less of them.

Another bonus is her collection of wonderful recipes to help readers put onto their plates the distilled wisdom accumulated during her years of investigation into eating well. Rosie is a truly good cook, her husband Earl (an MD) is a great eater, and one often finds their table replete with the culinary pleasures of healthful eating. The recipes offer a rainbow of choices that range from the simple/quick to the complex/involved. By themselves they are well worth the price of this book.

In her clarion call for enlightenment about the essential value of whole foods and PAX, Rosie Schwartz has given us the keys to the rich kingdom of a pleasurable healthy dinner table.

K. Dun Gifford
President, Oldways Preservation Trust, Boston, Massachusetts
February 2003

wisdom of the ages

The Oldways Preservation and Exchange Trust, based in Boston, is the group that created awareness both in the scientific community and for the public of the stellar nutritional and palate-pleasing attributes of the Mediterranean diet, a diet based on an abundance of vegetables, fruit, grains, nuts and seeds, with the predominant fat being olive oil. The Trust's efforts in creating awareness about the Mediterranean diet involved not only trumpeting its culinary delights but also stimulating scientific thought around the world and prompting researchers to discover the keys to this health-promoting diet. It was work that had begun almost a half century ago but somehow never attracted the interest it deserved.

In the 1950s, an American scientist, Ancel Keys, proposed that the plant-based diet of those who lived in the Mediterranean region offered protection against heart disease. In his groundbreaking study, published in the 1970s in the American Heart Association journal, *Circulation*, Keys compared the diets of seven countries— Greece, Italy, Yugoslavia, Finland, Japan, the Netherlands and the United States—and the rates of heart disease in these countries. It was the first international study of its kind and a scientific cornerstone that demonstrated the health advantages of the Mediterranean diet. But for decades that followed, while scientists investigated the dietary patterns of the region, its tantalizing dishes were savoured mainly by those only of Mediterranean heritage. North Americans who visited the region enjoyed the culinary offerings, but when they returned home, it was to meals they were accustomed to. Spaghetti and meatballs was as close to the Mediterranean that many home cooks aspired to.

In the early 1990s, everything changed. Oldways Preservation and Exchange Trust, together with the Harvard School of Public Health, began an initiative to scientifically evaluate the health attributes of the traditional foodways of the Mediterranean and introduce the cuisines of its various countries to people around the world.

As research uncovered the basic healthful components of the Mediterranean diet, the mystery remained of what exactly in these foods provided such powerful protection against disease. Unlocking the secret intrigued researchers and prompted a wave of scientific investigation into phytochemicals.

This research continues.

the power
of whole foods

certain foods are packed with healthy
nutrients ... but to what extent, and why,
is only now coming to light

Of course we've known for years—and so has your mother and her mother—that fruits and vegetables are packed with healthy nutrients. But to what extent, and how and why, is only now beginning to come to light in truly groundbreaking research spurred on by the Oldways Exchange and Preservation Trust.

In the 1990s, research on the possible effects of phytochemicals (newly discovered chemical compounds found in plant foods) started trickling in. The reports, which quickly became a steady stream, piqued my interest. Before then I had known very little about phytochemicals. I didn't know their names or that they existed in the thousands. It wasn't until I attended a conference organized by the Boston-based think tank and advocacy group Oldways Exchange and Preservation Trust that my curiosity turned to excitement and fascination. I wanted to know more.

During that landmark conference, scientist after scientist detailed the amazing health-promoting effects of a long list of plant foods. I might have doubted such widespread claims had I not known how credible these scientist are. Here were world-renowned researchers extolling the ability of nuts *to destroy cancer cells* and of berries *to protect the arteries*—all backed up with research studies based on sound scientific principles. We've always known there were health benefits to eating these foods, but now we were beginning to understand how and why, and in what form, and in which variety. It was a truly astonishing leap in the science of nutrition.

It was becoming clear from the research that certain foods contain a dazzling array of disease-fighting and health-promoting compounds *above and beyond* the known nutrients such as vitamins, minerals and fibre. Estimated in the thousands, these phytochemicals—"phyto" meaning from plants—are found in a host of foods, including fruits, vegetables, whole grains, legumes, nuts and seeds. It appears that consuming healthy food choices—and, for that matter, whole foods—can unleash a virtual arsenal of disease fighters. Substances with names such as carotenoids, phenols, flavonoids, isoflavones, terpenes and glucosinolates are among the diverse range of phytochemicals that are currently being investigated, with promising results.

At the conference, these very same foods were featured in satisfying dishes that allowed the delegates to dine literally to their heart's content. (The fare included a citrus avocado salad, fish with skordalia, which is a garlicky potato mixture, and tomatoes, a cucumber tomato salsa with won ton chips, vegetarian Chinese noodles with tofu peanut sauce, and a mixed berry tart with almond cream.) Since that conference, Oldways has held others, and has begun the PhytoVenture Initiative, a combined effort with scientists, chefs and the media to reveal more of nature's wonders—and to encourage us to change the way we eat and think about food.

a complexity of combinations

As scientists investigate the possible roles of these compounds, it is becoming increasingly clear that this area of research is a complex one. A specific phytochemical in a particular food may appear to have a certain effect, but when the compound is removed from the food and consumed on its own, it may be a different story. It may even have the opposite effect.

Take, for example, antioxidants. Research is just beginning to unravel the intricacies of oxidation, a process that occurs as a result of exposure to oxygen. The formation of rust and the browning of an apple are simple examples of oxidation. Without a doubt, oxygen—carried through the bloodstream by red blood cells—is vital to our survival. Oxidation, however, has been shown to result in the production of harmful compounds called free radicals. These free radicals are thought to play a major role in aging and in the development of various degenerative conditions and diseases. Heart disease, Alzheimer's, type 2 diabetes and certain cancers are on the list of diseases linked to oxidative damage. Oxidation is hastened by factors such as air pollution, radiation, cigarette smoke, sunlight, environmental chemicals and some foods.

Antioxidants, found in foods like colourful fruits and vegetables, whole grains and tea, seem to slow down or halt oxidation and counter the effects of free radicals (just as lemon juice slows down the browning of an apple slice).

Preventing oxidation may seem simple enough—just consume plenty of foods with antioxidant properties. But here's where it gets confusing: Some compounds may act as antioxidants and slow down oxidation when they're in the right environment—maybe when they're consumed with a mix of nutrients and phytochemicals or by the right person. But these same compounds, likely in the form of supplements, in other situations may act as *pro-oxidants* and actually speed up oxidative damage. Are you thoroughly confused yet? Well, even scientists themselves still don't have all the answers.

Research shows that there's much more to phytochemicals than their ability to act as antioxidants. As one group of scientists isolates a specific phytochemical or group of compounds in one food, other investigators at another facility may identify another. Still others may explore the action of both compounds jointly. Phytochemicals may be much more potent in their disease-fighting action when combined than when each is consumed on its own, as they are in supplement form. In scientific circles, this action is known as synergy—the sum of the parts is greater than each on its own. Add in the phytochemicals that may not yet have been identified and the arsenal against disease may be even greater in plant foods than we know.

For reasons such as these, it's time to look at the disease-fighting potential of foods as a whole instead of as the particular components that may be responsible—think of them as phytofoods instead of just phytochemicals. Get the whole package. Almonds are a perfect example. A study from Tufts University, in Boston, suggested that the nutrients found in almonds and in their skin together may offer better protection against heart disease than when those nutrients are consumed separately. Or take the tomato. News reports have touted the anti-cancer and heart-healthy attributes of the red pigment, or carotenoid, in tomatoes known as lycopene. Tomatoes also provide such nutrients as vitamin C, potassium and fibre. But a lesser-known fact is that the gel surrounding the tomato's seeds has a potent effect on decreasing the risk of blood clots forming and adhering to artery walls. (Blood clots can cause heart attack or stroke.) Combining certain "phytofoods" may boost disease-fighting capabilities even further. For instance, adding a splash of extra virgin olive oil to your tomato sauce aids lycopene absorption in the body. The olive oil, meanwhile, provides a range of other benefits (see page 209).

As scientists continue to unravel nature's secrets, the list of possibilities grows.

disease-fighting superstars

Excitingly, research on the effects of consuming whole foods—and consuming certain combinations of them—is revealing their starring role in combating lifestyle-related afflictions such as heart disease, stroke, type 2 diabetes, hypertension, certain cancers and even autoimmune diseases. And when it comes to their disease-fighting capabilities, the phytochemicals within these foods appear to have an effect at many different stages of the disease process.

The development of cancer is a perfect example. This is a complex illness that can sometimes be prevented at the outset or halted in its tracks. It's thought that some cancers or malignancies may be caused initially by exposure to a carcinogen (a cancer-causing agent) such as those found in tobacco, whereas other tumours may occur when inflamed cells mutate, or become abnormal and then cancerous. Genetic factors may also play a role in cell mutations or in how the body reacts to being exposed to a carcinogen. Stopping cancer cells from multiplying or having cancer cells simply die off are both part of the battle against cancer. Exciting research is showing that various phytochemicals may combat cancer at all these stages. Some may detoxify carcinogens and others may have an anti-inflammatory action. Still others may stimulate the body's immune system and release enzymes to stop cancer cell multiplication, or proliferation. And finally, some phytochemicals in vegetables, fruits, legumes, grains, nuts and seeds are simply powerful killers of cancer cells.

Like cancer, other prolific ailments of the twenty-first century, such as heart disease and stroke, are not so straightforward in their development. Both, though, were once thought to involve a very simple process: over years, arteries narrowed because of the build up inside them of cholesterol, until blood was no longer able to flow through. If the blocked artery was in the heart, a heart attack would take place. In the brain, it resulted in a stroke. Now the list of culprits and processes that may damage arteries has grown. Even in the cholesterol version of heart disease development, there are many factors that determine the risk of heart disease and stroke. While elevated blood cholesterol is linked to the narrowing of arteries, it's now recognized that inflamed arteries are much more susceptible to the cholesterol deposits, which result in plaque and hardened arteries. And not all cholesterol is as likely to be deposited and therefore damaging to the arteries. For example, artery walls are much more attracted to one type of cholesterol, called oxidized cholesterol.

The theory that most heart attacks are caused by progressive narrowing of the arteries has also taken a beating. Now it's thought that a piece of the artery wall may break off, forming a clot that can flow through the bloodstream and become lodged in a slightly narrowed artery, which leads to a heart attack or stroke.

It has become increasingly clear that susceptibility to heart disease and stroke can be increased by a long list of factors. And right up there high on the list is food. Some foods may pack a powerful blood-cholesterol-boosting wallop—take a double cheeseburger with a few slices of bacon on top. We've been hearing about such demons for ages—all the choices you're supposed to banish from your plate. But newer to the "dietribe" is the protective effect of an array of choices bursting with countless nutrients and phytochemicals. It's finally time to focus on what we should eat—*not on what we should consume less of.*

Just a few examples on the cholesterol front will demonstrate clearly how many ways a few heart-smart food choices can have an impact. The fibre in some grains like barley may bind with cholesterol, resulting in both being excreted from the body and lower blood cholesterol readings. Other compounds in the grain, known as tocotrienols, have been shown to blunt cholesterol production. The likelihood of clots forming may be decreased by yet other compounds in barley. The list goes on and, as it grows, the risk of artery disease drops.

Researchers are also focusing on how arteries respond to various scenarios. One of the factors is endothelial function—the health of the cells that line the artery walls. If a high-fat meal is consumed, for example, the blood flowing through the arteries can be fattier than usual. Arteries that have hardened through the years because of an accumulation of plaque are much less likely to relax, widen or dilate so the fatty blood can flow through. And the result, in someone with poor endothelial function, can be a blocked artery. People with pre-existing heart disease are at a much greater risk at various times, for example during stressful situations or after a fat-laden meal, simply because their arteries do not dilate or relax appropriately. But some phytochemicals may help. Recent studies have shown that phytochemicals in tea, for example, may actually increase the arteries' ability to relax or dilate—a process called vasodilation.

defenders of the plant world

While phytochemicals may be the new superstars in nutrition circles, their role in plant life is even more critical. The phytochemicals responsible for pigments, which give plants their colour, and those responsible for smells may both attract insects, which in turn leads to pollination. (No pollination means no reproduction.) Other phytochemicals are part of the plant's defence systems against various pests and diseases or even too much sunlight. Onions, for example, make you cry for a reason— it's a mechanism put in place to stop you from eating them. The sulfur compounds that lead to tears also repel the onion's natural predators. The bitter substances in citrus fruits are another example of a defence mechanism. To avoid being eaten, plants secrete a variety of toxins and natural pesticides. And some of these very same substances, such as flavonoids, isoflavones, terpenes and glucosinolates, have been shown to act as disease fighters in humans. In large doses, such as those found in supplements, however, these compounds may do to humans what small doses do to insects.

A scientific paper out of the School of Public Health of the University of California at Berkeley warns that overdoing certain phytochemicals—the flavonoids, which may have anti-cancer and heart-healthy actions in lower doses—could actually increase the risk of cancer. The scientists advise people not to consume flavonoids at doses beyond those that would be found in a typical vegetarian diet. As well, because these compounds easily cross the placenta, scientists urge particular caution for pregnant women.

making bitter better

Overdoing phytochemicals when choosing a variety of foods has historically been a difficult thing to do. Many of these substances, particularly the ones that are meant to deter pests from eating the plants, give foods a bitter taste. Excessive amounts of various phytochemicals in a food can make it unpalatable. In fact, extreme bitterness in a food has for humans been a natural safeguard against poisoning.

But the small amounts of bitter substances that are found in wholesome foods seem to offer benefit, so it's worth your while to get used to some of these flavours. Although over time, our palates tend to adjust, research does show that some people experience bitter tastes to a greater degree. They're more likely to remove every trace of the bitter white pith when they peel their oranges.

Instead of avoiding these bitter compounds if you find you don't like them, try adding tasty ingredients to them until you can actually enjoy them. Take the healthful broccoli rabe: by adding sautéed garlic, a splash of fruity extra virgin olive oil and a sprinkle of freshly grated Parmesan, you turn the humble rabe into an enticing treat.

As science provides more information about what causes unpleasant tastes in certain foods, producers are sometimes quick to remove them. As a result, many fruits and vegetables have been undergoing selective breeding or de-bittering processes to be more pleasing to consumers. The result? While there may be less bitterness, the product may also contain fewer protective substances. This comes at a detriment to both plants and humans. For plants, as their natural pesticides are removed, there may be a greater susceptibility to pests, which in turn can boost the use of chemical pesticides. At the same time, we may lose out by having less in the way of natural disease-fighting compounds in our food.

the science behind those studies

Observational studies are those in which scientists gather all the information they can about a particular subject from a specific group of people and then look for associations. This type of research is valuable as it provides scientists with great quantities of information—data that they can use to find associations between, for instance, lifestyle and dietary choices and the risk for various diseases. Observational investigations have revealed, for example, a link between eating tomatoes and a lower risk of cancer, and that people who eat lots of greens are less likely to suffer from macular degeneration, the leading cause of blindness in the elderly. The next step after making the association is to theorize what in these foods may be responsible for the protective effect—or to determine if there is even any protection at all.

But associations don't provide positive proof. Other aspects need to be considered. For example, let's say that in a group of women studied, those who consumed less fat had a lower risk of breast cancer. Scientists might then propose that a lower-fat diet may protect against this type of cancer. But there are other factors at play. Maybe those who opted for leaner choices also ate plenty in the way of fruits, vegetables and whole grains. Or it could be that they exercised more, weighed less or maybe took a multivitamin and mineral supplement, any of which might have an impact on cancer risk. So what's really responsible? Is dietary fat just a part of the picture, or is it a major factor in the odds of developing cancer?

A next step after doing these types of observational studies is to do clinical studies or controlled trials—that is, take similar groups of people and test the theories. That's how scientists find out the real story. Sometimes the results can shake up the scientific world.

Such was the case when researchers tested their theories about beta carotene, one of the pigments that provides the orange colour to vegetables and fruits such as carrots, sweet potatoes and mangoes. Dozens of studies conducted over many years in various parts of the world found that that people who ate more vegetables and fruit rich in beta carotene had a lower risk of developing lung cancer than those who consumed few of these foods. Eaters of foods rich in beta carotene also had higher concentrations of beta carotene in their blood. But the question scientists had to answer was whether the higher level of beta carotene in the blood was proof that the substance offers protection against lung cancer.

One of the first clinical trials was conducted in Finland. Former smokers—a group with a higher risk of lung cancer—were given either high doses of beta carotene supplements or a placebo. The scientific community was stunned when the supplement takers ended up with a higher incidence of lung cancer than those who took the pill! Theories abounded as to what may have caused this unexpected result. Maybe it was a fluke. Or could it be that a combination of compounds in these foods besides the beta carotene protected against the disease? The choice of the kind of beta carotene used—natural versus synthetic—also came into question. A similar study was later carried out in five U.S. cities using former smokers and asbestos workers as subjects. But the study was cut short when it was seen that the supplement takers once again were more likely to end up as lung cancer statistics.

The scientific community was humbled. "Remember the beta carotene studies" has become a standard response of many researchers when asked about the benefits of supplements over food. Instead, before recommending lycopene supplements for protection against prostate cancer or lutein to prevent various eye diseases, they routinely call for clinical trials in which benefits and safety issues are addressed.

Be aware that you won't hear anything about this as you venture down the supplement aisles. Or maybe even in your health-care professional's office. What you might get, however, is a brochure proclaiming the wonders of lutein for protecting your eye health. Supplements are bringing in big bucks for natural health and pharmaceutical companies even if reliable scientific studies haven't been done yet.

Another step after observational studies, and before clinical trials, is known as "in vitro" research—studies carried out in laboratory test tubes. But again, these don't yield a definitive answer. Animal and human research studies, which are called "in vivo" studies, have to follow. Whether research is carried out in vitro or in vivo is an important consideration when you evaluate just how much weight you should place on a study's findings. For example, in a test tube, a particular compound may deal a knockout blow to a clump of cancer cells, but when it comes to humans, it's possible that the compound isn't even absorbed by the body or is destroyed before it has a chance to perform its magic. In vitro research is certainly one of the critical initial steps in the scientific process, but when you're looking for definitive proof, in vivo—literally "in life"—research must be carried out.

In vivo studies can determine if these various compounds can be absorbed into the human body and if they actually perform their disease-fighting actions. In some cases, phytochemicals may pass through the body undigested or, even if they are absorbed, they may be bound up with other compounds, unable to battle disease. This concept is called bioavailability. And even bioavailability is not straightforward, as there seem to be differences in individuals in how compounds are digested and where they end up in the body.

In human studies, the many kinds of research can be complex. Peer-reviewed studies, double-blind, single-blind, randomized, non-randomized—they're enough to make your head spin. But getting some of the jargon straight might help you decide whether the research is real science or just science fiction.

sorting science facts from fiction

Some studies are better than others, so it's important to understand how results are arrived at. Here's a primer.

In studies published in peer-reviewed journals (studies in which the scientific methods used are reviewed by other scientists), there is much less likelihood of bias simply because those same reviewers have investigated how the study was conducted.

Biased studies happen all the time, but they don't get published in peer-reviewed journals. Manipulating a study to get a desired result is easy to do. If you want to say that your product prevents a particular problem, you simply choose a group of subjects who are more likely to develop that particular ailment and another group who you'd bet won't. You then give the product to the healthy group and the placebo, or sugar pill, to the sick or at-risk ones. Not surprisingly, at the end of the study, those taking your product are healthy. Although it sounds like an outrageous scenario, it happens all the time. This type of research is characterized as single-blind, non-randomized. It's single-blind because the study subjects didn't know what they were taking, but the researcher knew. When both the researcher and the subjects are in the dark, studies are called double-blind. Non-randomized means that who takes the product with the active ingredient and who's on the list for the placebo is decided ahead of time. When it's a random selection, there's a better chance of valid study results.

A gold standard of research trials—double-blind, randomized—is used for evaluating pharmaceutical agents. But when it comes to food and natural health products, the same standards and principles are all too often abandoned. Shoddy studies in which the so-called scientist sets out to prove a theory can indeed be made to appear legitimate. These sham studies can be printed in a format and style that makes the research look reliable. But it's whether—and where—the research has been published that gives legitimacy to the results. These days, plenty of well-known companies are offering up study results that aren't worth the paper they're printed on.

One product marketed as a herbal bar and supplement for men is a case in point. The manufacturer took a kitchen-sink approach to the prevention of prostate problems. "Prostate health the natural way," claimed the package. Among the ingredients were saw palmetto, panax ginseng, stinging nettle, hydrangea root, quercetin, lycopene and bee pollen—some of which are linked to preventing benign prostate disease and others to fighting prostate cancer. No matter that the conditions are unrelated and that no research has looked at the effects, either positive or potentially harmful, of combining all these herbs and phytochemicals. The recommended dosage was one bar and one capsule every day for the first month and then one bar and one capsule every second day thereafter.

The "clinical study" backing up the product's effectiveness was anything but convincing. The research was a single-blind study, and the urologist conducting the study also happened to be a partner in the company that manufactured the bars. On paper the study looked as impressive as any written up in a scientific format. But when asked why he didn't use a double-blind, randomized study, the urologist replied that nutraceuticals, or functional foods—products that may promote health or fight disease—are usually studied using single-blind research whereas pharmaceuticals, or prescription drugs, are tested with the double-blind investigations. (That's simply because in Canada it's a federal requirement to have valid research backing up the use of a drug.) But why not have valid and unbiased research for nutraceuticals and functional foods as well? It would certainly eliminate the slew of health-promoting imposters on store shelves. It would also elevate the status of products that may indeed play a role in preventing disease.

As for the ingredients in the bar, some were included to prevent benign prostate disease and others were added to decrease the risk of prostate cancer. Among those phytochemicals included was lycopene, the carotenoid that gives tomato its red colour. Yet scientists currently evaluating the link between tomato-based products and a lowered risk of prostate cancer have cautioned against using lycopene alone as a prostate cancer buster until studies show that it is the compound responsible for the tomato's anti-cancer effect.

If manufacturers want to provide the public with an array of food products with medicinal ingredients, they should either conduct unbiased, rigorous studies or wait until there is a scientific consensus on the merits of particular substances. Research on how these compounds interact when they're mixed into a "chemical soup" such as in the prostate bar is also necessary. In other words, as we enter a new food frontier, manufacturers must act responsibly. Until then, it's buyer beware.

To check the validity of a study, consult your health-care professional or surf the Web for sites linked to legitimate science and medical journals.

It's also important to understand that scientific research is a process. Many studies must be done to reach a consensus. One negative or positive study does not provide us with all the answers. They often give direction about how to attempt the next step in the research. So when you hear something that sounds like the opposite of what you heard the day before, don't be confused or despair. Understand that in an era in which interest in the keys to longevity is at an all-time high, every contradictory study makes the news. And if you are discouraged by all the conflicting reports, you'll just be more vulnerable to the quick-talking snake oil salespeople who will provide you with all "their" answers. Instead, allow more time for the scientific verdict to come in.

fruits

... of all origins are brimming with
disease-fighting capabilities

A fully ripened mango, dripping with juices, or strawberries fresh from a local berry patch—they're nature at its finest. Fruits of all origins, from apple trees, grape vines and melon patches, are brimming with both taste and disease-fighting capabilities. And because of its sweetness, fruit, unlike its vegetable counterpart, is often pleasing at first taste to the young palate. But with increasing age and busy lives, adults all too often forget about the pleasures of fruit.

For some a tart, crunchy apple is what fruit is all about. For others, a cinnamon-scented apple crisp may hold more appeal. Have it in its simplest form, just washed and maybe peeled, or make it into the fanciest of desserts. And if you are one of those who abhor the taste of anything sweet, instead of abandoning fruit, use it in savoury dishes. From appetizers to salads and soups to entrees, use spices and herbs to counter the sweetness, making the taste more appealing. Even for those with a penchant for sweets, this treatment can help to boost fruit consumption by offering an assortment of tastes. Arugula garnished with pears, blue cheese and dressed with a fruity extra virgin olive oil, couscous tossed with slivers of dried fruit, almonds and fresh herbs, fiery-hot fruit salsas mixed with jalapeño peppers, onions and chopped coriander, or chicken baked with apples and onions are just a few tempting examples. Instead of thickening a puréed butternut squash soup with a potato, use an apple instead. The possibilities are endless. Whatever your choice, eat a variety of whole fruits to gather all the benefits they offer.

Evidence continues to accumulate that foods rich in combinations of antioxidants, nature's own chemical brew, may unleash a powerful array of substances that slow oxidation and the production of damaging free radicals. (See below.) At the same time, scientists have developed tests to measure a food's antioxidant capacity and have started to tabulate and test their results.

ORAC: a true test of antioxidant power

ORAC—remember this term. You're going to be hearing a lot about it over the next few years. It stands for Oxygen Radical Absorbance Capacity and is a test-tube analysis that measures the total antioxidant power of foods and other chemical substances. The higher the ORAC score for a food, the greater its antioxidant capacity. It used to be that you would hear that a food was good for you because it was a super source of a certain nutrient, say fibre. Claims such as "Eat it. It's got lots of fibre" or "It's packed with calcium" may soon be replaced by "It's a high-ORAC food." As consumers have become more and more concerned with fighting disease and combating the effects of aging, antioxidants are getting lots of attention. At the same time, antioxidant supplements are being put through the scientific wringer with rigorous studies. And that research fails to support many of the claims being made for them.

But that hasn't stopped the skyrocketing sales of supplements. People often don't discern between foods rich in a particular nutrient and a pill containing just that nutrient on its own. Foods rich in vitamin C, for example, may also contain a vast array of antioxidants, possibly interacting with each other and needing each other for full benefit. But foods with similar vitamin C content may, when given the ORAC tests, all score differently. When you consider that numerous vitamin C-rich fruits and vegetables contain assorted compounds like flavonoids—with more than 4,000 of them thought to exist—the variation in antioxidant power does make sense. Taking a pill may provide you with only one or two of those many substances—the equivalent of taking a hand pistol into battle when you may be in need of an entire battalion. But you can bet that the manufacturers of supplements would like you to believe otherwise.

At the USDA Agricultural Research Service (ARS) Human Research Center, at Tufts University, in Boston, scientists also analyzed whether consuming foods high in ORAC scores translates into increased levels of antioxidants in the blood. Antioxidant substances may be very powerful in the test tube, but when it comes to their action in the human body, they may be duds. Factors such as whether they're actually absorbed are all important considerations. In the ARS studies, consuming high-ORAC foods indeed raised the antioxidant power of human blood by 10 to 25 percent. That means that antioxidants were hard at work in the body knocking out the action of damaging free radicals.

But does this translate into protection against known diseases such as heart disease and cancer—ailments that seem to result from free radical damage and oxidation? Earlier research on animals provided support for this thinking. Rats fed daily doses of blueberry extract for six weeks before being subjected to two days of pure oxygen suffered much less damage to the capillaries in and around their lungs. In those fed the blueberry extract, the fluid that can accumulate in excess in the pleural cavity surrounding the lungs was much lower than in those that weren't fed the extract.

The researchers later assessed the effect of high-scoring ORAC foods on certain areas in the body and the brains of animals. The top scorers, such as spinach and broccoli, yielded some pretty impressive results. Among them:

- Preventing some loss of long-term memory and learning ability in middle-aged rats.
- Maintaining the capability of brain cells in middle-aged rats to respond to a chemical stimulus—something that is usually reduced with increasing age.
- Protecting rats' blood vessels against damage by oxygen.

The ARS findings together with other research suggests that eating plenty of high-ORAC fruits and vegetables may slow the aging process in both body and brain. And the earlier you begin, the better.

In another study, Tufts researchers fed women a number of different antioxidant-rich options and found that a large serving of fresh spinach boosted their blood antioxidant scores up to 25 percent. Compared with scores when the women were given 1250 milligrams of vitamin C, the fresh spinach came out the winner. In yet another investigation, men and women had a 13 to 15 percent increase in the antioxidant power of their blood after they doubled their normal daily fruit and vegetable intake.

Back to the issue of supplements. The ARS scientists put 46 berry-based supplements to the test (berries are among the foods with stellar ORAC scores). Included in the testing were supplements of bilberry, cranberry, chokeberry and elderberry extracts. When they measured the ORAC readings of the supplements, they discovered that the total antioxidant capacity of 40 berry-based supplements ranged from 16 to 3,985 ORAC units. The great range in antioxidant power in supplements probably results from the processing techniques used.

TOP-SCORING FRUITS
ORAC units per 100 g (about 3 1/2 ounces)
Prunes 5,770
Raisins 2,830
Blueberries 2,400
Blackberries 2,036
Strawberries 1,540
Raspberries 1,220
Plums 949
Oranges 750
Red grapes 739
Cherries 670
Kiwifruit 602
Grapefruit, pink 483

So even if the benefits of supplements include everything their labels claim, the benefits most likely won't measure up to the power of simply eating fruits and vegetables. And since the contents of natural health products may not be regulated, there can be discrepancies from one brand to another, or possibly from one batch to another within the same brand. Quality assurance may be lacking.

berries

Blueberries, cranberries, blackberries, strawberries—whatever the berry, the wilder, the better. Wild versus cultured, that is. It seems that much of the hoopla surrounding berries is due to their colour: the more intensely coloured—as the wild ones are—the more benefits they contain.

A series of studies carried out at the USDA-ARS Human Research Center, at Tufts University, pointed to blueberries' benefits for an aging population. In one investigation, published in the *Journal of Neuroscience*, Dr. James Josephs and his colleagues found that rats fed an extract of blueberries, strawberries and spinach daily showed improvements in short-term memory. But only the blueberry extract improved balance and coordination. In a later study, older rats were fed, every day for two months, an amount of blueberries equivalent to half a cup for humans. Age-related declines in the ability to do motor tasks were reversed.

Scientists are working to isolate the specific compounds responsible for blueberries' effects, and they are focusing on a type of flavonoid called anthocyanins, the pigments that give the fruit their distinctive deep blue colour. Another class of compounds called hydroxycinnamates may work together with the anthocyanins to improve both motor and cognitive functioning.

The flavonoid content that likely propels the scores of berries like blueberries and blackberries upwards on the ORAC test may provide them with a host of other benefits. Research on cranberries and blueberries showed that the phytochemicals may protect against inflammation in the brain, one of the contributing factors in cognitive decline. Protection against LDL oxidation is another perk.

Berries also seem to shine in their roles as potent health protectors. Science is now backing up the health merits of cranberry juice, a long-time folk remedy for urinary tract infections. Proanthocyanidins, found not only in the juice but also in fresh, frozen and dried cranberries and other berries, appear to fight the bacteria responsible for these infections.

The anti-cancer actions of various berries range from strawberry extract as a cancer prevention (of esophageal cancer in animals) to raspberries' ability to halt the growth of cancer cells.

Added to their phytochemical totals are berries' rich nutrient profiles. From B vitamins to C, they're also packed with fibre. And they're not just a seasonal treat. Buy them frozen or dried as well (there's no real loss of nutrients in these forms).

citrus

Drinking a morning glass of orange juice used to be about meeting your quota of vitamin C. That was it. A lot of scientific research has gone into citrus since, and oranges, along with grapefruits, lemons, limes and tangerines, have made great gains in nutritional status. Among the phytochemical compounds elevating citrus's standing are beta carotene, flavonoids, limonoids, folate, potassium and dietary fibre.

The range of flavonoids varies not only from one citrus fruit to another but also within each fruit's varieties. For example, one type of grapefruit may contain more of the flavonoid naringin while another contains high amounts of hesperidin. And all may have varying actions. Blood oranges contain anthocyanins, the same flavonoids found in berries and thought to aid in boosting antioxidant power and protect against artery damage and certain cancers. Some of these compounds are tasteless to human beings, while others contribute to the bitterness in some citrus products. Limonoids, another class of phytochemical in citrus, are the culprit, but for citrus trees, these compounds act as pesticides, deterring insects from eating the fruit.

Although their bitterness may not be to everyone's liking, citrus fruits have been shown to provide an assortment of health benefits, including possible protection against breast and colon cancer. The effect of citrus fruits on breast cancer has been the focus of much research. Orange juice versus grapefruit juice, one flavonoid versus another, limonoid versus flavonoid—they're all the subject of scientific study. And by all reports, the results look promising.

All types of citrus fruit seem to show anti-cancer action in various types of breast cancer. But a red flag has been raised by the research. A number of scientists have found that high doses of one particular flavonoid, tangeretin, interferes with the cancer drug tamoxifen, making tangeretin something to avoid in supplement form. Checking supplement labels, even of vitamin and mineral preparations, for ingredients such as citrus bioflavonoids may be a wise idea if you are taking tamoxifen. On the other hand, research shows that consuming a variety of citrus fruits may boost the effectiveness of this drug.

Citrus is a terrific heart health ally. Besides its antioxidant protection against cholesterol buildup in the arteries, the phytochemicals together with citrus's soluble fibre provide quite a cholesterol-lowering punch. Although the juices do provide the antioxidant power supplied by the vitamin C, the fruit itself is higher in both phytochemicals and fibre. And don't forget about the peel. Adding some zest to your recipes is more than just a taste sensation. The peel is a rich source of some flavonoids.

Enjoy a variety of citrus to reap the potential benefits. But be aware that grapefruit juice may interact with some medications. While some medications may become more potent in their action, others may do the opposite. The best advice is to check with a pharmacist.

vitamin C—friend or foe?

British soldiers in the 1700s became known as limeys because of their habit of drinking lime juice on long voyages, when no fresh fruits and vegetables were available. They believed the acid in the limes prevented deadly scurvy. It was a few hundred years later that scientists discovered that it was the vitamin C in citrus fruit, and not the acid, that prevented this deficiency disease. The health-promoting reputation of vitamin C has come a long way since. Although countless studies have assessed its effect on the common cold, with results more often than not showing no preventive benefit, vitamin C may lessen the symptoms and severity of the infection. But C's main strength is its role as an antioxidant, preventing, or in some cases slowing the rate of, disease. Vitamin C-rich foods have been linked to protection against heart disease, stroke, certain cancers and other oxidative diseases. But there is a catch. It's thought that vitamin C, when taken as a supplement in large amounts, acts as a pro-oxidant, hastening ill health.

Whether antioxidant or pro-oxidant may depend on an individual's health, genetic makeup and sex. Men, for example, usually store higher levels of the mineral iron in their bodies than women do. (Too little iron stored in our bodies can lead to anemia and fatigue, whereas too much may lead to a greater rate of oxidation and its consequences.) Since vitamin C enhances iron absorption, men who consume mega-doses of vitamin C supplements may be putting themselves at a greater risk for developing cancer and heart disease. Likewise, people with an iron deficiency or low iron stores should make sure to include a vitamin C-rich food in a meal with iron from any plant source, including whole grains, leafy greens and legumes, to boost the iron absorption. For both men and women, fruits and vegetables that are naturally packed with vitamin C—no matter how many servings are eaten—do not present a risk of oxidation.

Although we should all get our fill of vitamin C-rich foods, it's especially important for certain segments of the population to focus on this nutrient. Among them are people with type 2 diabetes and smokers, both of whom require higher levels of vitamin C because of the high rate of oxidation their bodies may undergo.

apples

A few decades ago, as the then somewhat unsophisticated practice of nutritional analysis was in full swing, the age-polished saying "An apple a day keeps the doctor away" lost its sheen for many nutritionists. It was the orange, and other citrus fruits, that had the apple beat in many nutrient categories. But recent scientific findings have once again reinforced the wisdom of the past. That, and new methods of nutritional analysis that can measure what was previously undetectable.

Take fibre as an example. Old methods of nutrient analysis could measure only insoluble fibre, the kind that's found in wheat grains. Soluble fibre was unknown. Although apples contained some insoluble fibre, the amount was too minimal to be noted. So apples were thought to lack fibre—even though they are filled with pectin, a soluble fibre that lowers blood cholesterol and regulates blood sugar. And as for vitamin C, while apples are a source, they certainly didn't measure up to a morning glass of orange juice or a grapefruit half. Apples also seemed devoid of significant amounts of any vitamins or minerals. The apple didn't appear to offer much, nutritionally speaking. It just provided a wonderful sour or sweet crunch. Yet study after study showed that people who regularly ate apples had a lower risk of heart disease, stroke and other ailments. As scientists delved into apple-eating research, they began to uncover a variety of phytochemicals.

The first of these investigations, the Zutphen Elderly Study, was published in the journal *Lancet* in 1993. Scientists in the Netherlands measured the content in various foods of a range of flavonoids, such as quercetin, kaempferol, myricetin, apigenin and luteolin. They then assessed the flavonoid intake of more than 800 elderly men whose major sources of flavonoids were tea, onions and apples. The researchers tracked the men for a five-year period, during which time they documented the rate of heart attacks and deaths from coronary heart disease. When the researchers compared the results, men who had consumed the highest amounts of these phytochemicals were at the lowest risk of being a victim of heart disease.

Finnish scientists, in research published in 1996 in the *British Medical Journal*, also examined the connection between consuming flavonoid-rich foods and death from heart disease. In their study of more than 5,000 men and women, data was collected on healthy subjects between 1967 and 1972. For the next 20 years, the scientists tracked the deaths from heart disease and found that, once again, flavonoid intake was associated with a lower likelihood of dying from heart disease. And when foods rich in these compounds, like apples and onions, were also looked at, similar associations were found.

> **WHAT A BARGAIN!**
> According to Foodland Ontario, the province's promotion agency for produce, because apples were so versatile and durable and could be so easily preserved by drying, during the California Gold Rush their cost sometimes ended up more than $100 a bushel.

Apples are not just a winning choice for affairs of the heart. They may also offer protection against lung cancer. In Hawaiian research published in 2000 in the *Journal of the National Cancer Institute*, scientists examined not only the amount and types of flavonoids consumed but also the genetic propensity for risk of lung cancer. As some people are genetically susceptible to particular cancers, certain protective compounds in food may play a greater role in keeping them healthy. In the study, diets of almost 600 subjects with lung cancer were compared with those of 600 who were cancer free. Among the protective compounds were the flavonoids quercetin (found mainly in onions and apples) and naringin (from white grapefruit). Those who ate the most of these foods had the lowest risk of lung cancer. And those with a greater genetic predisposition seemed to reap more advantages from eating these foods. In Finnish research of almost 10,000 people, flavonoids were singled out as cancer fighting, but apples were specifically noted for their action against lung cancer risk.

The "apple a day" adage may hold even more importance for smokers. French scientists researching cell mutations linked to carcinogens from tobacco found that flavonoids such as quercetin can actually prevent cell mutation. After testing the urine of smokers for compounds that inhibit these cancer-causing mutations, it was concluded that, to prevent the bladder cancer that's more common in smokers, smokers should load up on quercetin-rich selections such as apples and onions. And for those at risk for asthma, similar recommendations were made by British researchers.

But according to researchers at the Federal Agriculture Lab in Guelph, not all apples are created equal when it comes to antioxidant content. Dr. Rong Tsao and his colleagues measured the antioxidant level of eight common varieties grown in Ontario. At the top of the list were Red Delicious apples, with the peel its richest source of antioxidants. Next came Spy, Ida Red and Cortland. Empire apples came in last, with less than half the antioxidant totals of the winner. Although these results were culled from only one study, they once again point to the importance of eating a variety of foods, even when it's one particular food.

Dutch researchers looked at the antioxidant concentration not only in assorted varieties of apples but also in fruits from different harvest years and in varying storage conditions. When apples from three different harvest years were analyzed, no difference in flavonoid concentration and antioxidant activity was observed. Other good news was that long-term storage, both at refrigerator temperature and under controlled atmosphere conditions, had no influence on flavonoid concentration or antioxidant activity.

Another area of research focused on the effect of apple juice on tooth enamel and dentin. It seems that regularly drinking apple juice or cola beverages promotes dental cavities and demineralization of teeth. Apple juice also doesn't provide the valuable fibre that the apple fruit contains. So eat apples rather than drinking apple juice—it's better for your teeth and for weight control.

Over the past few years, outbreaks of food poisoning in Canada and the U.S. have been linked to unpasteurized apple juice and cider. The microbes found in these outbreaks are *E. coli*, also the culprit in "hamburger disease," along with *Salmonella* and *Cryptosporidium*. *E. coli*, which can be deadly or leave its victims with permanent kidney damage, has been the most common source. Although the reported incidence is very low, the possible contamination of these beverages is still a very real risk, especially for the young, elderly and those with impaired immune systems. Contamination can occur if the apple falls to the ground and comes into contact with animal droppings or if the water used in processing contains microbes. In 2000, Health Canada began a campaign to get fruit producers to include "pasteurized" on labels. Pasteurization involves heating a product to a high temperature for a period of time in order to kill harmful micro-organisms. Most commercial apple juice brands bought in supermarkets or grocery stores have been pasteurized, but juice and cider purchased at roadside stands or farmers markets, or even at natural food stores, may not be. Check the label or ask the purveyor if you're unsure.

Apples, although a great "fast food" eaten as is, are terrific in both sweet and savoury dishes, ranging from appetizers, soups and salads right through to main courses and dessert. The number of varieties grown is tremendous, but those found in markets tend to be limited to those that "travel" well. Select the apple type according to how it's being used. Some are wonderful straight from the fridge; others are primarily for cooking. Some hold their shape when cooked; others don't.

When purchasing apples, look for firm fruit that is free of wrinkles, bruises and punctures. Once you have your apples home, to keep them crunchy, handle them with TLC, as they can bruise and then spoil more easily. Remove any bruised fruit from the bag and use for cooking, as bruised ones will shorten the shelf life of the others. Store apples in plastic bags in the refrigerator. Though a large bowl of rosy apples may indeed be a decorative touch in the kitchen, keep in mind that at room temperature apples soften 10 times faster than when stored in the fridge. And lastly, don't wash them until you're ready to use them.

Besides providing countless health perks, apples are a friend to fruit in need of ripening. Apples emit ethylene, a gas that speeds up the ripening process, so placing unripe fruit in a paper bag with an apple will help the fruit ripen sooner. But keep in mind that you might want to keep apples out of a fruit bowl mix where everything is at a perfect ripeness.

The flip-flopping fate of apples (a truly fibre-rich and nutritious food) is a cautionary tale about the shortcomings of science and the wisdom of variety. Over time, as further research uncovers more disease-fighting phytochemicals in fruits, as well as in vegetables, legumes, grains, nuts and seeds, previously ignored or neglected foods will be found to be important contributors to improved health. So, even if the apple is bumped off the top-ten list of health choices, be sure to include it in your diet anyway.

avocados

Over the past few decades, these wondrous fruits have too often been shunned. In the early days of cholesterol-consciousness, it was wrongly believed that they boosted blood cholesterol readings. Then, when low-fat eating seemed almost to be a religion, avocados, the only fruit containing significant amounts of fat, were considered sinful. Maybe it's just that they tasted that way. Just as our culinary horizons were expanding —when we no longer thought that a spicy guacamole was the only thing you could make with avocados—there was vindication.

It turns out these fruits are an excellent source of folate; they also provide an assortment of other nutrients—vitamins A and C, vitamin B-6, thiamine, magnesium and iron. They can also dethrone the well-known potassium king, bananas. Ounce for ounce, avocados have 60 percent more potassium than bananas. And to top off the abuse avocados have taken over the years, even their vitamin E content had been incorrectly reported. New data on California avocados shows that they have nearly twice as much vitamin E as previously described, making avocados the highest fruit source of the powerful antioxidant. The same study also revealed that avocados are the highest fruit source of lutein (see page 23).

The health profile of the avocado has been further raised as research continues to mount on the benefits of eating "fat smart" rather than "low fat." The monounsaturated fat the avocado contains promotes healthy HDL-cholesterol levels in addition to helping those with diabetes obtain better blood sugar regulation.

> **TOP FIVE FRUITS FOR VITAMIN E CONTENT**
>
> (per 100 g raw, edible portion fruit)
>
> | | |
> |---|---|
> | 1. Avocado | 4.31 IU |
> | 2. Kiwifruit | 1.67 IU |
> | 3. Nectarine | 1.33 IU |
> | 4. Grapes | 1.04 IU |
> | 5. Peach | 1.04 IU |
>
> Source: UCLA Center for Human Nutrition and USDA Nutrient Database for Standard Reference.

And the other nutritional goodies they contain, an assortment of phytochemicals, truly elevate avocados from dietary demons of the past to star status. Beta-sitosterol, one of a group of phytochemicals known as phytosterols, has been shown to decrease cholesterol absorption from the intestine. In animal studies, phytosterols have been found to inhibit the growth of tumours. Glutathione is another phytochemical in plentiful supply in these fruits. Acting as an antioxidant, it's been linked to the prevention of various types of cancers, including cancer of the mouth and pharynx, and heart disease.

But if your love of avocados has you thinking that you could live on avocados alone, think again. Science keeps on showing us that combos we've grown to love, like tomato salsas with guacamole, pack more than just a taste punch. (Maybe skip the fried nachos, though, and opt for quesadillas instead—see Cheese and Vegetable Quesadillas with Avocado and Tomato Salsa, page 90.)

A study from the University of California, Los Angeles, provides more proof about the value of whole foods and eating patterns. The research looked at intakes of the carotenoids lycopene and lutein, alone and together, and their protective effects against prostate cancer. Although lycopene-rich foods have been repeatedly associated with a lowered risk of prostate cancer, lutein-rich ones, like dark leafy greens and avocados, are new kids on the block. The initial stage of the investigation focused on men in a rural area of China where there was a low rate of prostate cancer even though the diet contained no tomatoes and no lycopene. Plenty of green vegetables on the menu, however, resulted in a high intake of lutein. The study was then expanded to include Chinese-American men and Caucasian men. The laboratory tests showed that lutein reduced the growth of prostate cancer cells by 25 percent, and lycopene reduced cell growth by 20 percent. But when lutein and lycopene were combined, prostate cancer cell growth was reduced by 32 percent. The findings indicated that both compounds together help protect against prostate cancer better than either substance alone.

The pleasurable health perks of avocados can be enjoyed all year long. With more than 60 varieties from California and Florida, whether they're round or pear-shaped, smooth-skinned or bumpy, green or purple, avocados all have one thing in common —a rich, smooth, buttery texture. The Florida varieties are lower in fat and calories, but they're a little less buttery-tasting as well.

When buying avocados, don't go by colour alone, as some varieties, like the Hass, will turn dark green

TOP FIVE FRUITS FOR LUTEIN CONTENT	
(per 100 g raw, edible portion fruit)	
1. Avocado	284 mcg
2. Plum	240 mcg
3. Kiwifruit	180 mcg
4. Pear	110 mcg
5. Grapes	72 mcg

Source: UCLA Center for Human Nutrition and USDA Carotenoid Database.

or black when ripe, whereas others may remain light green even when they're ripe. Instead, check the fruit for firmness. Those that are firm yet yield to gentle pressure are ready to be eaten. Firmer ones should be left to ripen for a few days. If you need to speed up the ripening, place the fruit in a closed paper bag and store at room temperature until ready to eat. Adding an apple to the bag can speed up the ripening process further. Don't buy those that are very soft to the touch, although slightly soft ones are a favourite ingredient of homemade skin treatments. Early research points to a component of avocados, avocado furan, having an anti-aging effect on the skin.

Avocados are a snap to peel once they've ripened. Start by cutting the avocado lengthwise around the seed. Rotate the halves in opposite directions to separate, and remove the seed. Then simply pull off the peel with your fingers. If you're using just a slice or two of the avocado, peel only that section. Rub the exposed remaining part with lemon or lime juice (to prevent discoloration) and store in the fridge. To use the whole fruit, cut the avocado lengthwise around the seed. Rotate the halves to separate them and remove the seed by sliding the tip of a spoon gently underneath and lifting it out.

Whether you're slicing, mashing or dicing, to retain the bright green colour and avoid any browning of the fruit, eat the avocado immediately or cover the cut surface with plastic wrap and store it in an airtight container. Although the darkened portions are still edible, they're not as appetizing to the eye. In recipes containing acidic ingredients such as lemon juice, the avocado will not discolour quickly, but if it does, just discard the top layer.

Add avocado slices to sandwiches, dice them for salads and salsas and mash them for dips. And instead of cream cheese, spread avocado, herbed or plain, on bread.

bananas

Few people realize that there is a vast assortment of banana varieties, with various tastes, textures and even colours. Even fewer people know that the banana variety we most often consume is called the Cavendish. In fact, there are many types of bananas, with various tastes, textures and even colours. Over the past few years, selections such as red and fingertip bananas—small, almost miniature, yet sweeter versions of the Cavendish—have been introduced into our market. Plantains, which have also become increasingly available, are now making appearances. Although bananas, plantains are not eaten raw; they must be cooked.

Regardless of their variety, bananas have a stellar reputation when it comes to their potassium content. Physicians often instruct people on blood pressure medication who have low levels of potassium to eat a banana a day. While plenty of other fruits and vegetables can match bananas in this department, they simply don't have as broad appeal or as high a profile.

Bananas contain much more than potassium, though. They're an excellent source of vitamin B-6, or pyridoxine, a nutrient that together with vitamin B-12 and folate, another B vitamin, is linked to lower homocysteine levels in the blood, leading to a reduced risk of artery disease. They're no slouch in the fibre department either, with almost 3 grams in a medium banana. And of that fibre, there's a proportion of inulin, the beneficial indigestible sugar with anti-cancer and cholesterol-lowering action.

Purchase bananas in varying stages of ripeness depending on when you plan to use them. Those that are green-tipped are best left to ripen at room temperature for a few days. They can be eaten as is but won't taste as sweet. To speed up ripening, place the bananas in a brown paper bag along with an apple and close. Keep the bag out of direct sunlight and the fruit will be ripen in a day or two.

Instructions on choosing and storing bananas used to be something to sing about. The Chiquita company, one of the big banana sellers, decided that a jingle was the easy way to teach Americans how to ripen and use bananas, an exotic and not well-known fruit at that time. Little did they envision the success of their campaign. The "Chiquita Banana" song hit the airwaves in 1944, and at its peak was played 376 times a day on radio. To this day, many people can sing or at least hum a few bars of the famous jingle. Miss Chiquita, with her maracas, would be singing, "I'm Chiquita banana and I've come to say ..." The jingle advises consumers not to put bananas in the refrigerator. The music has remained the same, but the lyrics have changed over the years.

And so have thoughts about storing bananas. Contrary to previous thinking, bananas can be refrigerated or frozen. The peels may blacken in the refrigerator, but the fruit is unaffected and still edible. Placing them in the fridge is a splendid way to keep bananas that are at the peak of their ripeness but not about to be eaten. But don't refrigerate unripe bananas; they will remain starchy and not become sweet even if left out for days at room temperature.

Yellow bananas that are free of flecks are perfect for eating out of your hand or to use in salads. To prevent browning when slicing them, dip in lemon, orange or pineapple juice. As bananas ripen further, the number of flecks increases and the fruit is sweeter, making them ideal for baking in pancakes, cakes, quickbreads, muffins, cookies or pies. When it comes to the perennial favourite, peanut butter and banana sandwiches, everyone has a personal preference as to how ripe a banana to use. Smoothies, however, usually taste better with riper fruit. Use bananas right out of the freezer for a thicker shake. To freeze bananas, peel and place in freezer bags in appropriate portions. For example, if your banana bread recipe calls for three bananas, freeze three together. When defrosting, do not discard the liquids that separate from the fruit; mash the fruit with the liquid and use in your recipe.

Bananas are a super fast-food snack—just a quick peel and you're ready to go. Or eat one right out of the freezer for a frozen ice-cream-like treat. Don't leave bananas out of your cooking repertoire, either. They make a simple, yummy dessert when roasted or broiled with a little brown sugar or honey, rum and butter or soft margarine. Serve on top of frozen yogurt. Or wrap the same combo in foil packets and place on the barbecue for a simple outdoor dessert.

pears

Including pears on the menu, with their significant amounts of soluble fibre, can lower blood cholesterol and may contribute to better blood sugar readings and appetite regulation, making them a terrific choice for helping to maintain a healthy body shape. In fact, their 4 grams put them high on the list of fruits with appreciable amounts of fibre. That's in addition to the vitamin C and potassium they contain.

The phytochemical mix contained in a pear depends on the variety. Among varieties studied, phenolic compounds such as the antioxidants catechins and procyanidins have been identified. In addition, the amounts of phytochemicals can vary depending on whether the fruit is ripe or unripe, and fresh or dried. As more research on phytochemicals is carried out, we will be hearing more about the health benefits of eating pears.

Produce markets in North America traditionally have sold only four or five varieties of the more than 4,000 available, although the assortment is increasing as consumers' tastes become ever more sophisticated. Pears are usually picked unripe because they ripen beautifully off the tree, and most of the fruit in the marketplace is unripe. Purchase your pears several days ahead of when they're to be eaten. Allow them to ripen for a few days at room temperature and then store them in the refrigerator. Or, for fast ripening, store them in a loosely closed brown paper bag at room temperature, out of direct sunlight. If you don't want them to ripen just yet, put the pears in the fridge and take them out a few days before you want to eat them. A ripe pear is fairly firm but when pressed gently at the stem end, yields a little. (Ripe pears bruise easily, and a few squeezes can turn them mushy.) Don't go by changes in colour when trying to determine ripeness, as some varieties don't change hues as they ripen.

When preparing pears for fruit salads, don't peel the fruit, for the peel contains valuable fibre. Pears are perfect for making sauces, crisps and purées. Pears make an elegant and nutritious dessert when poached in juices, wine or tea (see Cinnamon and Tea Poached Pears, page 244). And don't limit them to the dessert course. They partner well with savoury ingredients and are a delicious addition to soups, salads and main courses.

cherries

If life is a bowl of cherries, according to preliminary scientific research and a slew of anecdotal reports, partaking of the fruit may be beneficial indeed. These small red fruits not only provide vitamin C, thiamine and riboflavin, but are also the source of antioxidants such as melatonin. A study from Michigan State University found that anthocyanins, the flavonoids responsible for the red colour of cherries, besides having antioxidant action, appear to have an anti-inflammatory effect. For many people with arthritis who regularly consume cherry juice, this is not news. The beverage has apparently brought relief to countless people, but further research is required to back up the testimonials.

grapes

It stands to reason that grapes, especially purple ones, would be full of health-promoting compounds (see Red Wine, page 229). A plethora of studies have linked red wine—fermented grape juice—with a decreased risk of heart disease. Besides vitamin C, which acts as an antioxidant, grapes contain a variety of flavonoids with an impressive list of defensive manoeuvres against not only heart disease but a variety of cancers as well.

At the centre of much of the research is a phytochemical known as resveratrol, which may battle cancer at all stages of the disease, from neutralizing carcinogens to stopping tumour progression (see page 4). Since resveratrol is found in the highest concentration in the skins of grapes, red wine, which incorporates these skins when it is produced, is a richer source of resveratrol than white wine. Besides protecting against the oxidation of cholesterol and its becoming a more artery-clogging form, this compound has been shown to have a cholesterol-lowering action.

As well, grapes decrease the rate of platelet aggregation—the likelihood of blood clots forming, adhering to artery walls and eventually causing a heart attack or stroke —and improve endothelial function (see page 5). Getting good marks on endothelial function means blood flows through the arteries even when conditions may not be ideal—for example, after eating a high-fat meal.

Both the skins and the seeds of grapes are rich sources of phytochemicals, making purple grape juice, which contains both, one of the best grape products for phytochemical power. It appears that when extracts of grape seed and skin are

> **SERVING SIZE**
> Meeting your quota of fruits is not as difficult as you may think. Having 5 to 6 servings of fruits and vegetables doesn't necessarily mean 5 to 6 different items. One serving, for example, is just 1/2 cup (125 mL) of grapes; 1 cup (250 mL) is 2 servings.
>   One serving is
> - a medium-sized piece of fruit, such as an apple or an orange
> - 1/2 cup (125 mL) of canned, cooked or frozen fruit
> - 1/4 cup (50 mL) of dried fruit, such as raisins

consumed together, they are much more potent than when either extract is consumed alone.

The anti-cancer properties of grapes have been examined, with promising results, especially with breast and colon cancer. In animal studies, those that were fed purple grape juice had both smaller and fewer breast cancer tumours than those that were not given grape juice. But it seems that individual parts of grapes, such as the seeds, may not have the same ability to fight each type of cancer.

SOME ASSORTED FRUIT MORSELS

Apricot, Peach, Plum, Nectarine
- Vitamin C and potassium along with a variety of phytochemicals, including isoprenoids, carotenoids and antioxidant compounds that work synergistically.

Cantaloupe
- Vitamin C, folate, thiamine, niacin, beta carotene and beta-ionone. A rival for banana's super potassium content.

Cherimoya
- Vitamin C and iron.

Date

• Vitamin B-6, niacin, iron, magnesium and fibre.

Fig

• Calcium, iron, magnesium and fibre.

Gooseberry

• Vitamin C.

Guava

• Vitamin C, fibre and phytochemicals with potent anti-microbial and antioxidant activities.

Honeydew Melon

• Potassium, vitamin C, folate and thiamine.

Kiwifruit

• Potassium, vitamin C and magnesium. Contains both lutein and zeaxanthin and has high antioxidant power.

Kumquat

• An excellent source of vitamin C.

Lychee

• An excellent source of vitamin C. (Related to the latex family, making it a concern for those allergic to latex.)

Mango

• Vitamin C, vitamin E and thiamine, along with plenty of carotenoids.

Papaya

• Potassium, vitamin C, folate and the carotenoid beta-cryptoxanthin.

Passionfruit

• Vitamin C, iron and beta carotene. When eaten with its seeds, it's top-notch for fibre.

Persimmon

• Vitamin C, beta carotene and other antioxidants.

Pineapple

• Folate, thiamine, vitamin C, fibre and beta-ionone.

Pomegranate

• Fibre, vitamin C, niacin and packed with antioxidants. Its juice, especially when concentrated into pomegranate molasses, can give the power brokers of antioxidation, wine and tea a run for their money. (See Med-Rim Roasted Vegetables, page 88.)

Tamarillo
- Vitamin C, fibre and beta carotene.

Watermelon
- Potassium, vitamin C, vitamin B-6 and thiamine, along with the carotenoids beta carotene and lycopene.

food safety savvy

Food poisoning is frequently associated with the handling of food such as raw chicken and meat. But increasingly, foodborne illnesses are coming from another source. Fruits and vegetables can harbour a range of microbes, such as *Salmonella, Escherichia coli* (commonly known as *E. coli*) and *Cyclospora*, to name a few. In many cases, people are frequently unaware that they have been victims of food poisoning because symptoms may not appear until days after eating the culprit food. And more often than not, the illness may be mistakenly identified as the flu.

There's no doubt that our food supply has changed. *E. coli*, the potentially deadly bacterium found in undercooked meat, may make its way from fertilizers containing cow manure to crops in fields—even though most fertilizers are sterilized. The availability of imported foods from countries with lower agricultural standards (the same countries in which experienced travellers shun fresh fruits and vegetables for this very reason) has increased our risk of eating contaminated produce.

Washing all fruits and vegetables thoroughly, even those whose peel is not eaten, is one way to decrease the risk of foodborne illness. If you think this sounds a little obsessive, consider how many food handlers, supermarket staff and customers touch your fruits and vegetables before you buy them. And, unlike meat, poultry and fish, these foods are often not cooked before being eaten (it's the high cooking temperature that kills bacteria in meat). There have been reports of bacteria such as *Salmonella* being found on cantaloupe rinds as far back as 1991. In the spring of 2002, residents of a number of states, including California and Oregon, became ill after eating tainted cantaloupe.

If there are *Salmonella* bacteria on the rind, slicing through an unwashed cantaloupe can spread the bacteria to the melon flesh. Cutting a contaminated fruit can also lead to the very same cross-contamination in food that might occur by cutting raw chicken and then using the unwashed knife on another food. To ensure that your melon—or any other fruit with rind or a peel that isn't removed—is fit to eat, be sure to give it a good scrub before storing or cutting it.

FRUITS AND VEGETABLES CONTAINING VITAMIN C

(Fruits and vegetables containing at least 5 percent of the amounts recommended for daily consumption in 100 g)

Fruit	Vegetable
Apples	Arugula
Apricots	Asparagus
Avocados	Basil
Bananas	Beet greens
Blackberries	Broccoli
Blueberries	Brussels sprouts
Cantaloupe	Cabbage
Carambola	Cauliflower
Cranberries	Chard
Elderberries	Chicory greens
Gooseberries	Collard greens
Grapefruits	Dandelion greens
Guavas	Green onions
Kiwifruit	Kale
Kumquats	Kohlrabi
Lemons	Lettuce, dark varieties
Limes	Mustard greens
Loganberries	Okra
Lychees	Parsley
Mandarins	Parsnips
Mangoes	Peas, green
Melons	Peppers, green, red and yellow
Oranges	Plantain
Papaya	Potato, with skin
Passionfruit	Snow peas
Persimmon	Spinach
Pineapple	Sweet potato
Quince	Tomatoes
Raisins	Turnips
Raspberries	Watercress
Red currants	
Strawberries	

Being diligent in washing all your produce is critical to decreasing the likelihood of contamination and illness. *E. coli* has been detected in a variety of vegetables, including alfalfa sprouts and iceberg lettuce. Washing each individual leaf, rather than washing the whole lettuce at once, has been shown to significantly decrease bacteria counts. Mesclun or spring mixes, contrary to popular thinking, also require washing before being eaten.

Another common source of cross-contamination that leads to foodborne illness is your hands. Wash your hands often—before, during and after preparing food. Even wash your hands after unpacking fruits and vegetables from the market. Make sure to work up a good lather with plenty of soap, as it's the lather that lifts the germs off your hands.

The kitchen dishcloth, used to wipe counters and sinks where bacteria lurk, is another major source of bacterial contamination. Dishcloths should regularly be discarded or dipped in a solution of bleach and water. As well, regularly clean kitchen sinks and counters with a bleach and water solution, using about 1 tablespoon (15 mL) bleach for a quart (litre) of water. Wash cutting boards and knives in hot soapy water after every use.

A PITCHER'S GUIDE

It can be difficult to visit the greengrocer, witness the abundance of seasonal fruits and vegetables and not walk away without a bushel or more. But next time you're in the fresh produce section, try to restrain yourself. If your excess of tomatoes or peaches ends up developing white fuzzy beards, not only have you wasted your food dollars but you may be compromising your health as well. Certain moulds produce toxic substances called mycotoxins, which have been connected to an increase in certain cancers even when ingested only in small quantities but consistently over a number of years. In some foods, particularly soft ones, these mycotoxins can seep through the entire food, leaving no visible signs or obvious taste.

Here's a pitcher's guide, with examples below, of what you should toss and what you can cut. The general rule is that soft fruits and vegetables should be discarded, but you can cut the mould off hard produce. For safe measure, it's advised that you cut an extra inch (2.5 cm) around the mould. Of course, when in doubt, throw it out.

CUT	TOSS
Broccoli	Bananas
Carrots	Cucumbers
Cauliflower	Melons
Onions	Peaches
Potatoes	Tomatoes

QUICK FRUIT SOLUTIONS

- Top off your morning bowl of cereal with fresh or frozen berries. Add them to yogurt and savoury salads and stir into them into muffin and quick-bread batter.
- When time is in short supply for shopping and food preparation, or when the offerings at the greengrocer are limited, choose frozen fruit. The variety and taste of these products have vastly improved in the past few years, and they're frozen at the peak of their nutritional quality.
- If snacking on fresh fruit is not to your taste, and if you prefer savoury dishes, add sliced fruit to side dishes and salads.

Although these practices may sound extreme, after a while you'll find they are as routine as washing an apple or pear before eating.

recipes

orange, grapefruit and onion salad

A savoury way to sneak in some citrus. Getting in a variety of citrus provides an assortment of phytochemicals such as flavonoids and limonoids, substances linked to healthy hearts and a lower risk of certain cancers such as breast cancer.

MAKES 6 SERVINGS

2 tablespoons (25 mL) orange juice

1 tablespoon (15 mL) cider vinegar

1 tablespoon (15 mL) honey

1 teaspoon (5 mL) Dijon mustard

4 teaspoons (20 mL) extra virgin olive oil

Salt and freshly ground pepper, to taste

8 cups (2 L) mesclun mix

1 cup (250 mL) orange sections (about 2 small oranges)

1 cup (250 mL) grapefruit sections (about 1 large grapefruit)

1/2 cup (125 mL) red onion slices

In a small bowl, whisk together orange juice, vinegar, honey and mustard; add oil in a stream, whisking until emulsified. Whisk in salt and pepper.

In a large bowl, toss together mesclun, orange and grapefruit sections, and onion slices. Add dressing and toss to coat. Serve immediately.

PER SERVING NUTRITIONAL INFORMATION: Calories: 80, Protein: 1 g, Fat: 3 g, Saturated Fat: less than 1 g, Carbohydrate: 13 g, Dietary Fibre: 3 g

thai mango salad with roasted peanuts

This delicious salad is adapted from the Peanut Bureau of Canada. Its rainbow of colours supplies a super mix of phytochemicals. Top it off with peanuts and you're adding phytosterols and monounsaturated fat as well. Did I mention that the B vitamins like folate? A pretty impressive nutrient mix, indeed.

MAKES 4 SERVINGS

3 tablespoons (45 mL) peanuts, very coarsely chopped

1 lime

1 1/2 teaspoons (7 mL) sodium-reduced soy sauce or fish sauce

1 1/2 teaspoons (7 mL) sugar

1/2 small jalapeño pepper, seeded and minced (or 1/2 teaspoon/2 mL red pepper flakes)

1 tablespoon (15 mL) sesame oil

Salt

1 ripe but firm mango

1 red pepper, cut into thin strips

1 medium carrot, coarsely grated

1 green onion, thinly sliced

1/2 cup (125 mL) mixed chopped fresh mint and coriander

4 cups (1 L) baby spinach or mesclun mix

To toast peanuts, preheat oven to 350°F (180°C). Place nuts in a single layer on a baking sheet. Toast nuts 7 to 10 minutes, stirring occasionally, until fragrant. Set aside.

Zest lime finely and place in a measuring cup. Add juice from lime. Whisk in soy sauce, sugar and jalapeño pepper until sugar is dissolved. Gradually whisk in sesame oil until blended. Add salt to taste. Set aside.

Peel mango, then cut away chunks of fruit from pit. Cut into thin strips and place in a large bowl. Add red pepper, carrot, green onion, mint and coriander. Toss gently until combined.

Add spinach and dressing; toss until mixed. Serve on a platter or in a large salad bowl sprinkled with roasted peanuts.

PER SERVING NUTRITIONAL INFORMATION: Calories: 000, Protein: 136 g, Fat: 4 g, Saturated Fat: 1 g, Carbohydrate: 18 g, Dietary Fibre: 4 g

To: John
From: Tina
Linda & Eugene

anberry relish

...rom that of the Ocean Spray kitchens, is chock full of
...berries are linked to protection against a variety of ailments,
...t infections, certain cancers and heart disease.

...JT 2 1/2 CUPS/625 ML)

...kage fresh or frozen cranberries
...er, cut into quarters
...uarters
...
...opped fresh coriander
1/4 teaspoon (1 mL) ground cumin

Put all ingredients in a food processor. Process until the mixture is coarsely chopped.
Store in a non-metal bowl in refrigerator overnight to allow flavours to blend.

PER 1/4-CUP (50-ML) SERVING NUTRITIONAL INFORMATION: Calories: 75,
Protein: less than 1 g, Fat: less than 1 g, Saturated Fat: g, Carbohydrate: 19 g,
Dietary Fibre: 2 g

apple cheese quesadillas

A perfect breakfast dish. Double, triple or quadruple this recipe: everyone will want one. It's also a change-of-pace way to get in the apple's flavonoids along with the phytocompounds from whole wheat.

MAKES 1 SERVING

1 8-inch (20-cm) flour tortilla (preferably whole wheat)

1 teaspoon (5 mL) honey mustard

1/2 cup (125 mL) shredded light cheddar cheese

1/2 apple, cored and sliced

Spray tortilla with vegetable oil cooking spray. Place tortilla sprayed side down in a large nonstick skillet. Spread honey mustard on one half of the tortilla. Spread 1/4 cup (50 mL) cheese over the mustard. Arrange apple slices on the cheese, overlapping them. Top with remaining cheese. Fold other half of tortilla over and press firmly to spread filling evenly to edges. Place skillet over medium-high heat; cook for 3 to 4 minutes or until golden on bottom. Carefully turn quesadilla over and cook another 3 to 4 minutes or until golden.

PER SERVING NUTRITIONAL INFORMATION: Calories: 229, Protein: 14 g, Fat: 7 g, Saturated Fat: 3 g, Carbohydrate: 34 g, Dietary Fibre: 4 g

salmon kebobs with mango-papaya salsa

A dish that presents with pizzazz and top-notch nutrition.

MAKES 4 SERVINGS

SALSA

1 cup (250 mL) diced mango

1 cup (250 mL) diced papaya

1/2 cup (125 mL) diced red pepper

3 tablespoons (45 mL) finely chopped red onion

1 jalapeño pepper, seeded and finely chopped (optional)

3 tablespoons (45 mL) chopped fresh coriander

2 tablespoons (25 mL) fresh lime juice

2 teaspoons (10 mL) extra virgin olive oil

Salt, to taste

KEBOBS

1 teaspoon (5 mL) fresh lime juice

1 teaspoon (5 mL) extra virgin olive oil

2 red peppers, cut into 1-inch (2.5-cm) pieces

1/2 large sweet onion, cut in half lengthwise and separated into layers

1 pound (500 g) salmon, cut into 1-inch (2.5-cm) cubes

Soak 8 small or 4 large wooden skewers in water for 30 minutes (or use metal skewers). Preheat grill or broiler.

To make salsa, in a medium bowl, gently toss together mango, papaya, red pepper, onion, jalapeño pepper, if using, coriander, lime juice and olive oil. Season with salt. Set aside, or refrigerate if making ahead of time.

To make kebobs, in a small bowl, mix together lime juice and olive oil. Thread kebob ingredients on skewers, starting with red pepper followed by onion, salmon, red pepper and onion; repeat with remaining ingredients and skewers. Brush kebobs with lime juice mixture.

Grill kebobs for about 5 minutes on each side, depending on desired doneness. Serve immediately with salsa on the side.

PER SERVING NUTRITIONAL INFORMATION: Calories: 278, Protein: 24 g, Fat: 11 g, Saturated Fat: 2 g, Carbohydrate: 21 g, Dietary Fibre: 4 g

lemon chicken with dried figs

Originally the tree in the Garden of Eden was thought to be a fig tree. It was much later that legend changed it to an apple tree. Once you taste this recipe you'll know of Adam's temptations! And although figs have been around for a long time, scientists are just beginning to assess their phytopower. Keep in mind that they're a super fibre source.

MAKES 6 SERVINGS

6 skinless boneless chicken breasts

4 teaspoons (20 mL) extra virgin olive oil

1 cup (250 mL) chopped onions

2 cloves garlic, minced

1 cup (250 mL) slivered dried figs

1 cup (250 mL) defatted chicken broth

1/2 cup (125 mL) + 3 tablespoons (45 mL) chopped fresh coriander

2 tablespoons (25 mL) fresh lemon juice

Salt and freshly ground pepper, to taste

Preheat oven to 350°F (180°C). Prepare a baking dish large enough to hold the chicken in one layer by spraying with vegetable oil cooking spray.

Place chicken between sheets of wax paper and gently pound to flatten slightly.

Heat 2 teaspoons (10 mL) of the olive oil in a large skillet over medium-high heat. Add chicken and sauté until brown, about 5 minutes on each side. Remove from pan and place in baking dish; keep covered.

Add remaining 2 teaspoons (10 mL) olive oil to skillet; add onions and garlic. Reduce heat to medium and sauté until onions are soft, about 10 minutes. Add figs, broth, 1/2 cup (125 mL) of the coriander and the lemon juice; bring to a boil. Reduce heat and simmer, stirring occasionally, until figs are quite soft, about 15 minutes. Season with salt and pepper.

Spoon fig sauce over chicken breasts; cover baking dish and bake for 15 minutes or until chicken is cooked through. Serve garnished with remaining chopped coriander.

PER SERVING NUTRITIONAL INFORMATION: Calories: 303, Protein: 36 g, Fat: 9 g, Saturated Fat: 2 g, Carbohydrate: 20 g, Dietary Fibre: 4 g

sautéed maple apple slices

A quick sauté and you've got the taste of apple pie minus all the work and the fat. And lots of flavonoids and fibre, to boot. Serve over vanilla frozen yogurt.

MAKES 4 SERVINGS

2 tablespoons (25 mL) apple juice

1 teaspoon (5 mL) cornstarch

3 Golden Delicious apples

2 teaspoons (10 mL) fresh lemon juice

1 tablespoon (15 mL) soft margarine

3 tablespoons (45 mL) maple syrup

Cinnamon, for garnish

In a small bowl, blend apple juice and cornstarch. Set aside.

Peel and core apples and cut into 1/4-inch (5-mm) thick slices. Toss with lemon juice.

In a large skillet, melt margarine over medium-high heat; add apple slices and sauté about 5 minutes or until tender. Stir in maple syrup and continue to sauté for 2 minutes. Stir apple juice mixture; pour over apples. Continue to cook, stirring, until sauce is thickened and transparent. Serve sprinkled with cinnamon.

PER SERVING NUTRITIONAL INFORMATION (WITHOUT FROZEN YOGURT):
Calories: 115, Protein: less than 1 g, Fat: 3 g, Saturated Fat: 1 g, Carbohydrate: 23 g, Dietary Fibre: 2 g

honey-lime fruit salad

The honey-lime dressing is delicious on any combination of fresh fruit.

MAKES 6 SERVINGS

2/3 cup (150 mL) low-fat plain yogurt

1/4 cup (50 mL) honey

3 tablespoons (45 mL) fresh lime juice

2 tablespoons (25 mL) chopped fresh mint

1 teaspoon (5 mL) grated lime zest

6 cups (1.5 L) diced fresh fruit (such as cantaloupe, strawberries, papaya, mango)

In a small bowl whisk yogurt, honey, lime juice, mint and lime zest; set aside.

Just before serving, toss fruit with dressing. Dress only as much fruit as you are serving.

PER SERVING NUTRITIONAL INFORMATION: Calories: 112, Protein: 3 g, Fat: 1 g, Saturated Fat: less than 1 g, Carbohydrate: 27 g, Dietary Fibre: 2 g

wild blueberry and apple muesli

More and more research is linking blueberries to protection from cognitive decline. What a wonderful way to keep your mind sharp!

MAKES 2 TO 3 SERVINGS

1 medium apple, cored and coarsely grated

1 cup (250 mL) fresh or frozen wild blueberries

2/3 cup (150 mL) large-flake oats

1/2 cup (125 mL) plain low-fat yogurt

2 tablespoons (25 mL) toasted sliced almonds

2 tablespoons (25 mL) honey or equivalent low-calorie sweetener

1 tablespoon (15 mL) fresh lemon juice

In a medium bowl, combine apple, blueberries, oats, yogurt, almonds, honey and lemon juice. Stir to mix. Cover and refrigerate at least 1 hour or overnight. Adjust sweetening, if desired.

PER 3-SERVINGS NUTRITIONAL INFORMATION: Calories: 213, Protein: 6 g, Fat: 3 g, Saturated Fat: less than 1 g, Carbohydrate: 41 g, Dietary Fibre: 5 g

fresh strawberries with balsamic vinegar

So simple, yet so good. Strawberries are one of the top scorers when it comes to the ORAC test, which measures antioxidant power. If you have a top-quality aged balsamic vinegar, just a few drops will do the trick. For a variation, serve these berries over vanilla frozen yogurt or ice cream.

MAKES 4 SERVINGS

3 cups fresh strawberries, sliced
2 tablespoons (25 mL) balsamic vinegar
Sugar, to taste

Toss strawberries with balsamic vinegar. Season with sugar, if necessary, and serve.

PER SERVING NUTRITIONAL INFORMATION: Calories: 32, Protein: 1 g, Fat: less than 1 g, Saturated Fat: less than 1 g, Carbohydrate: 8 g, Dietary Fibre: 2 g

roasted amaretto peaches

Peaches are packed with beta-ionone, a cancer-fighting compound. These ones are also packed with a delicious taste!

MAKES 4 SERVINGS

2 tablespoons (25 mL) brown sugar
1 tablespoon (15 mL) soft margarine, melted
1 tablespoon (15 mL) amaretto liqueur
4 medium peaches, peeled, pitted and cut into 1/3-inch (8-mm) slices

Preheat oven to 425°F (230°C).

In a medium bowl, mix together sugar, melted margarine and amaretto. Add peach slices and toss to coat. Place peaches in a single layer in an 8-inch (2-L) square shallow baking pan. Bake for 25 minutes or until peaches are tender.

PER SERVING NUTRITIONAL INFORMATION: Calories: 86, Protein: 1 g, Fat: 3 g, Saturated Fat: 1 g, Carbohydrate: 16 g, Dietary Fibre: 2 g

very berry bread pudding

Evaporated 2% milk provides the richness in this bread pudding without all the fat of cream. Besides protecting the brain from cognitive decline, berries are packed with antioxidants having heart-healthy and anti-cancer effects.

MAKES 8 TO 10 SERVINGS

4 cups (1 L) 1/2-inch (1-cm) cubes of day-old bread

4 large eggs

2 egg whites

1 (385-mL) can evaporated 2% milk

3/4 cup (175 mL) sugar

2 tablespoons (25 mL) rum

2 teaspoons (10 mL) vanilla extract

1/2 teaspoon (2 mL) salt

3/4 cup (175 mL) fresh or frozen raspberries

3/4 cup (175 mL) fresh or frozen blueberries

Preheat oven to 350°F (180°C). Prepare an 8-cup (2-L) baking dish by spraying with vegetable oil cooking spray.

Put bread cubes in baking dish. In a large bowl, beat together eggs, egg whites, evaporated milk, sugar, rum, vanilla and salt until well blended. Add berries to bread cubes and stir to mix. Pour egg mixture over bread cubes and stir until bread is well coated and berries are evenly dispersed.

Bake for 60 to 65 minutes or until a knife inserted in centre comes out clean. Serve warm or cold.

PER 10-SERVINGS NUTRITIONAL INFORMATION: Calories: 170, Protein: 8 g, Fat: 3 g, Saturated Fat: 1 g, Carbohydrate: 28 g, Dietary Fibre: 1 g

vegetables

... provide a broad defense to the
ills that plague us

What could be more enticing than a bounty of vegetables—all the colours of the rainbow combined with an array of sensual and luscious flavours? What could be better tasting than a sliced summer tomato strewn with fresh fragrant basil and drizzled with a fruity olive oil? And what could be better for you than the cornucopia of phytochemical offerings that these foods provide?

Although research on phytochemicals is now being carried out on all plant foods, many of the first reports to catch the public's eye centred on vegetables. It was at first thought that colourful veggies were much more beneficial than their paler counterparts. There is some scientific backing for this thinking—yes, dark salad greens nutritionally outrank iceberg lettuce by leaps and bounds—yet studies show that phytochemicals are found in vegetables and fruits of all colours.

Intense colour, provided by a range of pigments such as carotenoids and anthocyanins, is certainly one way to identify phyto-rich foods. And eating an assortment of colours is a sure route to consuming a diversity of disease-fighting compounds. But don't just stick to those being touted in the media. Fruits and vegetables grown from seeds that have not been hybridized (a relatively modern technique in which grafting is used to produce hardier plants that are more disease resistant or that yield more uniform fruit) include purple carrots and yellow tomatoes. You might suspect that these are new hybrids, but they are in fact "heirloom" vegetables—part of the variety that nature used to offer and that are now making a comeback. Keep in mind that all varieties don't provide the same nutritional perks; one variety of carrot or tomato, say, is not nutritionally identical to another, so eating different kinds of each vegetable helps you to reap the most health benefits.

And just how packed these foods are with assorted phytochemicals is only now coming to light. The list of phytochemical compounds is growing at a frenzied pace. As each is identified, it's often assumed that that single compound alone is the active ingredient responsible for protection against disease. For example, scientists are investigating the action of lycopene, the red pigment in tomatoes, for its possible anti-cancer action. But contained in the same tomato is an assortment of compounds called isoprenoids, also having potent cancer-fighting qualities. It is tempting to trumpet lycopene, but the effects of isoprenoids, fibre and other nutrients need to be considered as well.

There's no question that vegetables are filled with compounds that have medicinal properties. For years, people taking medications such as warfarin, a blood thinner, have been counselled to monitor the dark leafy green vegetables they consume because of possible interactions. (Green vegetables may counter the blood-thinning properties of some medications. If varying amounts of these veggies are eaten from day to day, it can be difficult to determine the dosage of blood thinners required.) There has also been concern about possible interactions between the flavonoids contained in grapefruit juice and a long list of cholesterol-lowering and blood pressure medications.

But science is now demonstrating that it is the wealth of phytochemical compounds—not just one or two—contained in fruits and vegetables that offers enormous potential to fight many of the ills that plague us in North America. Hundreds of studies have looked into the connection between consuming fruits and vegetables and the rate of cancer—and the majority have shown protective effects. All indications are that regularly eating fruits and vegetables helps to prevent and to fight lung, colon, breast, cervical, esophageal, oral cavity, stomach, bladder, pancreatic and ovarian cancer. A review of 156 studies found that in 128 of them, people who didn't eat much in the way of fruits and vegetables had *twice the risk of developing cancer* compared with those who some would call "rabbit food eaters."

DASH your way to better health

There's no doubt that eating a variety of fruits and vegetables provides a host of health benefits. But with the U.S.-based DASH trial, scientists are beginning to come up with definitive advantages to certain eating patterns. DASH, an acronym for Dietary Approaches to Stop Hypertension, is a clinical study supported by the National Institutes of Health that was designed to test the effects of dietary patterns on blood pressure. The first stage of the DASH program enrolled more than 450 subjects, of which 133 had Stage I hypertension—blood pressure readings that were slightly elevated—but were not taking any medication for it. About half the participants were women and 60 percent were African-Americans, who develop hypertension earlier and more often than non-African-Americans.

First a little blood pressure primer. Blood pressure is the force of blood against the artery walls. It's measured in millimetres of mercury (mm Hg), and two readings are taken—systolic pressure (as the heart beats) over diastolic pressure (as the heart relaxes between beats). Both numbers are important gauges of disease risk. High blood pressure increases the risk of heart and kidney disease as well as stroke.

The investigation compared the effects on blood pressure of three diets: a control diet similar in nutrients to what many Americans consume; a diet high in fruits and vegetables; and a "combination" diet low in saturated and total fat and high in fruits, vegetables and low-fat dairy foods. Both test diets also included whole grains, poultry, fish and nuts.

On the fruits-and-vegetables diet and the combination diet, the subjects were to consume eight to ten servings of fruits and vegetables daily—that amounts to twice the average U.S. consumption. The combination diet also had two to three daily servings of primarily low-fat dairy foods—also about twice the dairy servings Americans currently eat. None of the three test diets were low-sodium but they did include slightly less sodium than the average diet. None of them was vegetarian or used specialty foods containing fat substitutes. And all the diets included typical fresh, frozen, canned and dried foods.

After eight weeks, the combination diet produced the largest drops in blood pressures. Overall, it lowered blood pressure by an average of 5.5 mm Hg for systolic and an average of 3.0 mm Hg for diastolic. For those with hypertension, the effect was much greater: the combination diet reduced their blood pressure by an average of 11.4 mm Hg for systolic and an average of 5.5 mm Hg for diastolic. Those on the fruits-and-vegetables diet also experienced a lowering of blood pressure—an average drop of 2.8 mm Hg for systolic and 1.1 mm Hg for diastolic.

The researchers also found that the reductions in blood pressure happened within just two weeks of starting on the eating programs—a pretty fast response—and were maintained throughout the test period. Lowered blood pressure could be seen right across the board—in men and women, and in all races. The researchers believe the combination diet can help prevent high blood pressure and may be an alternative to mild drug therapy in persons with Stage I hypertension. (They did stress, though, that patients should not stop taking blood pressure medication without first consulting their physician.)

Although the DASH study evaluated dietary patterns, not specific nutrients, the benefits of some nutrients do stand out. The fruits and vegetables provide plenty of potassium, a mineral that helps to regulate blood pressure. Their higher magnesium and fibre also aid blood pressure control. And then there's an assortment of phytochemicals, some of which science hasn't even begun to identify. In the combination diet, the added number of servings boosted calcium and potassium intakes, both nutrients that assist blood pressure control.

After the first stage of the research, the investigators estimated that if Americans were to follow the DASH diet—the combination diet—and experienced drops in blood pressure similar to those of the study participants, there would be about 15 percent less coronary heart disease and 27 percent fewer strokes in the U.S.

A later analysis of the DASH data evaluated the levels of homocysteine in the blood. High levels of homocysteine are linked to an increased risk of heart disease and stroke. The combination diet that was low in saturated and total fat and high in fruits, vegetables and low-fat dairy foods scored the best, significantly lowering homocysteine readings. The fruit-and-vegetable diet scored well but came in second. Both diets were also linked to higher levels in the blood of the B vitamin folate (also known as folic acid), a nutrient associated with reducing homocysteine.

The first stage of the DASH trial found that blood pressure could be reduced without lowering the amount of sodium in the diet, but the researchers wanted to see the effect of the combination diet together with less sodium being consumed. In the next stage of investigation, the DASH-Sodium study, 412 people ate either a typical U.S. diet (the control diet) or the DASH diet, low in saturated fat, cholesterol and total fat and with an emphasis on fruits, vegetables and low-fat dairy products. The DASH diet contains less red meat and fewer sweets and sugar-containing drinks than the typical American diet.

Participants in the DASH-Sodium study were each fed three different diets, each for 30 days. The amount of sodium varied in the 30-day periods—the first contained the average amount of sodium that Americans eat, the second contained an amount of sodium near the upper limit that's currently recommended by the National High Blood Pressure Education Program in the U.S., and the third contained a lower intake of 1500 milligrams—the equivalent of 2/3 teaspoon of table salt—per day.

At the start of the study, participants had normal to slightly elevated blood pressure, with 41 percent of those being elevated enough to classify as having high blood pressure. At the end of the study it was found that the DASH diet lowered blood pressure at each of the three levels of sodium intake. In addition, the lower sodium intakes resulted in lower blood pressures for both those on the typical diet and the DASH diet. And the findings applied right across the board—to men, women, African-Americans, whites and those with and without high blood pressure. Those on a lower-sodium diet—whether control or DASH—also had fewer headaches. (For low-sodium tips, see "DASHing with Less Salt," page 207.)

there's no place like the greengrocer's

All the research currently suggests that there is no replacement for vegetables—or, for that matter, fruits, whole grains, nuts, seeds or any plant foods. The following is what we know so far about the phytopower of various vegetables. Keep in mind that phytochemical research is in its infancy, so if a particular food doesn't seem chock full of phytochemicals, don't drop it from your menu. It's just possible that its mix of defenders against disease hasn't yet been revealed. And don't focus on one star food either. Varied combinations of vegetables may provide a broader defence. Variety is the spice of life and it may also be the route to a healthier one.

garlic and other members of the allium family

Can a clove of garlic a day keep the doctor away? Ancient herbalists thought so and often prescribed it to ward off an assortment of evils ranging from vampires to the common cold. Thousand of years later, its health benefits are again being recognized by modern medicine.

Allium vegetables are an example of how colour is not always a factor in disease prevention. Members of the allium family include garlic, leeks, onions, scallions, shallots and chives—all pale in colour. But among their purported enemies are some forms of cancer, high blood pressure and elevated blood cholesterol.

In 1989, in one of the early studies on allium vegetables, involving 1,600 people in China, it was reported that those who consumed the highest amounts experienced only 40 percent of the risk of stomach cancer of those who ate the least. The protective effects were seen for the whole family, and were not restricted to age or gender. Scientists have since concentrated more on the powerful effects of the "stinking rose," as garlic is sometimes called. Dozens of investigations have looked just at the garlic-cancer connection. A review of some of these studies, published in the *Journal of Nutrition* in 2001, found that a high intake of raw or cooked garlic, or both, is linked to protection against stomach and colorectal cancer. Five studies of garlic supplements did not show any link. (And because they may have a range of effects, garlic supplements can interact with medications.)

One of the ways garlic may protect against stomach cancer is through its antibacterial effect, particularly against the bacterium *H. pylori*, now thought to be a major cause of stomach ulcers. *H. pylori* has also been implicated in the development of gastric cancer. Wipe out the offensive bacteria and a reduced cancer risk may follow.

But garlic is not just a one-trick wonder. It contains many other sulfur compounds that perform disease-fighting actions. And if that's not enough, garlic also contains a different class of phytochemicals. Garlic is rich in the flavonol kaempferol, which may detoxify cancer-causing compounds. And as scientists discover more compounds in garlic, they're beginning to examine their effects, such as protection against breast cancer.

Garlic also gives new meaning to "the way to a man's heart is through his stomach." This bulb not only seems to provide benefits for the stomach but appears to be a tasty part of a heart-healthy diet as well. It's been linked to lowering blood pressure, decreasing the formation of blood clots and lowering blood cholesterol levels. Various components of garlic have also been shown to protect cholesterol from being oxidized, making it less likely to be deposited in the arteries.

If you've followed garlic's reputation over the years as various studies are published, you likely remember a slew of contradictory results. One problem with evaluating garlic's effects is that how garlic works depends very much on how it is prepared or which of its numerous phytochemicals have been activated. Japanese researchers suggest that the health benefits of garlic likely arise from a wide variety of bioactive components, possibly working synergistically. Because of the complex chemistry of garlic, it's possible that various ways of processing it can yield very different products. Garlic may show up at the examining table dressed as dehydrated garlic powder, garlic oil or aged garlic extract, all having different properties. Even simple changes in how you prepare garlic at home may affect its compounds. Maryland scientists examined the effect of how garlic is prepared on the amount of compounds it contains that fight breast cancer tumours. Heating garlic immediately after crushing it knocked out that particular anti-cancer effect, but when the crushed garlic was allowed to stand for ten minutes before microwaving, the anticarcinogenic activity was preserved.

That garlic breath drives away vampires is one thing, but the fact that it can be offensive to the people around us is quite another. Japanese researchers have come up with some promising findings that might allow us to reap the health benefits of garlic without the stinky side effects, garlicky breath and body odour. Foods that reduced the odours produced by garlic included mushrooms and various raw fruits and vegetables —yet another reason to eat your fruits and veggies. For one particular odour of garlic —diallyl disulfide—kiwifruit, spinach, parsley, basil, mushrooms, cow's milk and boiled rice worked the best. Choose them as a regular garlic chaser.

And while you're incorporating more garlic into your menus, don't forget about the other allium members. Onions have no shortage of beneficial sulfur compounds. Just cut into one—as your eyes begin to water, you'll get the picture. They're also chock full of heart-healthy flavonoids, as are other allium vegetables. (For more on flavonoids, see Tea, page 222.) All alliums are a super source of vitamin C. And garlic isn't top dog in the family when it comes to folate. Leeks, which are an excellent source of folate, take that honour. Onions aren't as rich in folate but they're still a source.

The good news about preparing onions is that sautéing doesn't lower the content of flavonoids or other compounds. Caramelized onions are just more proof that healthy eating can be fabulous tasting. Sweet varieties, such as red onions, are higher in the phytochemical anthocyanin, which is responsible for the red/purple colour. Enjoy them all—Vidalia, red, Spanish—and don't use them just as a seasoning, but elevate their status. Make onions a side dish. Invite other allium members to dinner too. Sprinkle chopped chives atop your mashed potatoes or toss them in salads. Include leeks in your soup or grill them on the barbecue.

garlic in oil: what's the stink about?

While garlic and oil, especially a wonderfully fruity olive oil, can be a marriage made in heaven, there can be trouble in paradise—very serious trouble indeed. When garlic, whether whole, chopped or minced, is mixed with oil and stored at room temperature or in the refrigerator for too long, it can be a source of a potentially fatal foodborne illness called botulism.

Botulism spores—*Clostridium botulinum*—are common in nature and aren't harmful to anyone over the age of one. They can cause illness only when they release their deadly toxins, and this occurs only when they're not in the presence of oxygen— such as when garlic, which contains botulism spores, is submerged in oil and left at room temperature. Garlic-oil combos became trendy when olive oil increased in popularity. Homemade flavoured oils were the rage before the potential for illness was identified.

Garlic-in-oil mixtures that are contaminated do not taste, smell or look spoiled. Do not even taste a product if you suspect a problem, because even a small dose of the toxin can be fatal.

Among the symptoms of botulism poisoning are dizziness, blurred or double vision, difficulty in swallowing, breathing and speaking, and a progressive paralysis.

These days, commercial products contain preservatives that prevent the growth of botulism spores. They didn't always, and outbreaks of botulism did occur. Be sure to check the label of any commercially prepared garlic-in-oil product for the presence of salts or acids, which are preservatives that make it safe.

Health Canada offers these tips if you make garlic-in-oil combos at home:

- Prepare garlic in oil fresh, and use it immediately.
- It's best to throw away any leftover garlic in oil. If you decide to store it, refrigerate it right away and use it within a week.
- Never store garlic in oil at room temperature. Throw away any that has been in the refrigerator for more than a week.

brassica a.k.a. crucifers

Brassica is the botanical name for an illustrious group of vegetables. Phytochemically speaking, cruciferous vegetables, as they're also known, are a powerful family containing a long list of extremely potent disease-preventing compounds. When you consider what a large family *Brassica* is, you can see that a variety of tastes awaits you: among the members are arugula, bok choy, broccoli, Brussels sprouts, assorted cabbages including Chinese, green, red and Savoy, cauliflower, collards, horseradish, kale, kohlrabi, mizuna (a type of lettuce), mustard greens, radish, rapini, rutabaga, turnips and watercress. Even wasabi, the hot Japanese horseradish, belongs to this clan.

And what a clan it is. These vegetables provide a cornucopia of phytonutrients and phytochemicals that may play a beneficial role in a variety of diseases. But where the family has really made its name is in the area of cancer prevention. As far back as 1982, the Committee on Diet, Nutrition and Cancer of the U.S. National Research Council conducted a comprehensive evaluation of brassicas, noting their outstanding anti-cancer action. Since then, hundreds of studies all over the world have connected the consumption of these vegetables with a decreased risk of a wide range of cancers, from breast, colon, thyroid, esophageal and kidney to a type of blood cancer known as multiple myeloma.

It seems that individual crucifers work in different ways, depending on which phytochemicals each contains. The parent compounds, called glucosinolates, are found in all crucifers and are somewhat responsible for their characteristic taste. But as they are different plants, each member of the family is metabolized differently, yielding an assortment of anti-cancer substances that work in diverse ways. For example, isothiocyanates may stop tumours from forming in the first place. Some isothiocyanates may stimulate enzymes in the body that fight cancer cells and others still may cause cancer cell apoptosis—somewhat like cancer cells committing suicide. Others substances produced from glucosinolates, called indoles, may also cause cancer cell death but protect against cancer-causing toxic substances, too. Researchers have found that indoles may protect against the effect of pesticides on breast cancer development. As well, some indoles may work in the liver to detoxify harmful substances. Others may affect estrogen metabolism, thereby reducing the risk of breast cancer. And many of these compounds also act as antioxidants—the list of possible actions seems endless.

Getting anything close to the number or range of phytochemicals found in this family in a pill form is impossible. Research is showing that eating a variety of brassicas, rather than a supplement, may provide a more varied arsenal of weapons against disease. For example, watercress contains high concentrations of the phytochemical phenethyl isothiocyanate, which in animal studies appears to be particularly effective at detoxifying a cancer-causing compound from tobacco. Broccoli, on the other hand, contains more than 100 of these isothiocyanates, some in greater amounts than others. One of them, sulforaphane, may offer a two-pronged protection against *H. pylori*, the bacterium responsible for many stomach ulcers but also linked to an increased risk of stomach cancer. Brassicas contain plenty of other phytochemicals as well, among them flavonoids and carotenoids.

As for the more traditional nutrients, like vitamins and minerals, each crucifer has impressive credentials. Broccoli and Brussels sprouts supply beta carotene, vitamins C and B-6, potassium and plenty of fibre. They're also super sources, along with cabbage and cauliflower, of the B vitamin folate. Green cabbage is one of the best of the bunch for its concentration of a powerful anti-cancer flavonol.

arugula

Known as rocket, rucola or arugula, this peppery green is bursting with nutrition. Besides being a member of the brassica clan and therefore affording the protection this family provides, it's packed with folate and carotenoids such as beta carotene and zeaxanthin. Add in the vitamin C and minerals—among them calcium and iron—it contains and it doesn't get much better for a vegetable often used as a salad green. Even if you're not familiar with it, if you eat commercial mesclun or spring mixes, arugula is often one of the greens in the mix.

Not everyone is an arugula fan. Its peppery and sometimes slightly bitter taste can have people turning up their noses. But learning to love it is definitely a worthwhile endeavour. Tasting small amounts over time can allow the palate to become used to the stronger flavours. Toss a few leaves into salads for a peppery bite, and gradually increase the amount. It's also delicious tossed with a fruity olive oil, sautéed with garlic and served with pasta and freshly grated Parmesan cheese. Or use it to top a pizza right after it has been taken out of the oven. Use arugula leaves instead of paler greens like lettuce to garnish a sandwich (see Chicken, Olive and Arugula Sandwiches, page 220).

Nowadays arugula can be found at the greengrocer and in supermarket produce sections. Choose bunches that are fresh looking. As arugula tends to be somewhat pricier than other salad greens, discarding lots of leaves from a wilted bunch can make it even more expensive. Arugula can be sandy, so give it a good wash. A salad spinner makes an easy job of washing fruits and vegetables.

greens

Beet greens, dandelion, mustard greens, endive, kale, Swiss chard and spinach are just a few of the many members of this stellar group. Some belong to other families but merit inclusion here because of looks—who says appearance doesn't matter? When it comes to their nutritional perks, they contain a virtual who's who of important vitamins. For example, greens are a super source of folate, which is the centre of much promising research. This B vitamin has been shown to offer protection against certain cancers, heart disease and stroke, as well as reduce the risk of such birth defects as spina bifida. They're also chock full of other B vitamins, along with vitamins E and C, both of which have been shown to have antioxidant action. As for fibre, they're a top contributor: just a cup of cooked spinach provides more than 5 grams. They're no slouch in the mineral department either, providing substantial amounts of potassium, iron and calcium.

Over the past few years, beta carotene, the yellowish-orange pigment found in such produce as carrots and mangoes but also in these leafy greens, has been a starring member of the carotenoid family. But with all the research on carotenoids currently under way, beta carotene will be forced to share the nutritional spotlight. Among the other powerful carotenoids to keep your eyes on and sink your teeth into are lutein and zeaxanthin. These two phytochemicals, found in dark leafy greens, appear to play important roles in maintaining optimal vision. Lutein is also being investigated for its protective role in certain cancers, like that of the colon, with some promising results so far.

The leading cause of blindness in the elderly is macular degeneration. The macula is the light-sensitive layer of tissue in the central part of the retina; its health is important for good central vision. In macular degeneration, the cells of the macula gradually die, leading to a progressive loss of central vision and an inability to see detail. Oxidative damage, caused by, among other things, smoking and exposure to light, is thought to increase the likelihood of developing this condition. As we get older and are exposed to more light through the years, there's a greater risk. These cases are referred to as age-related macular degeneration. Diet—including a low intake of certain carotenoids—is linked to the deterioration of the macula. Scientists have been testing their theories that antioxidants, including various vitamins and carotenoids, may counter the oxidative damage.

One of the first investigations, published in 1994 in the *Journal of the American Medical Association*, compared more than 350 subjects aged 55 to 80 who had recently been diagnosed with macular degeneration with a group with other eye diseases. A higher dietary intake of carotenoids was shown to be associated with a lower risk for macular problems. In fact, those with the highest intake of these plant pigments had the lowest risk, with lutein and zeaxanthin being particularly protective. The scientists also found that those who regularly consumed vegetables like spinach or collard greens had the lowest incidence of these problems.

Other studies show that subjects with high amounts of these two carotenoids in the blood supply around their macula are the least likely to suffer these degenerative changes. Further research has shown that produce rich in lutein and zeaxanthin may also minimize the risk of developing cataracts. Our mothers were right when they told us to eat our carrots —the body converts their beta carotene to vitamin A, which helps us to see at night. But now it's time to add dark leafy greens to the list of vegetables that promote good vision.

Researchers from the University of Utah Medical School found that people who consumed the highest amounts of lutein-rich foods were 17 percent less likely to develop colon cancer than those who ate the least. Lutein research even points to benefits in keeping arteries clear. For Canadians, inadequate lutein intake is a real concern. A McGill University study assessed 1,721 subjects and found that most were consuming inadequate amounts.

As for making up the shortfall by taking supplements, the research doesn't yet support any benefits. Lutein may be the disease-fighting component in these foods, but there may also be an undiscovered compound or mix of substances at work. In spite of the lack of research on lutein supplements, and in spite of some scientists' concern about their use, they are aggressively promoted to optometrists and ophthalmologists, and manufacturers of vitamin and mineral supplements are adding lutein to their formulations—and with no solid scientific evidence to back them up. High levels of lutein in the blood may simply be an indicator only of how much in the way of lutein-rich food is being consumed and not necessarily a measure of the actual protective compounds. Besides the possible adverse effects of taking these supplements (see page 8), there is also a question of how well the lutein in supplement form is absorbed. Until we have conclusive answers, it seems like a good idea to make like Popeye and eat your spinach—and kale, beet greens and all the rest.

tomatoes

The tomato's Italian name, *pomodoro*, provides a hint of its past. *Pomodoro*, meaning golden apple, suggests that tomatoes in ancient Rome were more commonly yellow than today's ubiquitous red. The phytochemical responsible for this familiar red, lycopene, started making the news in 1995, when Harvard researchers examined the food intake and risk of prostate cancer in almost 48,000 men in the Health Professionals Follow-up Study. The strongest protection appeared to come from eating tomatoes, tomato sauce, tomato juice and pizza—all rich sources of lycopene. (Interestingly, lycopene is better absorbed into the bloodstream from cooked or processed tomatoes than from raw tomatoes.) Researchers continued to track these men for years, and a follow-up in the *Journal of the National Cancer Institute* in March 2002 reported similar findings. A 1999 review of 72 studies on tomatoes, tomato-based products and levels of lycopene in the blood, also from Harvard, found that 57 reported a lower risk of various cancers in those who ate more tomatoes and tomato products.

Lycopene's action as an antioxidant doesn't just appear to provide a weapon against cancer. Dr. Venket Rao and colleagues, at the University of Toronto, showed that lycopene prevents LDL oxidation, making it a contributor to the fight against heart disease and stroke. And Finnish researchers found that low blood levels of lycopene in their middle-aged male subjects were associated with a greater likelihood of heart attack or stroke.

Tomatoes, of course, possess many more disease-fighting compounds than just lycopene. Tomato juice has been shown to contain a variety of carotenoids, including beta carotene, phytoene, phytofluene, zeta-carotene, gamma-carotene and neurosporene. Tomatoes also contain compounds that have an anti-clotting action in the blood, which leads to a reduced risk of heart attack and stroke. The good news here is that the anti-coagulant substances are found in the heat-stable gel surrounding tomato seeds, so whether your choice is a sliced tomato on a sandwich or a spicy tomato sauce, you'll reap the benefits, as long as you don't remove the seeds. Raw tomatoes are a super source of vitamin C, another antioxidant, and in potassium content, they rate up there with the top banana.

When selecting tomatoes, choose an assortment of colours and varieties, especially at different times of the year. When winter ones have lacklustre flavour and texture, try oven-drying plum tomatoes to intensify their sweetness (see Oven-Dried Tomatoes, page 94). And to boost their taste and nutritional value, enjoy them with a splash of extra virgin olive oil (see Olive Oil, page 208).

artichokes

For the uninitiated, fresh artichokes can be quite intimidating. If you have ever been pricked by a sharp leaf, you know the risks! But beneath the leaves and inedible, hairy thistle (or choke) lies a delectable reward, the heart, or the bottom as it's sometimes called. Even the leaves, though, can be quite meaty and are a pleasurable treat. It does require a little bit of patience, as you have to peel off each leaf and eat only one at a time, but it's a great exercise for those who eat at too fast a pace!

Artichokes, or rather "globe artichokes," which are the stem and unopened flower of a type of thistle, are not related to the tuberous vegetable known as the Jerusalem artichoke. They've been grown in the Mediterranean region as far back as the Greek and Roman civilizations and have in the more recent past become a popular California crop. Italy is the largest producer of artichokes and is definitely the place to be during the harvesting season if you love artichokes. They're on menus everywhere, with each eatery serving a family specialty.

Artichokes are an excellent source of folate, the B vitamin with a long and growing list of disease-fighting benefits. For women who consume adequate amounts of folate before becoming pregnant, there's a decreased risk of having a baby with neural tube defects such as spina bifida. Folate, together with two other B vitamins, vitamin B-12 and pyridoxine, or B-6, seems to play a major role in keeping arteries in good shape through its effect on lowering homocysteine (an amino acid, one of the building blocks of protein). Elevated levels of homocysteine in the blood have been implicated in a host of ailments, including heart and kidney disease, stroke and Alzheimer's disease. Reduced odds of developing colon cancer and breast cancer for women who consume alcohol is just another of folate's claims to fame. It also plays a role in maintaining healthy blood cells.

Vitamin C, magnesium, iron, potassium and phosphorus are other nutrients supplied by artichokes. And it's a great source of fibre, with more than 6 grams in a medium artichoke.

In ancient times, artichokes were thought to possess many medicinal attributes, among them a diuretic and a detoxifier for the liver. It was also thought to be an aphrodisiac. Science is now providing some of the reasons behind these age-old observations. In animal studies, high doses of artichoke extracts were found to decrease cholesterol synthesis, using the same mechanisms in the body as the cholesterol-lowering pharmaceutical agent statins do. In high doses—well beyond what a person could eat—the extracts were somewhat toxic, another example of how you can get too much of a good thing.

The phytochemicals in artichoke leaves—cynarin, caffeic acid, chlorogenic acid and luteolin—have been found to act as antioxidants. Another compound found in artichokes, a flavonoid known as silymarin, may offer protection against certain types of skin cancer such as basal and squamous cell. American researchers at the University of Colorado Health Sciences Center showed that the compound not only prevented the development of skin cancer cells in animals but in animals with tumours it also inhibited tumour growth. Japanese scientists are finding positive effects of silymarin on colon cancer cells.

Fresh artichokes are available almost all year long. Canned, frozen or marinated in oil and spices and packed in jars are other choices. Fresh ones vary in size from the large ones, over a pound each, to the baby variety that weigh only a couple of ounces. Select a size appropriate to your planned use of them. Large ones can be trimmed and steamed and the centre stuffed with a breadcrumb, herb and Parmesan mixture and then baked. Or they can be stuffed with various grain and vegetable combos. Baby ones are entirely edible and are yummy in salads and pastas or just simply sautéed with a fruity olive oil and garlic.

A word of warning about artichokes. Chemicals in them are not wine friendly. A bite of artichoke followed by a sip of certain wines can ruin the enjoyment of a fine wine.

TOP-SCORING VEGETABLES

ORAC units per 100 g
(about 3 1/2 ounces)

Kale 1,770
Spinach 1,260
Brussels sprouts 980
Broccoli florets 890
Beets 840
Red bell peppers 710
Onions 450
Corn 400
Eggplant 390

---

asparagus

Asparagus has been enjoyed for thousands of years. In fact, Roman treatises detailed instructions for its cultivation. Whether green or white, these stalks are a super source of folate and vitamin C. White and green asparagus are the same plant, but because it is grown shielded from sunlight, white asparagus doesn't manufacture the carotenoid beta carotene, the pigment responsible for the colour of green asparagus. Foods rich in beta carotene—also known as pro-vitamin A, because it turns into vitamin A in the body—are linked to protection against heart disease and certain cancers. Its main role in disease prevention appears to be in its action as an antioxidant.

As for fibre, about eight medium spears contains almost 3 grams, not a paltry amount at all. And contained in this fibre is an indigestible carbohydrate called inulin, a compound thought to provide a number of perks, among them lower blood cholesterol levels. Scientists are investigating the ability of inulin and other similar compounds known as oligosaccharides to decrease colon cancer risk.

In addition, asparagus provides glutathione, a very powerful antioxidant. Glutathione is also manufactured in the body by three amino acids that are easily obtained from food (as we age, it seems our ability to produce the compound may be decreased). Glutathione not only works on its own as an antioxidant but is also a part of various enzymes with potent anti-cancer effects.

For many years, fresh asparagus was a springtime treat, but with our global markets, it's now available almost year-round. Depending on how the asparagus is stored, that's not always a good thing. Look for stalks that are standing in water, ideally cold. Avoid those with tips that appear to be opening or that are wilting. And for even cooking, select spears that are uniform in width. If the spears are already bunched when you purchase them, start cooking the thicker ones first and then add the thin spears. It's a case in which thick and thin simply don't mix. Pencil-thin spears will become limp and unappetizing if overcooked.

Eat asparagus soon after you buy it. To store it at home—for only short periods—stand the stalks in a little water or wrap them in a damp paper towel, and keep them in the fridge. When preparing the vegetable, snap off the tough ends. Although some people prefer the tenderness of peeled asparagus, keep in mind that peeling it results in a loss of nutrients. Asparagus is wonderful steamed, microwaved, stir-fried, roasted and grilled. Boiling asparagus, however, can lead to nutrient losses, since vitamins such as folate are water soluble.

Some people complain about an odour they exude after eating asparagus. A sulfur compound, broken down by some of us, is the culprit. Whether this process occurs and whether you can detect the odour, even how you interpret the smell, depends on your genetic makeup. Almost half of the subjects in a British study described their urine as smelling like rotten cabbage after they ate asparagus. In other research, on Israeli and Chinese subjects, almost all reported on the malodorous consequences of eating the spear, though the Israelis found it to be less offensive. What's interesting about the phenomenon is that it was first noticed after sulfur-containing fertilizers were introduced at the start of the eighteenth century. But whatever the cause, there are no adverse effects associated with the odour.

beets

Nutritionally speaking, the "light" of this root vegetable has been hidden under a bushel far too long. Beets are an excellent source of folate, although they are often left off the list of folate stars. Potassium, vitamin C and fibre—more than 3 grams per cup—are among its other attributes. Beets don't contain many of the recognized phytochemicals, which might help to explain its undervalued stature. But as is the case with the ever-expanding phytochemical counts, if a plant food seems low on disease-fighting compounds, it's likely that the substances simply haven't yet been identified.

Israeli scientists recently identified a brand-new class of dietary antioxidants known as betalains that are found in red beets. These compounds are potent antioxidants in test tubes, even at low concentrations. Just as with any phytochemicals or antioxidants found naturally in plant sources, it's uncertain whether the compounds can be absorbed by the body. However, the latest news from researchers is promising: in a recent study, volunteers who consumed beet juice were able to absorb the betalains. Other research has identified small amounts of other antioxidants in beets. So it appears that it's now time to add beets to the list of antioxidant-rich veggies.

The disease-fighting fibre in beets has also received little attention. In a Japanese study, blood cholesterol levels in rats were reduced when they were fed beet fibre. The scientists speculated that compounds with a cholesterol-lowering ability are produced when fibre passes through the digestive tract and is fermented. Other Japanese scientists found that beet fibres led to a reduction of cholesterol production in the liver, where the waxy compound is made.

Beet fibre also seems to protect the colon against the development of precancerous cells. And for those undergoing radiation therapy, beet fibre may counter one of its more egregious side effects, diarrhea. Although beet-fibre research has been carried out only with rats, it may be worth exploring with humans for that reason alone.

There is one area in which beets can cause some distress. A proportion of people who eat beets are genetically predisposed to producing a red-coloured urine afterwards. For unknowing beet eaters, the sight of their red urine can trigger quite a scare—many a visit to a hospital emergency room has likely come about as a consequence of eating beets. Scientists have long been intrigued by the genetics behind the phenomenon but as of yet have no real answers. One theory is that everybody excretes varying amounts of beet pigments into their urine but that low concentrations are simply not detectable. Others speculate that the differences may be due to varying types of preparation. But whatever the cause, it seems that a lot of scientific investigation has gone into examining something of no real consequence. If you're new to the beet-eating scene, don't lose any sleep over red urine.

Beets, always undervalued for their nutrition, have also been often overlooked as a gourmet option. That's changing, however, as chefs have taken to preparing flavourful offerings such as roasted beet salads combined with goat cheese.

The best way to eat beets is fresh. And the best to buy are found in the late spring and summer, with their greens attached. Beets with their greens are not only the freshest but also the most value, since it is two nutritious veggies in one (see Greens, page 55). To retain the nutrients in the beets, cut the greens off and store them separately in the refrigerator.

When buying beets without the greens, go for firm ones that have their skins intact —with no cuts or bruises. Smaller beets are more tender than larger ones and are often the best choice for using raw in salads. Once you get them home, store beets in plastic bags in the vegetable drawer.

Red sugar beets are the ones available in most supermarkets and greengrocers. Yellow beets, more common in farmers' markets, may or may not contain the newly discovered antioxidants. (However, it may only be a matter of time before scientists discover some stellar attribute linked to yellow beets.) Both are delicious steamed, microwaved, baked or roasted. As with asparagus, the water-soluble B vitamin folate can be lost when boiled. Since beets take quite a while to cook—usually 35 minutes or longer for larger beets—make extra and then slice and store for later use in salads or to preserve as pickles.

Although canned beets are a convenient option and contain similar amounts of fibre to fresh ones, they provide only about half the levels of folate and potassium as their fresh counterparts.

carrots

Carrots were one of the first vegetables found to contain the pigment beta carotene. In fact, carotenoids—the colourful pigments in fruits and vegetables—and carotene are both named after the carrot. Its beta carotene, besides acting as an antioxidant, is also known as pro-vitamin A, meaning that once in the body, it's converted to vitamin A. And vitamin A is important for maintaining healthy night vision.

Carrots are also packed with alpha carotene, a carotenoid overshadowed by its cousin beta. Earlier research incorrectly proclaimed beta carotene as the compound in carrots that seemed to offer protection against lung cancer. After discovering the existence of alpha carotene, researchers awarded it the honour instead—a lesson in research to remember.

Carrots are also a super source of cholesterol-lowering soluble fibre.

mushrooms

Mushrooms have always been a dieter's best friend—they contain hardly any calories, depending on how they're prepared. Added to rice, pastas and grain pilafs, they allowed portions to grow at minimal caloric cost. Never considered nutritional heavyweights, mushrooms are in fact packed with the B vitamin riboflavin and potassium and contain significant amounts of niacin, folate, iron and phosphorus. But as the concept of phytofoods emerges—and research into phytochemicals escalates—mushrooms are now taking their place as a respected player.

Mushrooms have long been revered in Asian cultures as both food and medicine, with more than 50 species said to contain healing properties. Traditionally in these cultures, mushrooms are made into soup or tea or taken as a tonic or elixir. Studies conducted since the 1970s, mostly in Asia, have suggested that mushrooms may aid in the treatment of certain types of cancer, boost the immune system and reduce the risk of coronary heart disease. Shiitake, oyster and enoki mushrooms appear to contain the largest amounts of the active ingredients. Button mushrooms were until recently left out of the research loop. But now, they have been found to suppress an enzyme involved in estrogen metabolism that can increase the risk of breast cancer. The

California study suggested that consuming lots of button mushrooms may be a way to decrease the risk of breast cancer in post-menopausal women.

Dried mushrooms are convenient to have on hand and are super for adding flavour to a variety of dishes. For a meaty flavour, add just a handful of soaked dried mushrooms while cooking a pot of vegetable broth. Or boil a few in some water for an almost instant broth. Just be sure to strain the soaking liquid through a double thickness of cheesecloth before using—otherwise, along with a fabulous mushroom flavour, you'll likely get some sandy grit that's often carried on the dried mushrooms. Add the liquid to casseroles containing rice or barley or to mashed potatoes.

rhubarb

As kids, we used to pull rhubarb stalks from the garden, roll them in sugar and sit and munch. The sweet satisfaction of having picked them ourselves was enough for us to endure the tartness. Because of its sour taste, rhubarb is almost always sweetened, making it a natural for dessert. Often combined with berries, rhubarb makes for wonderful pies, crumbles and compotes. And if something's always on the menu for dessert, it's naturally thought of as a fruit. In fact, rhubarb is a vegetable. But unlike other veggies, the rhubarb's green leaves or tops are toxic and should not be eaten.

Rhubarb has a long history of medicinal use dating back to before the Middle Ages. It's still used as a herbal remedy.

Rhubarb's medicinal appeal in the past likely had to do with its ability to fight off infections. It has been shown to have both antibacterial and anti-fungal effects. It contains such nutrients as vitamin C, calcium, potassium and fibre, and the stalks are rich in phytochemicals.

One of these, the phytochemical galloyl ester, plays an important role in inhibiting cholesterol production. And there's more. Canadian research, from the University of Alberta in Edmonton, found that rhubarb lowered both the total amount of cholesterol in the blood and the harmful LDL cholesterol in people with high initial cholesterol. After one month of not eating any rhubarb and the diet remaining the same otherwise, the cholesterol levels jumped back up.

Rhubarb has also attracted the attention of scientists for its possible protection against cardiovascular disease. Asian research has identified a number of compounds in it with antioxidant activity. And if this isn't enough to make you plant a patch of rhubarb, Korean scientists have isolated three compounds in rhubarb that reduce the stickiness of blood, leading to a lower risk of blood clots.

One concern about rhubarb is its oxalate content. Oxalate is a compound thought to decrease calcium absorption and also boost the risk of kidney stones. The same

University of Alberta researchers who assessed the cholesterol-lowering ability of rhubarb also wanted to determine any drawbacks to increased rhubarb consumption, particularly effects on calcium absorption. In animal studies, they found that rhubarb did not decrease calcium absorption. The question of kidney stones is still one that needs to be answered.

The following are short nutritional profiles of other vegetables. Keep in mind that some may contain phytochemicals we've yet to identify. Remember, phytochemicals are part of all plants' reproductive and defence systems.

Celery
- This member of the same family as carrots, parsley and dill supplies folate and vitamin C along with antioxidant substances. Furanocoumarins, phytochemicals that may reduce the rate of blood clotting, have been found in celery.

Corn
- Folate, thiamine, phosphorus, fibre, lutein and zeaxanthin are among the corn's contributions.

Cucumber
- Unpeeled, this vegetable provides fibre. It's awaiting the uncovering of any major phytochemicals—stay tuned.

Eggplant
- This vegetable supplies the B vitamins folate and thiamine, but in order to obtain its phytochemical anthocyanin, you must eat the skin.

Fennel
- Vitamins C and A, calcium, iron, magnesium, fibre and compounds with antioxidant activity.

Fiddleheads
- Riboflavin, vitamin C and iron.

Green beans
- Folate, vitamins A and C and iron. Also a member of the pulse family.

Iceberg lettuce
- Small amounts of folate and vitamin K.

Jerusalem artichokes
- Thiamine, iron and phosphorus, along with fibre, much of it in the form of inulin, a fuel that helps to maintain healthy cells in the colon.

Jicama

• Vitamin C, potassium, iron and calcium.

Okra

• Folate along with the other B vitamins thiamine and B-6 in addition to vitamin C, magnesium and calcium. Super for its fibre content.

Parsnips

• Terrific for folate, fibre and potassium. Also contains vitamins C and E, magnesium and the phytochemicals furanocoumarins.

Peas

• Vitamin C, folate, niacin, vitamin B-6 and carotenoids along with iron, magnesium, phosphorus and fibre. Also a member of the pulse family.

Peppers

• Vitamin C, folate and iron. Red and orange varieties contain carotenoids. (For hot peppers, see page 206.)

Potatoes

• Vitamin C, thiamine, niacin and iron. Eat the skin to obtain the fibre.

Pumpkin

• Vitamin C, riboflavin, niacin, iron, calcium, fibre and beta carotene.

Romaine lettuce

• Folate, vitamin C, iron and, depending on the colour, beta carotene.

Squash, butternut and Hubbard

• Beta carotene, folate, vitamins C and B-6, magnesium and fibre.

Sweet potatoes

• Beta carotene, vitamins B-6 and C, and fibre.

Water chestnuts

• Plenty of potassium along with vitamins B-6 and riboflavin.

Zucchini

• Vitamin C, folate and lutein.

sprout advisory

Sprouts of all kinds have soared in popularity over the past few years. The standby bean sprout has been joined in the marketplace by a seemingly limitless variety of others, among them alfalfa, broccoli and radish sprouts. But before garnishing your sandwiches or salads with raw sprouts, be aware of the safety concerns.

According to Health Canada, between 1995 and 2001, around the world there were 13 outbreaks of foodborne illnesses linked to sprouts. The largest of these took place in Japan in 1996, when 6,000 people fell ill and 17 died after eating radish sprouts contaminated with *E. coli*. Outbreaks in two American states in 1997 were traced back to bean sprout seeds. In most of these cases of contamination, the illnesses were caused by *E. coli* or *Salmonella* bacteria. *E. coli* infections have been dubbed "hamburger disease" after a number of people in the U.S. became ill after eating undercooked hamburgers. *E. coli* infections can lead to permanent kidney damage requiring dialysis and, in severe cases, cause death.

Canada is not immune to foodborne illness from sprouts. Raw alfalfa sprouts (either alone or part of a sprout mixture) contaminated with *Salmonella* have been linked to outbreaks in British Columbia, Alberta, Ontario and Quebec.

It's believed that contaminated seeds may be the problem. Seeds may become contaminated by animal manure in the field or during storage. Put this together with the conditions required to grow sprouts, which are ideal for the rapid growth of bacteria, and you've got a recipe for food poisoning—especially given that most sprouts are eaten raw and therefore not exposed to the high temperatures needed to kill any bacteria that may be present.

Health Canada is working with sprout producers to come up with solutions to the problem. It points out that the consequences of eating raw sprouts are potentially more serious for anyone at risk for serious illness, such as young children, seniors and people with weak immune systems.

Health Canada advises that if you belong to one of the high-risk groups, you should avoid raw sprouts of any kind, especially alfalfa sprouts. It recommends checking for the presence of sprouts in salads and sandwiches bought in restaurants and delicatessens.

For those who insist on eating sprouts, Health Canada offers these tips:

- Make sure the sprouts you buy are crisp and have buds attached. Avoid dark or musty-smelling sprouts.
- Respect the best-before date. By law this date must be on prepackaged sprouts.
- Refrigerate the sprouts immediately after you get home.
- Reduce the risk of illness significantly by cooking sprouts before eating them.

smart soup strategies

If you're looking for an appetite tamer, nothing is more satisfying than a bowl of soup. Researchers from Pennsylvania State University compared the effect of three meals containing the same number of calories and ingredients on the amount of food eaten later in the day. Having a chicken rice casserole with or without water resulted in the same number of calories being consumed in the study period. But when the water was combined with the casserole ingredients to make a soup, the result was less food being eaten later on.

So if you're looking for some sound waist-management strategies, consider starting off your meal with a hot bowl of soup. Or have a soup packed with veggies to bridge a longer than usual gap between meals. Adding chunky vegetables may also be a wise tactic. According to French research, strained or puréed soups were found to have less of an effect on curbing appetites than those with larger pieces.

Homemade soups and stocks offer other advantages as well—especially when it comes to sodium counts. Many commercial soups are loaded with salt as a substitute for intense flavours. And all too often selections labelled "sodium-reduced" are anything but low in sodium. If you must, use these soups only as a soup "foundation." Adding a selection of items low in salt, to increase the yield of soup, can lead to a lower amount of sodium per serving. For example, simmering a cup of commercial broth with a cup of chopped vegetables results in less sodium per cup serving. It's also a tasty way of boost your vegetable intake.

Homemade soups can send sodium counts plummeting while keeping flavour intact. When making chicken, beef or vegetable broths or stocks, use a variety of ingredients to provide the complexity of taste. The use of minimal salt in the broth will then be less noticeable.

Here are a few tips for your stockpot:

- Rather than purchasing boneless chicken breasts, remove the bones yourself and accumulate them in the freezer for making stock. If you're less skilled with the boning knife, don't worry—leaving a little meat on the bones will add to the taste of your stock. When you've saved an adequate amount of chicken bones, cook up a batch of chicken stock, adding flavour boosters such as carrots, parsnips, celery, onions and fresh herbs. If the taste seems diluted, instead of adding salt, simmer the broth uncovered to reduce it and intensify the flavours. Freeze in various-sized containers, depending on how you plan to use it.
- Making vegetable broths is a terrific way to empty your vegetable bin. Carrots, celery, parsnips, onions, garlic, mushrooms, tomatoes and potatoes, along with such herbs as parsley and dill, are just a few of the many veggies and flavourings that can be simmered together for a rich-tasting broth. Avoid cabbages and other vegetables with strong tastes or aromas. Save the trimmings or odds and ends from different vegetables such as shiitake or portobello mushroom stems in a container in the freezer and add to the stockpot. For a meatier vegetable broth,

add a few dried black Chinese mushrooms reconstituted in boiling water and rinsed to remove any grit. Strain the soaking liquid and then add it to the broth as well. These mushrooms, which can be found in Asian grocery stores and some supermarkets, are a more economical choice for broth than other dried mushrooms. Simmer the broth over a low heat for a few hours and cool slightly before straining. By this point the vegetables likely won't be worth salvaging. Freeze the broth in various-sized containers, depending on how you plan to use it.

• Roast vegetables on a baking sheet until they're tender and then add them to a broth for a soup to savour.

• Don't waste valuable cooking time by preparing only small amounts of long-cooking soups. If a recipe calls for only small amounts of various vegetables, rather than wasting the rest, cook up extra at the same time. I sometimes make double batches in my largest pots.

• Be sure to have freezer containers and labels on hand. If your container supply is running low, once the soup is frozen, turn it out into a freezer-strength plastic bag and put back into the freezer.

recipes

cucumber and carrot raita

A savoury refresher packed with phytocompounds from almost all the ingredients.

MAKES 4 TO 6 SERVINGS (2 CUPS/500 ML)

Salt

1/2 cup (125 mL) grated cucumber

1 1/2 cups (375 mL) plain 1% or skim milk yogurt

3/4 cup (175 mL) grated carrot

2 tablespoons (25 mL) finely chopped onion

1/2 teaspoon (2 mL) ground cumin

2 tablespoons (25 mL) chopped fresh mint, for garnish

In a strainer or colander, sprinkle salt over cucumber; drain cucumbers 10 minutes. Rinse and squeeze out excess moisture.

In a bowl, combine cucumbers, yogurt, carrot, onion and cumin. Refrigerate for at least 1 hour. Serve garnished with chopped fresh mint.

PER 6-SERVINGS NUTRITIONAL INFORMATION: Calories: 43, Protein: 4 g, Fat: less than 1 g, Saturated Fat: less than 1 g, Carbohydrate: 7 g, Dietary Fibre: 1 g

ribollita

Ribollita is an Italian specialty that makes use of both leftover bread and soup.

MAKES 4 SERVINGS

6 cups (1.5 L) Mediterranean Vegetable Soup (page 75)

5–6 slices Italian bread, about 1 inch (2.5 cm) thick (enough to cover pan)

1/2 cup (125 mL) freshly grated Parmesan cheese

Prepare an 8-inch (2-L) square baking dish by spraying with vegetable oil cooking spray. Spread 1 cup (250 mL) of soup in the bottom of the baking dish. Place bread in a single layer over soup. Pour remaining soup over bread and sprinkle cheese evenly over top. Cover and let sit in the refrigerator for at least 1 hour or overnight.

Preheat oven to 350°F (180°C). Bake for 25 minutes, or until golden and bubbling.

PER SERVING NUTRITIONAL INFORMATION: Calories: 241, Protein: 13 g, Fat: 8 g, Saturated Fat: 3 g, Carbohydrate: 30 g, Dietary Fibre: 4 g

mushroom soup

For mushrooms lovers, this soup is as intense in mushroom flavour as it gets. And it's packed with a variety of mushrooms, so you get an assortment of phytochemicals that may provide an immune system boost as well as protect against certain cancers.

MAKES 4 TO 6 SERVINGS (6 CUPS/1.5 L)

2 teaspoons (10 mL) extra virgin olive oil

1/4 cup (50 mL) minced shallots

4 cups (1 L) chopped button mushrooms (about 3/4 pound/375 g)

3 cups (750 mL) chopped assorted mushrooms such as shiitake, portobello, oyster (about 1/2 pound/250 g)

1/3 cup (75 mL) dry sherry

6 cups (1.5 L) sodium-reduced vegetable or chicken broth

1 cup (250 mL) thinly sliced shiitake mushrooms (about 4 ounces/125 g)

Salt and freshly ground pepper, to taste

2 tablespoons (25 mL) chopped fresh parsley, for garnish

Heat oil in a heavy saucepan over medium heat. Add shallots and sauté until soft, 3 to 5 minutes. Increase heat to medium-high. Add chopped mushrooms; cook, stirring, until liquid is almost evaporated, 10 to 15 minutes. Stir in sherry and cook for 3 to 5 minutes, or until sherry evaporates. Add broth; bring to a boil, reduce heat and simmer for 20 minutes, stirring occasionally.

Add sliced shiitake mushrooms; continue to cook until mushrooms soften, about 10 minutes. Season with salt and pepper. Serve garnished with chopped parsley.

PER 1-CUP (250-ML) SERVING NUTRITIONAL INFORMATION: Calories: 55, Protein: 4 g, Fat: 2 g, Saturated Fat: less than 1 g, Carbohydrate: 7 g, Dietary Fibre: 2 g

broccoli cauliflower soup

Brassicas at their best. These vegetables contain a host of compounds that provide weapons to battle cancer at all stages, from possible prevention to halting the growth of tumours. If you want to freeze any soup, omit the milk and add after thawing and reheating.

MAKES 6 SERVINGS

2 teaspoons (10 mL) soft margarine

1 cup (250 mL) chopped onions

8 cups (2 L) broccoli florets (from about 2 bunches or 2 pounds/1 kg)

8 cups (2 L) cauliflower florets (from about 1 large head)

4 cups (1 L) sodium-reduced vegetable or chicken broth

2 bay leaves

2 teaspoons (10 mL) fresh thyme (or 3/4 teaspoon/7 mL dried)

2 cups (500 mL) 1% milk

Salt and freshly ground pepper, to taste

1/2 cup (125 mL) shredded light cheddar cheese

2 tablespoons (25 mL) chopped fresh basil, for garnish

Melt margarine in a large, heavy saucepan over medium heat. Add onions and sauté until soft. Add broccoli (reserving a few florets), cauliflower, broth, bay leaves and thyme. Bring to a boil, reduce heat and simmer, covered, for about 30 minutes, stirring occasionally. Discard the bay leaves.

Process the mixture in a food processor or in batches in a blender until smooth. Return to the saucepan. Add reserved broccoli florets and cook for 5 minutes. Add milk and cook until heated through. Season with salt and pepper. Serve garnished with cheddar cheese and fresh basil.

PER SERVING NUTRITIONAL INFORMATION: Calories: 149, Protein: 13 g, Fat: 4 g, Saturated Fat: 1 g, Carbohydrate: 21 g, Dietary Fibre: 7 g

savoury moroccan vegetable soup

This hearty soup is packed with flavour and plenty of colourful carotenoids, compounds linked to keeping arteries healthy and fighting cancer. And there's plenty of fibre to boot. Keep any extra in the freezer.

MAKES 10 SERVINGS

2 teaspoons (10 mL) extra virgin olive oil

2 cups (500 mL) diced onions

4 cloves garlic, finely chopped

1 tablespoon (15 mL) grated ginger

1/4 teaspoon (1 mL) red pepper flakes

Pinch saffron

1 (28-ounce/796-mL) can Italian plum tomatoes, coarsely chopped, with juice

1 (19-ounce/540-mL) can chickpeas, rinsed and drained

2 cups (500 mL) diced sweet potatoes

2 cups (500 mL) diced carrots

1 cup (250 mL) diced parsnips

1 cup (250 mL) diced celery

6 cups (1.5 L) sodium-reduced vegetable or chicken broth

1 cinnamon stick

Salt and freshly ground pepper, to taste

Zesty Charmoula Sauce (page 212)

Heat oil in a large, heavy pot over medium heat. Add onions and garlic; sauté until onions are soft, about 8 minutes. Add ginger, red pepper flakes and saffron; sauté another minute. Add tomatoes and their juice, chickpeas, sweet potatoes, carrots, parsnips, celery, broth, cinnamon stick, salt and pepper. Bring to a boil, reduce heat and simmer, covered, for 1 hour, stirring occasionally to break up tomatoes. Serve each portion topped with 1 teaspoon (5 mL) charmoula sauce.

PER SERVING NUTRITIONAL INFORMATION: Calories: 145, Protein: 5 g, Fat: 3 g, Saturated Fat: less than 1 g, Carbohydrate: 25 g, Dietary Fibre: 6 g

mediterranean vegetable soup

Like a minestrone but minus the beans and pasta, for a lighter touch. Tomato-based soups are an easy way to take in the carotenoid lycopene in a form that's more easily absorbed by the body than fresh tomatoes.

MAKES 6 TO 8 SERVINGS

1 tablespoon (15 mL) extra virgin olive oil

1 cup (250 mL) chopped onions

4 cloves garlic, finely chopped

1 cup (250 mL) diced carrots

2 stalks celery, diced

1 medium zucchini, diced

1 cup (250 mL) green beans, trimmed and cut into 1/2-inch (1-cm) lengths

1 (28-ounce/796-mL) can plum tomatoes with juice, puréed

5 cups (1.25 L) sodium-reduced vegetable or chicken broth

2 tablespoons (25 mL) chopped fresh basil

2 tablespoons (25 mL) chopped fresh parsley

1/4 teaspoon (1 mL) each salt and freshly ground pepper

2 cups (500 mL) coarsely chopped spinach or Swiss chard

Heat oil in a large, heavy pot over medium heat. Add onions and garlic; sauté until soft, about 5 minutes. Add carrots, celery and zucchini; cook, stirring frequently, until soft, about 10 minutes. Add green beans, puréed tomatoes, broth, basil, parsley, salt and pepper. Bring to a boil, reduce heat and simmer, covered, for 30 minutes, stirring occasionally.

Stir in spinach and continue to cook another 20 minutes. Season to taste with salt and pepper.

PER 8-SERVINGS NUTRITIONAL INFORMATION: Calories: 76, Protein: 4 g, Fat: 3 g, Saturated Fat: less than 1 g, Carbohydrate: 12 g, Dietary Fibre: 3 g

southwest tortilla soup

A meal in a bowl with as many flavours as there are phytonutrients—lycopene, lutein and lignans, to name a few—and monounsaturated fat.

MAKES 4 SERVINGS

2 teaspoons (10 mL) extra virgin olive oil

1/2 cup (125 mL) chopped onions

2 cloves garlic, minced

1 tablespoon (15 mL) tomato paste

1/2 teaspoon (2 mL) chili powder

1/4 teaspoon (1 mL) ground cumin

1 1/2 cups (375 mL) canned tomatoes, coarsely chopped, with juice

4 cups (1 L) homemade or sodium-reduced vegetable or chicken broth

1 medium zucchini, diced

1 cup (250 mL) fresh or frozen corn kernels

2 tablespoons (25 mL) fresh lime juice

Salt and freshly ground pepper, to taste

1 cup (250 mL) shredded light cheddar cheese

2 tablespoons (25 mL) chopped fresh coriander, for garnish (optional)

1/2 cup (125 mL) coarsely broken baked corn tortilla chips

Heat oil in a large saucepan over medium-low heat. Add onions and garlic; sauté until onions are soft, about 8 minutes. Stir in tomato paste, chili powder, cumin, tomatoes and their juice, and broth. Bring to a boil, reduce heat and simmer for 10 minutes, covered and stirring occasionally. Add zucchini and corn; simmer another 10 minutes. Stir in lime juice, salt and pepper. (Soup can be made to this point and refrigerated. Reheat before serving.)

Serve soup sprinkled with cheddar cheese and coriander, if using, and topped with tortilla chips.

PER SERVING NUTRITIONAL INFORMATION: Calories: 209, Protein: 14 g, Fat: 6 g, Saturated Fat: 2 g, Carbohydrate: 26 g, Dietary Fibre: 4 g

gazpacho

Always keep some of this refreshing soup in the fridge during the summer. Using raw garlic maximizes its cancer-fighting potential.

MAKES 6 SERVINGS

4 large ripe red tomatoes (about 2 pounds/1 kg), cut into eighths

2 red peppers, cut into eighths

1 English cucumber, cut into 2-inch (5-cm) pieces

2 cloves garlic, chopped

1 medium red onion, cut into eighths

1/4 cup (50 mL) chopped fresh flat-leaf parsley

1/4 cup (50 mL) chopped fresh coriander

2 tablespoons (25 mL) extra virgin olive oil

2 tablespoons (25 mL) red wine vinegar, or to taste

Salt and freshly ground pepper, to taste

Place half the tomatoes, half the red peppers and half the cucumber in a food processor. Add garlic, onion, 3 tablespoons (45 mL) each of the parsley and coriander, the olive oil and vinegar. Process to a smooth purée. Place in a large bowl.

Process remaining tomatoes, red peppers and cucumber until smooth. Stir into purée. Season with salt, pepper and more vinegar, if desired.

Refrigerate at least 1 hour or overnight. Serve garnished with remaining chopped parsley and coriander.

PER SERVING NUTRITIONAL INFORMATION: Calories: 97, Protein: 2 g, Fat: 5 g, Saturated Fat: 1 g, Carbohydrate: 12 g, Dietary Fibre: 3 g

cabbage, beet and apple slaw

For coleslaw lovers, here's a colourful slaw that's packed with all kinds of phytopower. For example, there are anti-cancer compounds from the cabbage and onions, heart-healthy flavonoids from the apple and onions, and beet's contribution of cholesterol-lowering fibre.

MAKES 6 TO 8 SERVINGS

6 cups (1.5 L) thinly sliced cabbage

3/4 cup (175 mL) coarsely shredded carrots

3/4 cup (175 mL) coarsely shredded raw beets

1/4 cup (50 mL) finely chopped red onions

1 large or 2 small apples, shredded

6 tablespoons (90 mL) light mayonnaise

1/4 cup (50 mL) plain low-fat yogurt

3 tablespoons (45 mL) cider vinegar

1 1/2 tablespoons (20 mL) honey

Salt and freshly ground pepper, to taste

In a large bowl, combine cabbage, carrots, beets, onions and apple. To prepare the dressing, in a small bowl whisk together mayonnaise, yogurt, vinegar and honey. Pour over vegetables and toss until well mixed. Season with salt and pepper.

PER 8-SERVINGS NUTRITIONAL INFORMATION: Calories: 90, Protein: 2 g, Fat: 4 g, Saturated Fat: 1 g, Carbohydrate: 13 g, Dietary Fibre: 3 g

arugula oven-dried tomato salad

Lycopene and lutein—compounds that fight both heart disease and cancer—together in a taste bonanza!

MAKES 4 SERVINGS

2 large bunches arugula, stems trimmed

1 cup (250 mL) Oven-Dried Tomatoes (page 94), cut into 1/4-inch (5-mm) slices

2 tablespoons (25 mL) extra virgin olive oil

1 tablespoon (15 mL) balsamic vinegar

Salt and freshly ground pepper, to taste

1 ounce (25 g) Parmigiano-Reggiano cheese

In a large bowl, gently toss together arugula, tomato slices, olive oil and balsamic vinegar. Season with salt and pepper. Place on salad plates. Using a vegetable peeler, shave some cheese onto each plate. Serve immediately.

PER SERVING NUTRITIONAL INFORMATION: Calories: 110, Protein: 3 g, Fat: 9 g, Saturated Fat: 2 g, Carbohydrate: 4 g, Dietary Fibre: 1 g

spinach, orange and red onion salad

Chock full of heart-healthy nutrients like the B vitamin folate.

MAKES 4 SERVINGS

4 teaspoons (20 mL) extra virgin olive oil

1 tablespoon (15 mL) each frozen orange juice concentrate and balsamic vinegar

1/8 teaspoon (0.5 mL) each salt and freshly ground pepper

5 cups (1.25 L) spinach

2 small oranges, peeled, quartered and sliced

1/2 cup (125 mL) red onion slices

Salt and freshly ground pepper, to taste

In a small bowl, whisk together olive oil, orange juice concentrate, balsamic vinegar, salt and pepper. Place spinach, oranges and red onion in a large bowl. Add dressing and toss to coat. Adjust seasoning with salt and pepper. Serve immediately.

PER SERVING NUTRITIONAL INFORMATION: Calories: 103, Protein: 2 g, Fat: 5 g, Saturated Fat: 1 g, Carbohydrate: 16 g, Dietary Fibre: 5 g

enlightened potato salad

This is an example of how to boost the phytopower in old favourites like potato salad. Mustard, horseradish, celery, onions, peppers and dill—all contribute their own phytopower to the mix.

MAKES 6 SERVINGS

1/4 cup (50 mL) plain low-fat yogurt

3 tablespoons (45 mL) light mayonnaise

2 teaspoons (10 mL) grainy mustard

1 teaspoon (5 mL) prepared horseradish

1 1/2 pounds (750 g) Yukon Gold potatoes (about 4 medium), unpeeled

3 large eggs, hard boiled

1 red pepper, diced

3/4 cup (175 mL) diced celery

1/3 cup (75 mL) chopped red onions

Salt and freshly ground pepper, to taste

1/4 cup (50 mL) chopped fresh dill

To prepare dressing, in a small bowl whisk together yogurt, mayonnaise, mustard and horseradish. (Dressing may be prepared ahead of time, then covered and refrigerated.)

Cook potatoes in a large pot of boiling water until just tender, 25 to 30 minutes. Drain potatoes and, when cool enough to handle, peel if desired, and cut into slices 1/4 inch (5 mm) thick. Dice egg whites, reserving yolks for another use.

In a large bowl, toss together potatoes, egg whites, red pepper, celery, red onions and dressing. Season with salt and pepper. Just before serving, toss with chopped dill.

PER SERVING NUTRITIONAL INFORMATION: Calories: 138, Protein: 5 g, Fat: 3 g, Saturated Fat: 1 g, Carbohydrate: 24 g, Dietary Fibre: 3 g

mushroom spinach salad with poppy seed dressing

Considering spinach's nutritional profile, you can't have too many spinach salad recipes. Using a fruity extra virgin olive oil adds not only taste but also a variety of antioxidant compounds.

MAKES 4 SERVINGS

2 tablespoons (25 mL) extra virgin olive oil

1 tablespoon (15 mL) minced red onions

1 tablespoon (15 mL) orange juice

5 teaspoons (25 mL) apple cider vinegar

4 teaspoons (20 mL) sugar

2 teaspoons (10 mL) poppy seeds

1 teaspoon (5 mL) Dijon mustard

1/4 teaspoon (1 mL) salt

1/8 teaspoon (0.5 mL) freshly ground pepper

2 large eggs, hard-boiled

6 cups (1.5 L) spinach

1 cup (250 mL) sliced mushrooms

1/3 cup (75 mL) thinly sliced red onions

In a food processor, combine oil, minced onions, orange juice, vinegar, sugar, poppy seeds, mustard, salt and pepper until well mixed. Set aside.

Coarsely chop 1 egg and 1 egg white, reserving remaining yolk for another use. In a large bowl, toss together spinach, mushrooms, sliced onions and egg. Add dressing; toss to mix and serve immediately.

PER SERVING NUTRITIONAL INFORMATION: Calories: 115, Protein: 5 g, Fat: 8 g, Saturated Fat: 1 g, Carbohydrate: 5 g, Dietary Fibre: 2 g

oven-baked zucchini sticks

Your family will forget the deep-fried appetizers after they taste these crispy zucchini sticks. And it's a yummy way to get in lutein, the carotenoid noted for keeping eyes healthy, decreasing the risk of colon cancer and protecting arteries.

MAKES 4 SERVINGS

3 medium zucchini (about 1 1/4 pounds/625 g)

3/4 cup (175 mL) fresh breadcrumbs (preferably made from whole grain bread)

1/4 cup (50 mL) freshly grated Parmesan cheese

1 tablespoon (15 mL) chopped fresh oregano (or 1 teaspoon/5 mL dried)

1/2 teaspoon (2 mL) freshly ground pepper

1/4 teaspoon (1 mL) salt

1 tablespoon (15 mL) extra virgin olive oil

Enlightened Horseradish Sauce (recipe follows)

Preheat oven to 450°F (230°C). Prepare a large baking sheet by spraying it with vegetable oil cooking spray.

Cut zucchini into 1- x 1/4- x 1/4-inch (2.5-cm x 5-mm x 5-mm) pieces.

In a plastic bag, mix together breadcrumbs, Parmesan cheese, oregano, pepper and salt. In a large bowl, toss together zucchini and olive oil until the zucchini is evenly coated. Place zucchini, a handful at a time, in the plastic bag and shake to coat. Place zucchini in rows on prepared baking sheet, taking care not to crowd. Repeat with remaining zucchini.

Bake for 20 minutes. Turn zucchini and bake another 12 to 15 minutes or until zucchini sticks are golden brown. Serve immediately with Enlightened Horseradish Sauce.

PER SERVING NUTRITIONAL INFORMATION: Calories: 163, Protein: 8 g, Fat: 6 g, Saturated Fat: 2 g, Carbohydrate: 20 g, Dietary Fibre: 2 g

ENLIGHTENED HORSERADISH SAUCE

Serve with Oven-Baked Zucchini Sticks or as a sandwich spread or dip. Horseradish, unbeknownst to many people, is a member of the brassica family, known for its cancer-fighting effects.

MAKES 4 SERVINGS

2 tablespoons (25 mL) plain low-fat or skim milk yogurt

1 tablespoon (15 mL) prepared horseradish

4 teaspoons (20 mL) light mayonnaise

Salt and freshly ground pepper, to taste

In a small bowl, mix together yogurt, horseradish, mayonnaise, salt and pepper.

PER SERVING NUTRITIONAL INFORMATION: Calories: 22, Protein: 1 g, Fat: 2 g, Saturated Fat: less than 1 g, Carbohydrate: 1 g, Dietary Fibre: less than 1 g

sweet potato baked fries

These are a beta carotene-rich alternative to traditional fat-laden french fries. Science is showing that there are many reasons to boost your beta, including protection against heart disease, stroke and some cancers.

MAKES 4 SERVINGS

2–3 large sweet potatoes (about 1 1/2 pounds/750 g), peeled, if desired
2 tablespoons (25 mL) vegetable oil
Salt, to taste

Preheat oven to 450°F (230°C). Generously coat a large baking sheet with vegetable oil cooking spray.

Cut a slice off the long side of a sweet potato and place on a cutting board cut side down. The sweet potato should sit evenly. Cut lengthwise into 1/4-inch (5-mm) slices. Place two or three slices on top of each other and cut into matchsticks. Repeat with remaining sweet potatoes.

Place matchsticks in a large bowl and toss with vegetable oil until well coated. Place potatoes in a single layer on prepared baking sheet, lined up in rows for easier turning; do not crowd. If a second pan is necessary, be sure to rotate the pans in the oven for even browning.

Bake for 25 to 30 minutes or until the fries are crispy, turning every 10 to 12 minutes. Season with salt, if desired.

PER SERVING NUTRITIONAL INFORMATION: Calories: 202, Protein: 2 g, Fat: 7 g, Saturated Fat: 1 g, Carbohydrate: 33 g, Dietary Fibre: 4 g

swiss chard with raisins and pine nuts

A combination of North African and Italian flavours that is delicious hot or cold. Terrific atop toasted slices of crusty whole grain bread and served as crostini. Nuts, greens, raisins and olive oil—you couldn't ask for a tastier heart-healthy combo!

MAKES 4 SERVINGS

3 tablespoons (45 mL) raisins

2 tablespoons (25 mL) extra virgin olive oil

2 cloves garlic, chopped

1 bunch Swiss chard (about 1 1/4 pounds/625 g), stems trimmed and leaves coarsely chopped

2 tablespoons (25 mL) pine nuts, toasted (see page 190)

Salt and freshly ground pepper, to taste

Place raisins in a small bowl. Add enough warm water to cover; let stand 20 minutes. Drain well.

Heat oil in a large, heavy pot over medium heat. Add garlic and sauté until fragrant, about 1 minute; do not let brown. Add Swiss chard; sauté until chard is wilted and tender, about 5 minutes. Stir in pine nuts and raisins. Season with salt and pepper. Remove from heat. Serve hot or cold.

PER SERVING NUTRITIONAL INFORMATION: Calories: 134, Protein: 4 g, Fat: 9 g, Saturated Fat: 1 g, Carbohydrate: 11 g, Dietary Fibre: 3 g

roasted sesame cabbage and onions

If using one large baking sheet, centre rack in middle of the oven. For two sheets, be sure to rotate pans halfway through the cooking. Keep any leftover in the fridge, as this cabbage-onion combo is delicious hot or cold. And with both these vegetables and their phytomix, it's a powerful cancer-fighting combo.

MAKES 4 SERVINGS

8 cups (2 L) thinly sliced cabbage (about half a cabbage)

2 cups (500 mL) thinly sliced onions

1 tablespoon (15 mL) vegetable oil

2 tablespoons (25 mL) rice wine vinegar

1 1/2 tablespoons (20 mL) sodium-reduced soy sauce

1 tablespoon (15 mL) mirin (sweet Japanese rice wine)

1 1/2 teaspoons (7 mL) sesame oil

Salt and freshly ground pepper, to taste

Preheat oven to 450°F (230°C). Spray 1 large or 2 medium baking sheets with vegetable oil cooking spray.

Combine cabbage and onions in large bowl. Add vegetable oil; toss to coat. Spread vegetables on baking sheet; roast for 15 minutes. Using a spatula, stir to ensure that the slices are evenly roasted. Bake another 10 to 15 minutes or until edges of cabbage are browned.

Place cabbage in a large bowl. Combine vinegar, soy sauce, mirin and sesame oil. Pour over cabbage; toss well. Season with salt and pepper. Serve hot or cold.

PER SERVING NUTRITIONAL INFORMATION: Calories: 114, Protein: 3 g, Fat: 6 g, Saturated Fat: 1 g, Carbohydrate: 14 g, Dietary Fibre: 5 g

shiitake mushroom and potato cakes

Here's an Asian twist for potato lovers. Shiitake mushrooms rank among the tops in this vegetable category for providing phytochemicals that may aid in the treatment of certain cancers, lower the odds of developing heart disease and boost the immune system. And they taste oh so wonderful!

MAKES 8 CAKES

1 tablespoon (15 mL) vegetable oil

2 teaspoons (10 mL) grated ginger

2 cloves garlic, minced

2 cups (500 mL) finely diced shiitake mushrooms

1 cup (250 mL) sliced shiitake mushrooms

2 baked potatoes, peeled and chopped (about 2 cups/500 mL)

1 green onion, chopped

2 tablespoons (25 mL) chopped fresh coriander

1 tablespoon (15 mL) sesame oil

Salt and freshly ground pepper, to taste

Heat 1 teaspoon (5 mL) of the vegetable oil in a large nonstick skillet over medium-high heat. Add ginger and garlic; sauté for 30 seconds, being careful not to burn. Add mushrooms; continue to sauté until the mushrooms are soft, about 5 minutes. Remove from heat and allow to cool.

In a large bowl, stir together cooled mushrooms, potatoes, green onion, coriander and sesame oil. Season with salt and pepper. Form into 8 patties.

Wipe clean the skillet. Heat 1 teaspoon (5 mL) of the vegetable oil in the skillet over medium heat. Add 4 patties and cook for 4 minutes on each side or until golden brown. Remove from skillet and keep warm. Repeat with remaining oil and patties. Serve warm.

PER PATTY NUTRITIONAL INFORMATION: Calories: 76, Protein: 1 g, Fat: 3 g, Saturated Fat: less than 1 g, Carbohydrate: 11 g, Dietary Fibre: 1 g

med-rim roasted vegetables

Pomegranate molasses, packed with colourful anthocyanins, is used regularly in the Middle East to season dishes. A taste of these veggies and you'll know why. Look for pomegranate molasses in Middle Eastern markets.

MAKES 6 SERVINGS

2 large sweet potatoes (about 1 1/2 pounds/750 g), peeled and cut into 1/4-inch (5-mm) slices

1 pound (500 g) carrots, peeled, halved lengthwise and cut into 1 1/2-inch (4-cm) pieces

1 pound (500 g) parsnips, peeled, halved lengthwise and cut into 1 1/2-inch (4-cm) pieces

1 tablespoon (15 mL) extra virgin olive oil

2 tablespoons (25 mL) pomegranate molasses

1/4 teaspoon (1 mL) ground cumin

Salt and freshly ground pepper, to taste

Preheat oven to 450°F (230°C). Spray a large baking sheet with vegetable oil cooking spray.

Combine sweet potatoes, carrots and parsnips in a large bowl. Add oil; toss to coat thoroughly. Spread on baking sheet. Roast, without stirring, for 25 minutes.

Return vegetables to the bowl. Stir together pomegranate molasses and ground cumin. Add to vegetables and toss to coat. Return vegetables to baking sheet and roast for another 25 minutes or until vegetables are tender and golden brown. Season with salt and pepper.

PER SERVING NUTRITIONAL INFORMATION: Calories: 244, Protein: 4 g, Fat: 3 g, Saturated Fat: less than 1 g, Carbohydrate: 52 g, Dietary Fibre: 9 g

shakshuka

This Israeli specialty elevates eggs to irresistible fare. This recipe is an adaptation from chef Moshe Basson of Eucalyptus Restaurant in Jerusalem.

MAKES 2 SERVINGS

2 teaspoons (10 mL) extra virgin olive oil

1 cup (250 mL) chopped onions

1 red pepper, diced

2 cups (500 mL) diced plum tomatoes (about 1 pound/500 g)

1/4 teaspoon (1 mL) ground cumin

Salt and freshly ground pepper, to taste

3–4 eggs

Heat oil in a saucepan over medium-high heat; add onions and sauté for 5 minutes or until soft. Add red pepper and continue to sauté another 5 minutes. Stir in tomatoes and cumin. Reduce heat to medium-low and cook, covered and stirring occasionally, for 20 minutes. Season with salt and pepper.

Breaks the eggs into the pan and let them poach, covered, until set, about 4 minutes. Serve immediately.

PER SERVING NUTRITIONAL INFORMATION: Calories: 263, Protein: 13 g, Fat: 13 g, Saturated Fat: 3 g, Carbohydrate: 26 g, Dietary Fibre: 5 g

cheese and vegetable quesadillas with avocado and tomato salsa

Elegant enough for company but easy enough for a fast dinner for the family. With the whole wheat tortillas, vegetables and salsa, these quesadillas offer a rich array of antioxidants.

MAKES 4 APPETIZER SERVINGS OR 2 MAIN-COURSE SERVINGS

1 cup (250 mL) shredded light cheddar or Monterey Jack cheese

3 large flour tortillas (preferably whole wheat)

1 small red pepper, diced

1/3 cup (75 mL) chopped green onions (green tops only)

Avocado and Tomato Salsa (recipe follows)

Preheat oven to 400°F (200°C). Prepare a baking sheet by spraying with vegetable oil cooking spray.

Divide cheese into six equal portions. Spray one flour tortilla with vegetable oil cooking spray and place sprayed side down at one end of the baking sheet. Spread one portion of the cheese on one half of the tortilla, leaving a 1/2-inch (1-cm) border at edge. Top with one-third of the red pepper and one-third of the green onions. Top with a second portion of the cheese. Fold tortilla over filling and press down so that tortilla will remain folded. Repeat with remaining two tortillas, filling up the baking sheet.

Bake for 12 to 15 minutes or until tortillas are slightly browned. Allow to cool slightly before cutting each quesadilla into four wedges. Serve with salsa on the side.

PER APPETIZER SERVING NUTRITIONAL INFORMATION: Calories: 258, Protein: 14 g, Fat: 11 g, Saturated Fat: 4 g, Carbohydrate: 32 g, Dietary Fibre: 7 g

PER MAIN-COURSE SERVING (WITH 1/2 CUP/125 ML SALSA) NUTRITIONAL INFORMATION: Calories: 416, Protein: 25 g, Fat: 15 g, Saturated Fat: 6 g, Carbohydrate: 59 g, Dietary Fibre: 10 g

AVOCADO AND TOMATO SALSA

The combos of beneficial compounds in this dish can't be beat. Carotenoids, the pigments that provide the colour to fruit and vegetables, are plentiful, as are nutrients like folic acid and vitamin E. And it's delicious, to boot!

MAKES 4 SERVINGS

1 medium avocado (preferably California), peeled and diced

1 medium tomato (about 6 ounces/175 g), diced

3 tablespoons (45 mL) finely chopped red onion

2 tablespoons (25 mL) chopped fresh coriander

1 teaspoon (5 mL) finely chopped jalapeño pepper

5 teaspoons (25 mL) fresh lime juice

2 teaspoons (10 mL) extra virgin olive oil

Salt, to taste

In a medium bowl, toss together avocado, tomato, red onion, coriander, jalapeño pepper, lime juice and olive oil; season with salt. (May be made a few hours ahead and refrigerated, covered.)

PER SERVING NUTRITIONAL INFORMATION: Calories: 101, Protein: 2 g, Fat: 9 g, Saturated Fat: 2 g, Carbohydrate: 6 g, Dietary Fibre: 4 g

eggplant, roasted red pepper and goat cheese sandwiches

A delicious way to dress up a sandwich for lunch. Keep in mind that in order to take in the phytochemical anthocyanin, you must eat the eggplant skin.

MAKES 4 SERVINGS

1 eggplant, cut lengthwise into slices 1/2 inch (1 cm) thick

8 ounces (250 g) soft low-fat goat cheese

8 thick slices whole grain bread

2 red peppers, roasted, peeled and cut into halves

8 large basil leaves

Salt and freshly ground pepper, to taste

Preheat grill to medium-high heat (or preheat broiler). Spray eggplant slices with olive oil cooking spray. Grill eggplant until golden, about 4 minutes per side. Let cool.

Spread goat cheese over four slices of bread. Top with eggplant slices, roasted pepper halves and basil. Season with salt and pepper. Top with remaining slices of bread.

PER SERVING NUTRITIONAL INFORMATION: Calories: 345, Protein: 19 g, Fat: 9 g, Saturated Fat: 4 g, Carbohydrate: 51 g, Dietary Fibre: 9 g

pasta with butternut squash and sage

Italians have a way with seasonal cooking. If you love the various squash and pasta offerings at Italian eateries, you'll be wild about this dish. It's also a tasty way to tempt non-squash eaters to eat this vegetable. It's packed with beta carotene, folate, vitamins C and B-6, magnesium and fibre.

MAKES 8 APPETIZER SERVINGS OR 5 TO 6 MAIN-COURSE SERVINGS

4 cups (1 L) 2-inch (5-cm) pieces butternut squash (about 1 1/4 pounds/625 g)

1 tablespoon (15 mL) extra virgin olive oil

1 medium onion, chopped

2 cloves garlic, chopped

1 1/2 cups (375 mL) sodium-reduced vegetable or chicken broth

2 tablespoons (25 mL) finely chopped fresh sage

1 pound (500 g) short pasta such as fusilli or penne (preferably whole wheat)

2 tablespoons (25 mL) chopped fresh flat-leaf parsley

1/2 cup (125 mL) freshly grated Parmesan cheese plus additional for sprinkling

Salt and freshly ground pepper, to taste

Finely chop squash pieces in a food processor; set aside.

In a large nonstick skillet over medium heat, heat oil. Add onion and garlic; sauté until onions are soft, 8 to 10 minutes. Add squash and broth. Bring to a boil, reduce heat to medium-low and simmer, covered and stirring occasionally, until squash is tender, about 20 minutes. Stir in sage and simmer 10 minutes more.

Meanwhile, cook pasta in a large pot of boiling salted water until just tender. Drain pasta and return to pot. Add squash mixture, parsley and 1/2 cup (125 mL) Parmesan, stirring until mixed. Season with salt and pepper. Serve sprinkled with additional Parmesan.

PER APPETIZER SERVING NUTRITIONAL INFORMATION: Calories: 247, Protein: 11 g, Fat: 4 g, Saturated Fat: 1 g, Carbohydrate: 44 g, Dietary Fibre: 5 g

PER 6 MAIN-COURSE SERVINGS NUTRITIONAL INFORMATION: Calories: 329, Protein: 15 g, Fat: 6 g, Saturated Fat: 2 g, Carbohydrate: 58 g, Dietary Fibre: 7 g

linguine with oven-dried tomatoes

A lycopene-packed pasta dish with fresh tomatoes that's fabulous tasting throughout the year.

MAKES 4 TO 6 SERVINGS

3/4 pound (375 g) linguine (preferably whole wheat)

4 teaspoons (20 mL) extra virgin olive oil

3 cloves garlic, chopped

1 recipe Oven-Dried Tomatoes (recipe follows)

2 bocconcini balls, diced

2 tablespoons (25 mL) chopped fresh basil

Salt and freshly ground pepper, to taste

1/4 cup (50 mL) freshly grated Parmesan cheese

Cook pasta in a large pot of boiling salted water until just tender; drain.

In a large skillet over medium heat, heat 2 teaspoons (10 mL) of the olive oil. Add garlic and sauté for 30 seconds or until fragrant. Lower heat to medium-low and continue to sauté for 2 minutes, being careful not to brown the garlic. Increase heat to medium; add tomatoes and heat, stirring, until mixture is just beginning to simmer. Add drained linguine and toss. Remove from heat. Add bocconcini, tossing to distribute the pieces evenly. Toss with remaining 2 teaspoons (10 mL) olive oil and the basil. Season with salt and pepper. Serve sprinkled with Parmesan.

PER 6-SERVINGS NUTRITIONAL INFORMATION: Calories: 302, Protein: 14 g, Fat: 7 g, Saturated Fat: 2 g, Carbohydrate: 49 g, Dietary Fibre: 9 g

OVEN-DRIED TOMATOES

Use these in salads, sandwiches and pastas.

MAKES 3 CUPS (750 ML)

2 pounds (1 kg) plum tomatoes

Preheat oven to 325°F (160°C). Place a rack on a baking sheet.

Cut tomatoes into wedges (quarters for small tomatoes and sixths for larger ones). Arrange tomatoes on rack in a single layer. Bake for 1 1/2 hours to 2 hours or until tomatoes are dried slightly but still soft to the touch. Be careful not to overdry. Remove from oven and allow to cool; cut tomatoes into 1/2-inch (1-cm) pieces.

PER 1/2-CUP (125-ML) SERVING: Calories: 31, Protein: 2 g, Fat: less than 1 g, Saturated Fat: less than 1 g, Carbohydrate: 7 g, Dietary Fibre: 2 g

portobello mushroom burgers with herb mustard mayonnaise

Even meat eaters will forgo burgers made of meat once they taste these. Eating less grilled meat may reduce the risk of certain cancers, but when you substitute mushrooms and their anti-cancer effects, the odds drop even further.

MAKES 2 SERVINGS

2 teaspoons (10 mL) extra virgin olive oil

2 teaspoons (10 mL) balsamic vinegar

1 1/2 teaspoons (7 mL) finely chopped garlic

2 portobello mushrooms, 4–5 inches (10–12 cm) in diameter, stems removed

Salt and freshly ground pepper, to taste

1/4 cup (50 mL) light mayonnaise

1 teaspoon (5 mL) Dijon mustard

1 tablespoon (15 mL) chopped fresh parsley

2 slices red onion (1/2 inch/1 cm thick)

2 whole grain crusty rolls

2 slices light provolone cheese

2 slices tomato (1/2 inch/1 cm thick)

Leaf lettuce or arugula

In a shallow bowl, whisk together olive oil, balsamic vinegar and 1 teaspoon (5 mL) of the garlic. Add mushrooms and sprinkle with salt and pepper. Turn mushrooms to coat. Allow to marinate for about 20 minutes.

To make herb mustard mayonnaise, mix together mayonnaise, mustard and remaining 1/2 teaspoon (2 mL) chopped garlic. Add pepper to taste. Set aside. (Can be made earlier and refrigerated.)

Preheat grill or broiler to medium-high. Place mushrooms on grill, gill side down. Brush onion slices with marinade and place on grill, taking care to keep onion slices intact. Grill vegetables for 6 minutes. Turn vegetables over; grill for another 6 minutes or until tender. If desired, rolls can be toasted over grill for the last minute.

Spread herb mayonnaise on rolls. Place mushrooms on bottom half of each roll; top with cheese, grilled onion slices, tomato slices and lettuce. Top each with top half of roll. Serve immediately.

PER SERVING NUTRITIONAL INFORMATION: Calories: 254, Protein: 14 g, Fat: 12 g, Saturated Fat: 4 g, Carbohydrate: 26 g, Dietary Fibre: 7 g

fish and vegetable chowder

A satisfying meal in a bowl. Plenty of protein but without the accompanying saturated fat, and with an assortment of phytochemicals, such as the sulfur compounds in onions and the carotenoids in the carrots. Serve with crusty whole grain bread and a salad.

MAKES 4 SERVINGS

2 teaspoons (10 mL) vegetable oil

1/2 cup (125 mL) chopped onions

1/2 cup (125 mL) diced celery

1/2 cup (125 mL) diced carrots

2 medium potatoes, diced

1/2 teaspoon (2 mL) dried thyme

2 cups (500 mL) sodium-reduced vegetable or chicken broth

1 pound (500 g) fish fillets (such as sole, haddock, cod or whitefish), cut into small pieces

1 cup (250 mL) frozen corn kernels

1 1/2 cups (375 mL) 1% milk

Salt and freshly ground pepper, to taste

2 tablespoons (25 mL) finely chopped fresh parsley, for garnish

Heat oil in a large, heavy saucepan over medium heat. Add onions, celery and carrots; sauté until vegetables are soft, about 5 minutes. Add potatoes, thyme and broth; bring to a boil. Reduce heat and simmer, stirring occasionally, until potatoes are almost softened, about 15 minutes. Stir in fish and simmer for 5 minutes. Stir in corn and simmer another 2 to 3 minutes. Stir in milk; cook until heated through. Season with salt and pepper. Serve garnished with chopped parsley.

PER SERVING NUTRITIONAL INFORMATION: Calories: 274, Protein: 29 g, Fat: 5 g, Saturated Fat: 1 g, Carbohydrate: 29 g, Dietary Fibre: 3 g

grilled fish with caramelized onions

Halibut, salmon, or swordfish is delicious with this type of preparation. And remember, sautéing doesn't diminish the rich flavonoid content of the onions.

MAKES 4 SERVINGS

1 tablespoon (15 mL) extra virgin olive oil

1 large onion, thinly sliced

1 teaspoon (5 mL) sugar

1/3 cup (75 mL) orange juice

1/4 cup (50 mL) balsamic vinegar

Salt and freshly ground pepper, to taste

4 fish fillets, each about 6 ounces (175 g)

Heat olive oil in a large, heavy skillet over medium-high heat. Add onions and sauté until translucent, about 10 minutes. Add sugar and stir through. Reduce heat to medium and continue to cook another 5 minutes, stirring occasionally, until onions are very soft. Add orange juice and vinegar; stir through. Continue cooking until the liquid evaporates. Season with salt and pepper. Remove from heat and keep warm.

Meanwhile, preheat grill. Brush fish with olive oil and grill until cooked through. Serve fish topped with caramelized onions.

PER SERVING NUTRITIONAL INFORMATION: Calories: 246, Protein: 36 g, Fat: 7 g, Saturated Fat: 1 g, Carbohydrate: 7 g, Dietary Fibre: 1 g

roasted halibut with roasted tomato garlic sauce

Garlic, tomatoes and olive oil—an unbeatable phyto match that's simple to prepare. The flavourful sauce, also wonderful with grilled chicken, can be made ahead of time and heated just before serving. Any firm white fish fillets work well in this recipe.

MAKES 4 SERVINGS

SAUCE

1 medium head garlic

1 tablespoon (15 mL) + 1 teaspoon (5 mL) extra virgin olive oil

1 1/2 pounds (750 g) plum tomatoes, quartered (6 to 8 tomatoes)

2 tablespoons (25 mL) balsamic vinegar

Salt and freshly ground pepper, to taste

4 halibut fillets, each about 5 ounces (150 g) and 3/4 inch (2 cm) thick

2 teaspoons (10 mL) each extra virgin olive oil and balsamic vinegar

Fresh basil leaves, for garnish

Preheat oven to 450°F (230°C).

To make tomato sauce, cut top 1/8 inch (3 mm) off the head of garlic. Remove any loose skins. Place garlic, cut side up, on a double thickness of foil. Sprinkle with 1 teaspoon (5 mL) of the olive oil. Wrap in foil and bake about 40 minutes or until garlic is soft and forms a paste when a clove is squeezed. Unwrap garlic and allow to cool.

In the meantime, place tomato quarters in an 8-inch (2-L) square baking dish; sprinkle with remaining 1 tablespoon (15 mL) olive oil and 2 tablespoons (25 mL) of the balsamic vinegar. Roast 40 minutes or until tomatoes are very soft and break up easily when stirred.

Place tomatoes in a food processor. Squeeze garlic from cloves into the bowl; purée the mixture until smooth. Season with salt and pepper. Remove from food processor and keep warm if using immediately. Otherwise refrigerate and reheat when ready to use.

While tomatoes are roasting, in a shallow dish marinate fish in 2 teaspoons (10 mL) each olive oil and balsamic vinegar for 20 minutes. Place fish on a baking sheet and sprinkle with salt and pepper. Roast for 15 minutes or until fish is cooked through.

Divide sauce among 4 plates, top with roasted halibut and garnish with fresh basil leaves.

PER SERVING NUTRITIONAL INFORMATION: Calories: 205, Protein: 27 g, Fat: 7 g, Saturated Fat: 2 g, Carbohydrate: 7 g, Dietary Fibre: 1 g

grilled salmon and mediterranean vegetable salad

For maximum taste in this easy dish, use good-quality olive oil and balsamic vinegar. The grilled vegetables make a saucy and tasty accompaniment to the salmon. And there are plenty of nutritional perks. A fruity extra virgin olive oil along with the vegetables will provide an assortment of antioxidants, while the salmon supplies omega-3 fatty acids with their anti-inflammatory effects—all of which may benefit those with arthritis.

MAKES 4 SERVINGS

3 tablespoons (45 mL) balsamic vinegar

2 tablespoons (25 mL) extra virgin olive oil

4 salmon fillets, each about 6 ounces (175 g)

Salt and freshly ground pepper, to taste

3 medium or 2 large tomatoes, cut into 1/3-inch (8-mm) slices

1 red pepper, cut into 1/3-inch (8-mm) strips

1 medium red onion, cut into 1/3-inch (8-mm) slices

1/2 cup (125 mL) chopped fresh basil

Prepare grill racks by brushing lightly with vegetable oil or by spraying with vegetable oil cooking spray. Preheat grill.

In a shallow dish, whisk together 1 tablespoon (15 mL) each of the balsamic vinegar and olive oil. Add salmon fillets and turn to coat. Sprinkle with salt and pepper. Allow to marinate for 10 minutes.

Meanwhile, place tomatoes, red peppers and red onions on a platter and spray with vegetable oil cooking spray. Place vegetables on the grill sprayed side down. Grill for 3 to 4 minutes or until grill marks are evident. Turn vegetables over and grill another 3 to 4 minutes. Remove from grill and place in a medium bowl.

Add remaining 2 tablespoons (25 mL) balsamic vinegar, 1 tablespoon (15 mL) olive oil and the basil. Toss to coat, separating onions into single rings; season with salt and pepper. Set aside.

Place salmon skin side up on grill. Grill for 3 to 4 minutes. Using a spatula, carefully turn the salmon and grill another 4 to 5 minutes or until cooked through.

Place grilled vegetable salad on plates and top with salmon. Serve immediately.

PER SERVING NUTRITIONAL INFORMATION: Calories: 288, Protein: 31 g, Fat: 13 g, Saturated Fat: 2 g, Carbohydrate: 10 g, Dietary Fibre: 2 g

california fish tacos

In Southern California, it seems that almost every eatery serves up some version of fish tacos. A taste of these will tell you why. And nutritionally speaking, the combos are top-notch. Research shows that eating lycopene—from the tomatoes—combined with lutein—from the avocado—provides a great disease-fighting blend.

MAKES 4 SERVINGS

SALSA

1 medium avocado (preferably California), peeled and diced

1 medium tomato, finely diced

1/2 cup (125 mL) finely diced cucumber

1/4 cup (50 mL) finely chopped red onion

3 tablespoons (45 mL) chopped fresh coriander

2 tablespoons (25 mL) fresh lime juice

2 teaspoons (10 mL) extra virgin olive oil

1 teaspoon (5 mL) finely chopped jalapeño pepper

Salt, to taste

4 large flour tortillas (preferably whole wheat)

4 tilapia fillets, each 4–5 ounces (125–140 g)

2 teaspoons (10 mL) extra virgin olive oil

Salt and freshly ground pepper, to taste

To prepare salsa, in a medium bowl, toss together avocado, tomato, cucumber, red onion, coriander, lime juice, olive oil, jalapeño pepper and salt. Set aside. (May be made a few hours ahead and refrigerated, covered.)

Preheat oven to 325°F (160°C). Preheat grill or broiler.

To warm the tortillas, place one tortilla on a large piece of foil. Sprinkle with a drop or two of water. Continue stacking and sprinkling tortillas. Close the packet tightly so the air will not escape. Heat in the oven for 10 minutes.

Coat fish with 2 teaspoons (10 mL) olive oil. Sprinkle with salt and pepper. Grill or broil for 10 minutes per inch (2.5 cm) thickness, turning the fish over at half time.

Place tortilla on a plate; spread 1/2 cup (125 mL) salsa in centre of tortilla. Place tilapia on salsa; fold sides of tortilla over filling. Fold up bottom and continue to roll up to enclose filling. Serve immediately.

PER SERVING NUTRITIONAL INFORMATION: Calories: 395, Protein: 26 g, Fat: 12 g, Saturated Fat: 2 g, Carbohydrate: 47 g, Dietary Fibre: 8 g

asian beef and broccoli wraps

A change-of-pace way to eat a stir-fry. And the ingredients, which help to extend portions, are filled with phytochemicals.

MAKES 4 WRAPS

3 tablespoons (45 mL) each sodium-reduced soy sauce and dry sherry

1/2 teaspoon (2 mL) Chinese chili sauce

1 pound (500 g) lean well-trimmed boneless beef, sliced into 1/4-inch (5-mm) thick strips

4 large flour tortillas (preferably whole wheat)

1 tablespoon (15 mL) cornstarch

3 tablespoons (45 mL) hoisin sauce

1 teaspoon (5 mL) sesame oil

2 teaspoons (10 mL) each vegetable oil, minced garlic and grated ginger

1 cup (250 mL) thinly sliced onions

3 cups (750 mL) broccoli florets (reserve stalks for another use)

1/4 cup (50 mL) sodium-reduced beef broth

In a large bowl, mix together 1 tablespoon (15 mL) each soy sauce and sherry; stir in chili sauce. Add beef; toss to coat. Marinate for 15 minutes at room temperature or up to 8 hours covered in the refrigerator.

Preheat oven to 325°F (160°C). Place one tortilla on a large piece of foil. Sprinkle a drop or two of water on tortilla. Continue stacking and sprinkling with remaining tortillas. Close the packet tightly so that the air will not escape. Heat in oven for 10 minutes. Meanwhile, in a small bowl, mix together cornstarch and 1 tablespoon (15 mL) of the soy sauce to make a paste. Mix in remaining 1 tablespoon (15 mL) soy sauce, remaining 2 tablespoons (25 mL) sherry, hoisin sauce and sesame oil; set aside.

Heat vegetable oil in a wok or large nonstick skillet over high heat. Add garlic and ginger; stir-fry until fragrant, about 30 seconds. Remove beef from marinade using a slotted spoon and add to wok; stir-fry until beef is no longer pink. Add onions and broccoli; stir-fry another 3 minutes. Stir in beef broth; cover and allow to steam for 3 minutes or until heated through.

Stir soy sauce-cornstarch mixture and add to wok. Cook, stirring, until sauce is thickened. Place mixture in the centre of each tortilla and roll tortilla tightly around filling. Serve immediately.

PER SERVING NUTRITIONAL INFORMATION: Calories: 342, Protein: 31 g, Fat: 10 g, Saturated Fat: 3 g, Carbohydrate: 33 g, Dietary Fibre: 4 g

whole grains

... play a major role in
disease prevention because of their
antioxidant capacity

Grains, and the science surrounding them, have really been put through the mill lately: First we're told that foods made from grains make us fat, then we're told they don't— because, actually, they contain very little fat. And now, once again, grain foods are the fat culprit. Here's an example. Not so long ago health and food experts touted the benefits of pasta, and so we piled it onto our plates accordingly. But then the good-for-you mantra flipped. In fact, the thinking was wrong: pasta was bad and should be eaten only in very limited quantities. So what's the real scoop? Well, it's simple: some grains are good for us and don't promote obesity. The advantages grains provide— including protecting against such diseases as type 2 diabetes, heart disease and cancer —depend very much on how they are processed. Whole grains have it. Refined ones just don't measure up.

It used to be thought that the only significant difference between refined and whole grains was in their fibre content. There may have been a few nutrient shortfalls in refined grain products, but since they are generally enriched with nutrients, that concern was no big deal. But scientific research over the past few years has exploded that myth. It's the entire package, not just fibre and a few added nutrients, that packs a wallop. Whole grains have the entire package, including a fibre-rich outer coating of bran, a central endosperm and a nutrient-packed inner germ, which together make up the kernel of the grain. During the milling process, the bran and germ are removed from refined grains and only the endosperm, the least nutritious part of the grain, remains. And although both whole grains and refined grains provide plenty of carbohydrates, because of their speedy digestion and the fast rate with which they are absorbed into the bloodstream, refined grains are linked to easier weight gain. Whole grains, on the other hand, take more time to digest, which leads to greater satiety, which means we may eat less.

Whole grains also contain vitamins—including a number of B vitamins and vitamin E—minerals and an assortment of phytochemicals, among them saponins, lignans, phytosterols and tocotrienols. The fibre in whole grains has long been known as a boon to bowel regularity and reduces the incidence of a host of bowel ailments, including diverticular disease and hemorrhoids. Newer research links fibre to protection against a variety of chronic diseases as well. Even so, most people consume only about half of the recommended 25 to 30 grams a day.

Some of the earliest research on grains was carried out by the British scientist Denis Burkitt in the 1970s. Burkitt identified a higher prevalence of certain diseases, such as heart disease and stroke, in countries whose populations consumed refined grains. Burkitt eventually became known as the father of fibre for making the link between fibre and good health. But it seems that fibre—or the lack of it—was just the tip of the refined-grain iceberg.

In the Iowa Women's Health Study, published in 1998, scientists found whole grain intake was associated with a reduced risk of dying from heart disease. More than 34,000 post-menopausal women between 55 and 69, and free of heart disease, were tracked for nine years. The results were striking: women who rarely consumed whole grain foods had a 50 percent greater chance of dying from heart disease than those who consumed the most whole grain foods. Recognizing that there were other factors involved in the development of heart disease, the scientists recommended further research.

And there was plenty to come. In 1999, a group of University of Kentucky experts in the field of whole grains reviewed 29 published reports on the subject and found that whole grain consumption was consistently linked to protection from heart disease. But they didn't find such a strong association between the protective effect and the fibre alone. In other words, just adding fibre to white bread, as some companies are now doing, is not the way to prevent heart disease.

The effect of whole grains on the risk of stroke has also been extensively studied. At Harvard University, where researchers followed more than 75,000 women in what is known as the Nurses' Health Study, whole grains again were shown to offer protection. But whole grains don't benefit only women. An eight-year Harvard-based follow-up study of close to 45,000 men also gave grains top marks.

Whole grains may protect against heart disease in numerous ways, among them reducing blood cholesterol levels and acting as antioxidants—which in turn protects against clogging arteries—and decreasing the likelihood of developing blood clots. But each of these benefits occurs as a result of a number of components present within the whole grain. The fibre may reduce the level of cholesterol already in the blood, some phytochemicals may cause the liver to produce even less cholesterol and other compounds may lead to less dietary cholesterol being absorbed. And there are even more ways that blood cholesterol profiles can be improved by choosing whole grains.

One way is to select foods with a low glycemic index, or GI. This term has become a buzzword for those who shun carbohydrate-rich foods. The term, first used at the University of Toronto, is a measure of how fast carbohydrates are released into the bloodstream after being eaten compared with the rise in blood sugar caused by quickly released carbs such as sugar or white bread. The more like sugar the food is in the speed of its release into the bloodstream, the higher its glycemic index. And among those foods with a high glycemic index are refined grains.

A rapid increase in blood sugar levels can lead to a higher risk of certain diseases. It may result in higher levels of insulin, the hormone that regulates blood sugar. High insulin levels have been linked to hypertension, artery damage and increased risk for certain types of cancer. Research from Harvard Medical School and Brigham and

Women's Hospital, published in November 2002, links consuming an excess of high-GI foods with an increased risk for blood clots leading to heart attacks or strokes.

High-GI foods may take more of a toll on those who are apple-shaped and carry excess weight around the middle. When extra fat is in the abdomen, insulin may not be not as effective in lowering blood sugar levels—in other words, insulin sensitivity is diminished. Being sedentary also decreases insulin sensitivity. Over time, this decrease results in a condition known as insulin resistance. And eventually, if things continue along in the same way—insulin resistance combined with abdominal fat and inactivity —blood sugar levels rise above normal and type 2 diabetes becomes the diagnosis. High levels of the blood fat triglycerides and low HDL levels are typically partnered with these high blood sugar readings.

So although quickly digested foods don't cause type 2 diabetes, they're associated with the potentially harmful consequences. As a result of their research, published in the *American Journal of Clinical Nutrition,* the Harvard scientists suggest that consuming low-GI foods leads to improvements in blood sugar control and even a lower risk of type 2 diabetes and heart disease. They examined whole grain intake and the risk of type 2 diabetes in almost 43,000 men over a period of 12 years. The men who ate several servings of whole grain products daily had a significantly lower risk of developing type 2 diabetes. And even those who were obese reaped benefits from the whole grains—especially those who were active. Compared with their sedentary obese counterparts, they had a 52 percent lower risk of diabetes. But, once again, it isn't just the GI effect that the scientists believe is responsible. Whole grains contain higher amounts of the mineral magnesium than refined grains. Magnesium plays a role in blood sugar regulation as well as in decreasing the risk for high blood pressure.

A new area of research on a number of disease fronts focuses on a compound in human blood called enterolactone. It seems that high levels of enterolactone in our blood may protect against heart disease and certain cancers, among them breast and prostate. It's speculated that a number of phytochemicals in whole grains may contribute to boosting enterolactone levels. But raising enterolactone levels doesn't happen overnight. In one study, most of the increase was seen in the two weeks after the initiation of a diet rich in whole grains. It's an interesting area of study and one to keep an eye on.

The whole grain connection extends to colon and other digestive cancers, breast cancer and prostate cancer—the most common types in North America. And the mechanisms at work are potentially numerous. Whole grains, while less championed than colourful fruits and vegetables, play a major role in disease prevention because of their antioxidant capacity.

searching for the whole-y grain

Getting whole grains into your shopping basket and onto your plate provides you with a strong defence against a range of diseases. And whole grain choices abound in the marketplace these days. The multicultural mix of foods available, combined with an interest in healthy eating, has led to an unprecedented number of choices in whole grain products.

Among the fabulous range of available choices are whole grain pitas and flatbreads, and breads from artisanal bakers, who use whole grain flours that haven't been seen in bakers' ovens for decades. Yet, despite what we know, and despite our changing attitudes towards what we eat, supermarket shelves continue to overflow with the ever-popular refined-grain white bread, alongside brown breads—some of which are nutritional, some of which are not. A loaf might be darker than its white-bread cousin simply because it contains caramel-type colouring or molasses with just a dash of whole grains thrown in. You also can't judge a bread by its name. Product names containing words such as "oats" and "wheat" conjure up visions of the heartiest of whole grains, but in some cases nothing could be further from the truth. Even labels such as "multigrain" or "100% wheat" are meaningless without the word "whole" in front of them.

But most kids and many adults avoid the whole grain selection. One reason might be that whole grains, unlike their refined counterparts, often have a nutty taste and coarser texture, which some people might not initially find pleasing. But over time, even if you've been a white bread eater all your life, your palate can become accustomed to whole grains, and chances are that eventually you will prefer the nuttier taste of a whole grain product over a bland refined one. For parents who might be trying to convert their youngsters, it can take a lot of patience, but the payoff is worthwhile. Making deals can make the switch easier. Alternating the purchases of bread between white bread and a variety of whole grain loaves may eventually result in a family who prefers the taste of whole grains. Sometimes buying products containing a mix of whole and refined grains can be a nutrient-boosting compromise.

When purchasing whole grains, read labels. Look for the word "whole" on the ingredient list. Opt for "whole wheat" over just "wheat," "brown rice" over "enriched white," "whole rye" over "rye," and a mix of rye and wheat and so forth. No one will notice if you switch the regular couscous for the whole wheat kind. The list of easy whole grain switches is endless. And the options keep increasing, even at the corner grocery store, as assorted grains go mainstream.

The old standbys, like oats, wheat and barley, have been the focus of much scientific study. As these grains become everyday fare, the phytochemical power of less common alternatives such as amaranth, teff, spelt, sorghum and triticale will start to be unveiled as researchers delve into their natural mix of protective compounds.

The following is just a glimpse into the field of grains and what each has to offer.

oats

Oats used to be plain old-fashioned comfort food. A bowl of oatmeal topped with some brown sugar and a favourite fruit was considered stick-to-the-ribs fare. Then, in the late 1980s, researchers discovered that the outer coating of the grain, the oat bran, lowered cholesterol. Suddenly oat bran was the darling of the processed-food industry. It could be found listed on all sorts of ingredient labels, from fat-laden cookies to savoury snacks. Oat bran shortbread cookies loaded with butter and fried oat bran puffs and chips were touted by the food industry as top nutritious fare. No matter that the products were short on many other nutritious ingredients and filled with cholesterol-elevating fats. The thinking was that oat bran was an artery cleaner of sorts. It wasn't long after, in 1990, that the oat bran bubble burst. A study that discounted the bran's effectiveness in lowering blood cholesterol appeared in the *New England Journal of Medicine* and quickly made the front pages of newspapers across North America. Almost overnight, oat bran was on the outs.

Nevertheless, oat bran and oats remain a top source of soluble fibre, a nutrient that can reduce the amount of artery-clogging fat in the blood. But oat bran is so much more than a one-nutrient wonder. Researchers continue to uncover an assortment of benefits. Since the cholesterol-reducing properties of oats were first demonstrated, in 1963, at least 50 other studies on the effects of oats on blood fats have followed. It was previously thought that soluble fibre lowered cholesterol through one mechanism only. Bile acids, compounds that are essential to the digestive process and are made from cholesterol, are trapped in a gel formed by the soluble fibre and then excreted from the body. As the body makes more bile acids for digestion, more cholesterol is removed from the blood. But new research reveals that the fibre may actually inhibit both cholesterol production and absorption—an all-out assault.

Oat products such as oat bran and oat flakes may have an impact on heart disease in a variety of ways. People concerned about blood cholesterol, diabetes, high blood pressure and obesity—all risk factors for heart disease—should consider becoming oat fans, if they aren't already.

One of oat's claims to fame is its beta-glucan content. Beta-glucan is the main type of soluble fibre found in oats—it's what brought the grain into the limelight in the first place. In spite of its earlier bad press, enough solid evidence of its ability to lower blood cholesterol has accumulated that the U.S. Food and Drug Administration (the equivalent of our Health Canada) approved the use of a health claim for oats and heart disease: "Soluble fiber from foods such as oat bran, rolled oats or oatmeal, and whole oat flour, as part of a diet low in saturated fat and cholesterol, may reduce the risk of heart disease." The recommended intake for a cholesterol-lowering effect is 3 grams of oat beta-glucan per day, which can be obtained by eating 1 1/2 cups (375 mL) of cooked oatmeal (3/4 cup/175 mL of uncooked oatmeal) or 3 packets of instant oatmeal. And it seems the more in need of cholesterol lowering you are, the greater the impact of oats on the readings. Some studies have shown that oats not only lower levels of the artery-clogging LDL cholesterol but may also boost the level of the protective HDL cholesterol.

For people with type 2 diabetes, oats may offer a sort of back-door approach to decreasing the risk for heart disease. Both the higher levels of blood sugar and insulin, which can go hand in hand with type 2 diabetes, may boost the risk of heart disease and stroke. Now the good news. Putting foods rich in soluble fibre on the menu may not only reduce blood cholesterol, which can be elevated in people with diabetes, but may also lead to better blood sugar regulation and lower insulin levels. More than 12 published studies report that oats, consumed as oat bran, oatmeal or beta-glucan formulations, reduce blood sugar and insulin levels.

Partaking of foods with plenty of soluble fibre also appears to result in healthier blood pressure readings. How fibre works in lowering blood pressure isn't clear as of yet but it may be the result of its effect on insulin readings. More and more research is pointing to high insulin levels as a culprit in many ailments, including high blood pressure. The list of soluble fibre's advantages includes easier waist management. Studies show that foods rich in soluble fibre can keep you feeling fuller for longer. In one investigation, obese subjects who were placed on a calorie-restricted diet that included an oat-based soup as the main meal once or twice daily lost significant amounts of weight after 23 weeks.

Oats are no slouch when it comes to insoluble fibre either. Almost half their fibre is the insoluble type, with almost 2 grams of insoluble fibre per ounce (30 grams) of dry rolled oats. And if you're not yet sold on oats, here are a few more reasons to sow yours. The grain is loaded with phytochemicals. Among them are unique antioxidants, called avenanthramides, as well as the vitamin E-like compounds tocotrienols and tocopherols. These may all protect cholesterol from being oxidized, making it less likely to be deposited on artery walls. Oats also appear to have a beneficial effect on endothelial function (see page 5), allowing artery walls to respond to various stresses in a healthier way.

And if you think that oats are just for breakfast, think again. A hot bowl containing oats is super for lunch or dinner. No, not a bowl of cereal! Because of the type of fibre oats contain, they can be used to thicken soups. Use oats as a filler for burgers and meatloaf and as a crumb topping for savoury dishes. And when it comes to dessert and in-between-meal eats, the possibilities are endless. As a crunchy topping for fruit crisps and in cookies, muffins and quickbreads, oat flakes can't be beat. And for a change of pace, try oat groats. Groats are the whole grain product before it is flaked, or rolled, to become oat flakes or oatmeal. Use them as a substitute for barley or rice in a savoury pilaf or with veggies in a cold summer salad.

The more processed or finer the oats are, the faster they are digested and incorporated into the bloodstream as sugar. If possible, avoid instant oatmeal—the fastest to prepare and the quickest into the bloodstream—and quick oats. Rolled oats or large flaked oats are the best choice when looking for an oat cereal that produces the slowest rise in blood sugar. And by cooking large-flake oatmeal in the microwave, which takes just a minute or two, you get the best of both worlds—the benefits of quick-cooking oats with the benefits of slower digestion.

wheat

Bulgur, couscous, farina, wheat berries, wheat bran, wheat germ and 100% whole wheat bread or cereal, and even just plain white bread are all made from the same grain. But how much they yield in the way of health advantages depends on the wheat product you choose. Though many appear to offer top-notch nutrition, many in fact don't. Couscous is one such example. Although it is made from wheat, most commercial varieties are not whole grain. Because of its prevalence in Middle Eastern cooking, it seems suitably ethnic and healthy. But unless the label has the words "whole grain," couscous, like white bread, is simply refined wheat, which is neither very healthy nor exotic.

Whole grain wheat, or whole wheat as it's better known, contains the bran as well as the germ, both of which are available as commercial products. Wheat bran, which is brimming with insoluble fibre, has long been a recognized aid to bowel regularity. This type of fibre increases the bulk of bowel material while softening its texture, leading to an increased transit time of waste products through the bowels. The effect is to reduce pressure on the bowel walls and prevent pockets from developing, lowering the odds of a common North American ailment, diverticular disease.

Wheat bran doesn't only provide relief from constipation. Analysis of the bran shows that fibre makes up less than half of it. The other half contains a range of phytochemicals, including lignans, flavonoids and a compound called phytic acid. These compounds may offer protection against colon and breast cancer. Keep in mind that a fibre supplement may certainly provide a remedy for constipation but it won't likely have disease-fighting perks. As always, a rounded diet is your best bet.

Phytic acid and its relatives, phytates, have long been known to lower the absorption of minerals such as iron and zinc. Rather than avoiding phytates, a smarter nutritional move is simply to eat more foods rich in minerals to compensate for the losses.

The germ of the wheat kernel—that is, wheat germ—is a concentrated form of compounds that offer a defence against artery disease. Among these are B vitamins, iron, manganese, zinc, magnesium, phosphorus, copper, potassium and fibre.

Wheat bran and wheat germ can be used in cooking and baking. Try them in place of breadcrumbs, as a filler for burgers, for casserole toppings and as a coating for baked chicken, fish and vegetables. They add a nutty taste in toppings for fruit crumbles. Because of its unsaturated fat content, wheat germ can go rancid at room temperature, so keep it in the fridge.

Using whole wheat products gives you both the bran and germ all in one. When purchasing cereals, breads and crackers, don't just go by the name of the product, which may imply that it's made from the whole grain when instead it contains mainly refined flour. Read labels and look for "whole wheat" or "100% whole wheat." Some old favourites contain a mix of both whole and refined wheat.

wheat berries

All the goodness of wheat is found in the berries, which aren't berries at all but the whole kernels. Enjoy them as a cooked cereal, incorporated into baked goods and made into savoury dishes such as soups, poultry stuffing, pilafs and grain salads. Wheat berries are available in hard or soft varieties; the hard requires a longer cooking time.

bulgur

Bulgur is made from whole wheat berries that have been steamed, hulled and then cracked. As a result of these processes, bulgur can be prepared in a flash. Look for it in three different grinds—fine, medium and coarse. Use the fine or medium for tabbouleh (see recipe on page 120) and the medium or coarse for side dishes such as pilaf and stuffing.

couscous

Couscous, the name used for the smallest size of cracked wheat, requires no cooking (just pour boiling water or stock over couscous, and let it sit until the liquid is absorbed). Although the refined varieties are more common, make a special effort to find whole wheat couscous. The two types taste very much alike but their nutritional counts don't compare.

barley

This fibre-filled ancient grain supplies trace minerals such as zinc, manganese, magnesium, phosphorus, copper and iron, plus some B vitamins. Barley commonly appears in soups but, considering its wonderfully chewy texture, surprising versatility and nutritional perks, it's underused. Barley's flavour and texture, combined with mushrooms and onions in a pilaf, makes for delectable comfort food. Served cold with chopped herbs and veggies, it yields a palate-pleasing salad (see Citrus Barley Salad, page 118).

Barley's soluble fibre has been given all the credit for its potential to lower blood cholesterol, but according to research by University of Wisconsin scientist Dr. Charles Elson, there's more to the grain than meets the eye. Compounds known as tocotrienols, also found in a host of other grains, suppress the production of cholesterol. When barley with the tocotrienols removed was fed to laboratory animals, cholesterol levels were significantly higher than when the whole grain was provided.

The most nutritious barley is the hulled variety, readily available in natural food stores. Next on the nutrition scale comes pot barley, which is less polished and slightly higher in nutritional value than pearled barley, the most common type.

buckwheat

Truth be told, buckwheat is not actually a grain. Although it resembles grain and is prepared like grain, it is, in fact, a seed. It has no ties to wheat despite its name but is a member of the rhubarb family. It is included here because its seeds are made into a flour or cooked as groats.

Buckwheat blinis, the Russian pancakes traditionally and decadently topped with sour cream and caviar, and soba noodles, a Japanese favourite, are both buckwheat flour products. When the seeds are roasted, the bran remains intact, resulting in groats. Better known as kasha, these groats, with their distinctive nutty flavour, are commonly found in Eastern European and Russian cuisines. Kasha varnishkes— groats cooked with noodles and onions—are a perennial favourite in some households (see recipe on page 125).

Kasha, ground to varying consistencies, has long been found in stores selling kosher products. Unroasted groats are a newer addition to natural and specialty food stores. Buckwheat provides minerals such as magnesium and manganese and noteworthy amounts of soluble fibre. Its protein, like that of soy, appears to provide a cholesterol-lowering kick. Add in the phytochemicals such as flavonoids, flavones and phytosterols and you have to wonder why buckwheat is not trumpeted as a heart-healthy food more often.

cornmeal

Cornmeal is available in yellow, white and blue, though the first two are more common. For a higher carotenoid content, including beta carotene, opt for the yellow over the white. And for the most nutrition, look for stone-ground varieties. Dried corn is ground using either stones or, for most commercial products, machinery, but the machine milling removes much of the hull and germ, resulting in less nutrition and flavour. The stone ground, with its coarser texture, has a shorter shelf life. Interchangeable in recipes, each supplies B vitamins—thiamine, riboflavin, niacin and vitamin B-6—iron, magnesium, phosphorus, zinc and copper. Among its phyto-chemicals are tocotrienols, with their cholesterol-lowering ability and anti-cancer action. And cornmeal is ranked as one of the grains with the highest levels of antioxidant power.

Cornmeal is a favourite for some as their morning bowl of cereal or as an ingredient in baked goods (see Orange Cornmeal Bread, page 128). And if you've never tried the Italian way of preparing cornmeal, the savoury polenta, you're missing out on a taste treat.

Hominy—or, when ground, hominy grits—is a staple in the southern U.S. It is made from corn but is completely refined.

And don't forget about popcorn. It can be a super snack option—just pay attention to how it's prepared. Beneath the terms "unbuttered" and "air-popped" can lurk a fat-laden selection. Because of the fat used in popping the corn, even "unbuttered" movie theatre popcorn can provide more than 500 calories and 20 grams of fat in a medium bag. Cheese-flavoured air-popped varieties have been known to clock in with fat counts similar to those of potato chips. "Light" microwave or air-popped, with only 30 calories and over 1 gram of fibre per cup, is a satisfying and nutritious option.

farro

Farro is experiencing a comeback. It is one of the original grains of the Mediterranean, an early wheat variety that was the standard ration of the Roman legions. Like barley, it's somewhat chewy, making it an ideal candidate for pilafs and grain-veggie salad combos. As it's just making its return to dinner plates, it hasn't yet been the subject of much scientific research. But considering it's a whole grain product, it's likely packed with the best that nature has to offer.

quinoa

Quinoa (pronounced keen-wah) is not a grain. It's a seed, a member of the same family to which green leafy vegetables such as Swiss chard and spinach belong. This ancient grain-like product is brimming with assorted nutrients, among them riboflavin, folic acid, magnesium, zinc, iron and potassium. It's also top-notch in the protein department. To protect it from being eaten by insects and birds, the outer coating of the seed is packed with disease-battling and blood-cholesterol-lowering phytochemicals called saponins. Researchers from Rutgers University Department of Food Science have isolated another dozen of these saponins, some of which have been shown to strengthen the immune system in addition to having anti-fungal properties.

With its short cooking time, quinoa can be used like rice and barley in salads, pilafs, casseroles and vegetable soups. (See Sesame Quinoa Salad, page 121, and Savoury Quinoa Pilaf, page 127.) Cooked in fruit juice, it makes a tasty foundation for desserts.

And here's an interesting note for Jewish people who observe the dietary laws of Passover, during which time the use of grain products is limited: Because it's not a true grain, quinoa can be certified kosher for Passover, making it a high-protein and high-fibre option for this festival.

rice

Brown rice has come a long way since the 1960s, when it was the hippies' food of choice. Newer quicker-cooking varieties make it a more convenient option nowadays. It's also a more nutritious selection than its refined white counterpart. Among its nutrient contributions are niacin and vitamin B-6, vitamin E, magnesium, manganese, phosphorus and selenium. Brown rice adds not only more fibre than white rice but also the perks of rice bran oil and its unsaturated fat. Wisconsin researchers examined the effects of the various components of rice bran on blood sugar and cholesterol in subjects with type 1 (or insulin-dependent) diabetes and type 2 (or non-insulin-dependent) diabetes. And the results were impressive. Not only did rice bran have a heart-healthy effect on cholesterol and triglycerides but, in addition, it led to better blood sugar readings. Research from India, as well as showing that rice bran had a favourable effect on blood cholesterol profiles, showed that it had antioxidant powers too.

rye

If you're seeking a whole grain rye, forget about the kind that sandwiches the corned beef at the deli. While offering some whole rye, more than 50 percent of the bread is refined white flour. True, it's a better option than sliced white bread, but it still doesn't provide the nutrition and nutty taste of the whole grain. Rye is a good cold-weather crop, and in northern Europe wholemeal rye, as it's usually called there, is a common bread, cracker and flatbread.

Finnish scientists compared the blood and urine concentrations of enterolactone in healthy subjects after they ate their usual wholemeal rye and after they ate refined-wheat bread (a.k.a. white bread). Levels of enterolactone, which may protect against some forms of cancer and heart disease, appear to rise with consumption of lignans. But in this study, even the scientists were taken aback at the levels. Their data indicated about five to ten times the expected rise in enterolactone, leading them to postulate that there may be synergistic effects of different compounds like fibre and lignans. Another Finnish study had subjects eat either whole grain rye or white bread, and then compared a number of measures speculated to be risk factors for diseases such as colon cancer. Once again, the rye won out.

recipes

mushroom barley soup

The full-bodied flavour is worth the longer cooking time. Keep a container or two of this soup in the freezer, as it freezes well. The barley and vegetables offer a potent cholesterol-lowering punch, while the mushrooms offer anti-cancer action, making this soup more than just delicious comfort food.

MAKES 8 SERVINGS

1 1/2 cups (375 mL) boiling water

1 ounce (30 g) dried mushrooms (such as porcini)

2 teaspoons (10 mL) vegetable oil

1 large onion, chopped

2 large stalks celery, diced

1 parsnip, diced

1 cup (250 mL) diced carrots

2 cups (500 mL) sliced button mushrooms (about 1/2 pound/250 g)

3/4 cup (175 mL) barley (preferably pot barley)

8 cups (2 L) sodium-reduced beef, chicken or vegetable broth

Salt and freshly ground pepper, to taste

In a medium bowl, pour boiling water over dried mushrooms; soak for 25 minutes. Remove mushrooms, reserving soaking liquid, and squeeze out excess water. Coarsely chop mushrooms and set aside. Strain soaking liquid through a cheesecloth-lined strainer or a coffee filter and set aside.

Heat oil in a stockpot over medium-high heat; add onion and sauté until soft, 5 to 7 minutes. Add celery, parsnip, carrots, soaked mushrooms and button mushrooms; sauté another 5 minutes. Stir in barley, broth and reserved mushroom liquid. Bring to a boil and simmer, covered and stirring occasionally, for about 1 1/2 hours or until barley is tender. Season with salt and pepper.

PER SERVING NUTRITIONAL INFORMATION: Calories: 150, Protein: 10 g, Fat: 2 g, Saturated Fat: less than 1 g, Carbohydrate: 24 g, Dietary Fibre: 5 g

citrus barley salad

This recipe will sell you on using barley in other dishes besides soup. Keep some cooked barley on hand in the freezer and just toss it together in this salad. The cholesterol-lowering fibre of the various ingredients combined with the assortment of antioxidants makes this a terrific heart-healthy choice.

MAKES 6 TO 8 SERVINGS

3 cups (750 mL) cooked barley (preferably pot barley)

1 red pepper, diced

1 cup (250 mL) diced English cucumber

1/2 cup (125 mL) diced red onions

1/2 cup (125 mL) diced celery

1/2 cup (125 mL) diced carrots

1/4 cup (50 mL) chopped fresh coriander

1/4 cup (50 mL) chopped fresh mint

1/2 cup (125 mL) orange juice

2 tablespoons (25 mL) fresh lemon juice

2 tablespoons (25 mL) extra virgin olive oil

1 teaspoon (5 mL) honey

Salt and freshly ground pepper, to taste

In a large bowl, combine barley with red pepper, cucumber, red onion, celery, carrot, coriander and mint. Whisk together orange juice, lemon juice, olive oil and honey. Pour over barley and vegetables; toss until coated. Season with salt and pepper.

PER 8-SERVINGS NUTRITIONAL INFORMATION: Calories: 129, Protein: 2 g, Fat: 4 g, Saturated Fat: 1 g, Carbohydrate: 23 g, Dietary Fibre: 5 g

couscous, chickpea and vegetable salad

The vitamin C-rich tomatoes and red pepper are super in their ability to boost the absorption of iron from the whole wheat couscous and the chickpeas. And between the couscous and the chickpeas, there's plenty of both insoluble and soluble fibre—a bonus for healthy bowels, blood sugar and cholesterol.

MAKES 4 TO 6 SERVINGS

1/2 cup (125 mL) couscous (preferably whole wheat)

1/8 teaspoon (0.5 mL) salt

1 cup (250 mL) boiling water

1 (19-ounce/540-mL) can chickpeas, rinsed and drained

1 red pepper, diced

1 cup (250 mL) chopped green onions

1 cup (250 mL) diced tomatoes

1 cup (250 mL) diced cucumber

3/4 cup (175 mL) chopped fresh assorted herbs (parsley, coriander, dill, mint)

2 tablespoons (25 mL) extra virgin olive oil

2 tablespoons (25 mL) fresh lemon juice

1 clove garlic, finely chopped

Salt and freshly ground pepper, to taste

Place couscous and salt in a large bowl; pour boiling water over couscous and stir with a fork. Cover and let sit for 5 minutes, then fluff with a fork. Allow to cool.

Add chickpeas, red pepper, green onions, tomatoes, cucumber and herbs to the couscous and toss to mix.

In a small bowl, mix together olive oil, lemon juice and garlic. Pour over couscous mixture and toss to coat evenly with dressing. Season with salt and pepper. Refrigerate for at least 2 hours to allow flavours to blend.

PER 6-SERVINGS NUTRITIONAL INFORMATION: Calories: 194, Protein: 7 g, Fat: 6 g, Saturated Fat: 1 g, Carbohydrate: 30 g, Dietary Fibre: 6 g

tabbouleh salad

This salad is a snap to make. Why buy prepared tabbouleh when you can quickly whip up a phyto-packed one in no time flat? And it's a yummy way to take in an assortment of heart-healthy and anti-cancer substances. The phytate from the bulgur protects bowel health while the vegetables and herbs offer a variety of antioxidants.

MAKES 4 SERVINGS

1/2 cup (125 mL) medium or fine bulgur

3/4 cup (175 mL) finely diced English cucumber

3/4 cup (175 mL) finely diced tomatoes

2/3 cup (150 mL) finely chopped fresh parsley

1/3 cup (75 mL) finely chopped fresh basil

1/3 cup (75 mL) finely chopped fresh mint

1/3 cup (75 mL) finely chopped green onions

2 tablespoons (25 mL) fresh lemon juice

2 tablespoons (25 mL) extra virgin olive oil

Salt and freshly ground pepper, to taste

Rinse bulgur by placing it in a sieve and running water through it. Place in a large bowl; cover with 1 inch (2.5 cm) water; soak for 45 to 60 minutes or until bulgur is soft. Drain bulgur in a sieve and squeeze out excess water.

Place bulgur in a large bowl. Add cucumber, tomatoes, parsley, basil, mint, green onions, lemon juice and olive oil; toss to mix well. Season with salt and pepper. Let stand for 10 to 15 minutes before serving.

PER SERVING NUTRITIONAL INFORMATION: Calories: 174, Protein: 4 g, Fat: 7 g, Saturated Fat: 1 g, Carbohydrate: 24 g, Dietary Fibre: 6 g

sesame quinoa salad

Deconstructed sushi is what my daughter Alyssa called this after she tasted it. And it certainly made a quinoa fan of her. Quinoa is chock full of saponins, compounds shown to both lower cholesterol and boost immune system functioning.

MAKES 6 SERVINGS

1 cup (250 mL) quinoa

1 English cucumber, diced

1 red pepper, diced

1/3 cup (75 mL) chopped green onions

1 tablespoon (15 mL) toasted sesame seeds

2 tablespoons (25 mL) sodium-reduced soy sauce

2 tablespoons (25 mL) rice wine vinegar

1 1/2 tablespoons (20 mL) sesame oil

2 teaspoons (10 mL) vegetable oil

2 teaspoons (10 mL) grated ginger

1 teaspoon (5 mL) sugar

Salt, to taste

In a sieve, rinse quinoa under running water. Transfer quinoa to a medium saucepan and add 2 cups (500 mL) water. Bring to a boil over medium-high heat; reduce heat and simmer, covered, for 10 to 15 minutes or until liquid is absorbed. Allow to cool.

Toss quinoa, cucumber, red pepper, green onions and sesame seeds in a large bowl. Whisk together soy sauce, vinegar, sesame oil, vegetable oil, ginger and sugar in a small bowl. Pour over quinoa and vegetables and toss well to coat. Season with salt.

PER SERVING NUTRITIONAL INFORMATION: Calories: 134, Protein: 4 g, Fat: 6 g, Saturated Fat: 1 g, Carbohydrate: 18 g, Dietary Fibre: 2 g

farro with tomatoes and basil

Antioxidant-rich with lots of fibre, combined with great taste—what more can you ask for? If you can't find farro at a local health food or specialty store, you can substitute wheat berries, but cooking times will be shorter. Use a top-quality olive oil for maximum taste.

MAKES 4 TO 6 SERVINGS

1 cup (250 mL) farro, washed and picked over

1 cup (250 mL) diced tomatoes

1/4 cup (50 mL) chopped fresh basil

2 tablespoons (25 mL) chopped pitted black olives

2 tablespoons (25 mL) extra virgin olive oil

Salt and freshly ground pepper, to taste

Soak farro in enough cold water to cover for at least 2 hours. Drain. In a medium saucepan, combine farro and 3 cups (750 mL) cold water. Bring to a boil; reduce heat to low and cook, covered, until farro is soft, about 45 minutes. Drain.

In a large bowl, toss together farro, tomatoes, basil, olives and olive oil. Season with salt and pepper. Serve immediately.

PER 6-SERVINGS NUTRITIONAL INFORMATION: Calories: 95, Protein: 2 g, Fat: 5 g, Saturated Fat: 1 g, Carbohydrate: 11 g, Dietary Fibre: 3 g

spaghetti with roasted garlic, tomato and balsamic sauce

This intensely flavoured sauce is so simple to make. You can put the sauce through a food mill for a smoother finish, but you'll be minus the fibre of the skin and seeds. The combination of cooked tomatoes and olive oil makes for greater absorption of the lycopene. You can make the sauce ahead and store it in the refrigerator; reheat it while you cook the spaghetti.

MAKES 4 TO 6 SERVINGS

1 medium head garlic

2 tablespoons (25 mL) extra virgin olive oil

2 pounds (750 g) plum tomatoes, quartered (10–12 tomatoes)

1 pound (500 g) spaghetti (preferably whole wheat)

2 tablespoons (25 mL) balsamic vinegar

Salt and freshly ground pepper, to taste

1/3 cup (75 mL) freshly grated Parmesan cheese

Fresh basil leaves, for garnish

Preheat oven to 450°F (230°C).

Cut top 1/8 inch (3 mm) off the head of garlic. Remove any loose skins. Place garlic, cut side up, on a double thickness of foil. Sprinkle with 1 teaspoon (5 mL) of the olive oil. Wrap in foil and bake about 40 minutes or until garlic is soft and forms a paste when a clove is squeezed. Unwrap garlic and allow to cool.

In the meantime, place tomato quarters in a 3-quart (3-L) baking dish; sprinkle with 2 teaspoons (10 mL) of the olive oil; roast 40 minutes.

During the last few minutes of roasting the garlic, cook spaghetti in a large pot of boiling salted water until just tender; drain.

Place tomatoes in a food processor. Squeeze garlic from skins into the bowl; add remaining 1 tablespoon (15 mL) olive oil and the balsamic vinegar. Purée the mixture until smooth. Season with salt and pepper.

Toss sauce with spaghetti. Serve sprinkled with freshly grated Parmesan and garnished with fresh basil.

PER 6-SERVINGS NUTRITIONAL INFORMATION: Calories: 366, Protein: 15 g, Fat: 8 g, Saturated Fat: 2 g, Carbohydrate: 64 g, Dietary Fibre: 11 g

whole wheat pasta with rapini

Also known as broccoli rabe, rapini is traditionally combined with pasta, as in this classic dish from Puglia. Greens, whole wheat and garlic—a perfect combination for healthy blood pressure readings. The rapini is also chock full of anti-cancer compounds, like all its relatives from the brassica family.

MAKES 4 TO 6 SERVINGS

3/4 pound (375 g) whole wheat penne or other short pasta

2 bunches rapini, trimmed and chopped

2 tablespoons (25 mL) extra virgin olive oil

2 cloves garlic, finely chopped

1 teaspoon (5 mL) anchovy paste

1/4 cup (50 mL) freshly grated Pecorino Romano cheese

1/4 cup (50 mL) freshly grated Parmesan cheese

Salt and freshly ground pepper, to taste

Cook pasta in large pot of boiling salted water until it begins to soften, 8 to 10 minutes. Add rapini and cook until pasta is just tender, another 3 to 5 minutes. Drain.

While pasta is cooking, heat oil in a small, heavy saucepan over medium heat. Add garlic and sauté until it begins to soften, about 1 minute. Stir in anchovy paste. Remove from heat and keep warm.

Place pasta and rapini in a large bowl; toss with the oil and garlic mixture. Sprinkle with cheeses and toss again. Season with salt and pepper. Serve immediately.

PER 6-SERVINGS NUTRITIONAL INFORMATION: Calories: 296, Protein: 14 g, Fat: 8 g, Saturated Fat: 2 g, Carbohydrate: 47 g, Dietary Fibre: 5 g

kasha varnishkes

No chicken fat like the way it used to be traditionally prepared, but plenty of taste and nutrition! Add in the heart-healthy phytochemicals flavonoids, flavones and phytosterols, along with the cholesterol-lowering fibre, and you certainly have a heart-smart offering.

MAKES 6 TO 8 SERVINGS

1 cup (250 mL) whole kasha

1 egg white

1 tablespoon (15 mL) extra virgin olive oil

2 cups (500 mL) thinly sliced onions

1/2 cup (125 mL) diced red peppers

2 cups (500 mL) sodium-reduced vegetable or chicken broth

2 cups (500 mL) bow-tie pasta

1/2 teaspoon (2 mL) salt

Freshly ground pepper, to taste

Chopped fresh parsley, for garnish

In a small bowl, stir together kasha and egg white. Prepare a large skillet by spraying with vegetable oil cooking spray. Heat skillet over medium-high heat. Add kasha mixture and stir for 1 minute. Transfer kasha to a large bowl and set aside.

Heat oil in same skillet over medium-high heat. Add onions; sauté until lightly browned, about 3 minutes. Add red peppers; sauté until tender, about 3 minutes longer. Stir in kasha and broth. Bring to a boil; reduce heat to low and cook, covered, until broth is absorbed, about 12 minutes.

Meanwhile, cook bow-tie pasta in a large pot of boiling salted water until just tender; drain.

Toss pasta with kasha mixture; season with salt and pepper. Serve garnished with chopped fresh parsley.

PER 8-SERVINGS NUTRITIONAL INFORMATION: Calories: 152, Protein: 5 g, Fat: 3 g, Saturated Fat: less than 1 g, Carbohydrate: 28 g, Dietary Fibre: 2 g

oat groat pilaf with wild mushrooms

Comfort food at its best. Groats are the least processed of the various oat products, making them a grain product with a lower glycemic index, which leads to better blood sugar readings. Add in the soluble fibre and this is a cholesterol-lowering savoury treat. Look for oat groats in a natural food store.

MAKES 4 TO 6 SERVINGS

3 1/2 cups (875 mL) sodium-reduced chicken or vegetable broth

1 cup (250 mL) oat groats, rinsed

2 teaspoons (10 mL) extra virgin olive oil

1 cup (250 mL) chopped onions

4 cups (1 L) sliced mushrooms

1/2 cup (125 mL) red wine

Salt and freshly ground pepper, to taste

2 tablespoons (25 mL) chopped fresh parsley, for garnish

Bring broth to a boil in a medium saucepan. Stir in groats. Return to a boil, reduce heat, cover and simmer for 55 to 60 minutes or until groats are tender. Remove from heat and let stand for 10 minutes.

Meanwhile, heat oil in a large skillet over medium heat; add onions and sauté for 5 minutes. Stir in mushrooms; cook another 10 minutes. Add wine and cook until it is almost evaporated, 3 to 4 minutes. Add groats to skillet and toss. Season with salt and pepper. Garnish with chopped parsley and serve immediately.

PER 6-SERVINGS NUTRITIONAL INFORMATION: Calories: 167, Protein: 10 g, Fat: 4 g, Saturated Fat: 1 g, Carbohydrate: 24 g, Dietary Fibre: 3 g

savoury quinoa pilaf

This is a fibre-packed change of pace from rice pilafs. Quinoa's saponins together with its fibre make the grain a cholesterol-watcher's delight.

MAKES 4 TO 6 SERVINGS (4 CUPS/1 L)

3/4 cup (175 mL) quinoa

2 teaspoons (10 mL) extra virgin olive oil

1/2 cup (125 mL) chopped onions

2 cups (500 mL) sliced mushrooms (about 1/2 pound/250 g)

2 1/2 cups (625 mL) sodium-reduced vegetable or chicken broth

1 tablespoon (15 mL) fresh lemon juice

1 teaspoon (5 mL) lemon zest

3/4 cup (175 mL) green peas (cooked fresh or thawed frozen)

2 tablespoons (25 mL) chopped fresh dill

Salt and freshly ground pepper, to taste

Rinse quinoa well and pat dry. In a large saucepan over medium heat, toast quinoa, stirring occasionally, for 5 to 8 minutes or until golden. Transfer quinoa to a bowl; set aside.

In the same saucepan, heat oil over medium heat; add onions and sauté until soft. Add mushrooms; cook 10 minutes more. Add quinoa and broth. Bring to a boil, reduce heat and cook, covered, until liquid has evaporated, about 15 minutes. Add lemon juice, lemon zest and peas. Stir until just heated through. Stir in dill, salt and pepper. Serve immediately.

PER 6-SERVINGS NUTRITIONAL INFORMATION: Calories: 127, Protein: 5 g, Fat: 3 g, Saturated Fat: less than 1 g, Carbohydrate: 21 g, Dietary Fibre: 3 g

orange cornmeal bread

Here's a corn bread without all of the typical fat—perfect for muffin and quick-bread lovers. Both the cornmeal and the orange provide cholesterol-lowering and anti-cancer action.

MAKES 18 SERVINGS

1 1/4 cups (300 mL) all-purpose flour

3/4 cup (175 mL) yellow cornmeal (preferably stone-ground)

1 tablespoon (15 mL) baking powder

1/2 teaspoon (2 mL) baking soda

1/4 teaspoon (1 mL) salt

1 large seedless orange, peeled and white pith carefully removed

3/4 cup (175 mL) sugar

1 teaspoon (5 mL) orange zest

1 egg

1 egg white

1/3 cup (75 mL) buttermilk

2 tablespoons (25 mL) vegetable oil

Preheat oven to 350°F (180°C). Prepare a 9- x 5-inch (2-L) loaf pan by spraying with vegetable oil cooking spray.

In a food processor, process the flour, cornmeal, baking powder, baking soda and salt until mixed. Transfer to a large bowl.

Cut the orange into about 8 pieces and place with sugar and orange zest in the food processor; pulse until orange is finely chopped. Add the egg, egg white, buttermilk and oil; process until combined. Add to dry ingredients, stirring just until blended; do not overmix.

Pour into loaf pan and bake for 38 to 40 minutes or until tester comes out clean. Cool for 10 minutes; remove from pan and cool completely on a wire rack.

PER SERVING NUTRITIONAL INFORMATION: Calories: 109, Protein: 2 g, Fat: 2 g, Saturated Fat: less than 1 g, Carbohydrate: 21 g, Dietary Fibre: 2 g

carrot zucchini bran muffins

Beta carotene, lutein and whole grains—all in one delicious package.

MAKES 12 MUFFINS

3/4 cup (175 mL) bran cereal

3/4 cup (175 mL) buttermilk

1 cup (250 mL) all-purpose flour

1/2 cup (125 mL) whole wheat flour

1/2 cup (125 mL) sugar

1 tablespoon (15 mL) baking powder

1/4 teaspoon (1 mL) salt

1 teaspoon (5 mL) cinnamon

1/2 cup (125 mL) raisins

1 cup (250 mL) grated carrots

1 cup (250 mL) coarsely shredded zucchini (about 2 medium)

1 egg

1 egg white

1/4 cup (50 mL) vegetable oil

1 teaspoon (5 mL) vanilla extract

Preheat oven to 400°F (200°C). Grease a muffin pan.

In a medium bowl, stir together bran and buttermilk; set aside for 10 minutes to soften bran.

In a large bowl, stir together all-purpose flour, whole wheat flour, sugar, baking powder, salt, cinnamon and raisins. Add carrot and zucchini; stir until well mixed.

In a medium bowl, lightly beat egg and egg white. Beat in vegetable oil and vanilla. Add bran and mix well. Add to the dry ingredients, stirring just until blended; do not overmix. Spoon into muffin cups. Bake for 18 to 20 minutes or until tester comes out dry.

PER MUFFIN NUTRITIONAL INFORMATION: Calories: 165, Protein: 4 g, Fat: 5 g, Saturated Fat: 1 g, Carbohydrate: 30 g, Dietary Fibre: 3 g

pumpkin oat streusel muffins

Nuts and oats provide a cholesterol-lowering punch while the pumpkin's carotenoids protect against the cholesterol being oxidized, making it less artery clogging.

MAKES 12 MUFFINS

STREUSEL

1/4 cup (50 mL) oats (any variety)

1 tablespoon (15 mL) each firmly packed brown sugar and melted soft margarine

1/8 teaspoon (0.5 mL) pumpkin pie spice

MUFFINS

1 cup (250 mL) all-purpose flour

1/2 cup (125 mL) whole wheat flour

1 cup (250 mL) oats (any variety, uncooked)

3/4 cup (175 mL) firmly packed brown sugar

1 tablespoon (15 mL) baking powder

1 1/2 teaspoons (7 mL) pumpkin pie spice

1/2 teaspoon (2 mL) baking soda

1/4 teaspoon (1 mL) salt

2 tablespoons (25 mL) coarsely chopped nuts

1 cup (250 mL) canned or cooked pumpkin purée

3/4 cup (175 mL) skim or 1% milk

1/3 cup (75 mL) vegetable oil

1 egg, lightly beaten

Preheat oven to 400°F (200°C). Line 12 medium muffin cups with paper baking cups or lightly grease bottoms only.

To make the streusel, in a bowl combine oats, sugar, margarine and pumpkin pie spice; stir well. Set aside.

To make the muffins, in a large bowl combine all-purpose flour, whole wheat flour, oats, sugar, baking powder, pumpkin pie spice, baking soda, salt and nuts; stir well. Whisk together pumpkin, milk, oil and egg; add to dry mixture, stirring just until dry ingredients are moistened. Fill muffin cups almost full. Sprinkle streusel evenly over batter, patting gently. Bake 22 to 25 minutes or until golden brown. Let muffins stand a few minutes before removing from pan. Serve warm.

PER MUFFIN NUTRITIONAL INFORMATION: Calories: 199, Protein: 5 g, Fat: 8 g, Saturated Fat: 1 g, Carbohydrate: 31 g, Dietary Fibre: 2 g

apple oatmeal pancakes

With their apple and oats, these pancakes are perfect fare for the cholesterol conscious—and anyone else for that matter!

MAKES ABOUT 12 PANCAKES

1 1/4 cups (300 mL) buttermilk

2/3 cup (150 mL) quick-cooking rolled oats (not instant)

1 large egg, lightly beaten

2/3 cup (150 mL) firmly packed grated peeled apple, excess juice squeezed out

2 tablespoons (25 mL) firmly packed light brown sugar

1/2 cup (125 mL) whole wheat flour

1/4 cup (50 mL) all-purpose flour

1 teaspoon (5 mL) cinnamon

1 teaspoon (5 mL) baking soda

1/2 teaspoon (2 mL) salt

4 teaspoons (20 mL) vegetable oil

Low-fat plain yogurt flavoured with cinnamon and honey

In a bowl, whisk together 1 cup (250 mL) of the buttermilk and the oats; let stand for 15 minutes.

In a large bowl, stir together the egg, apple and brown sugar. Add the whole wheat flour, all-purpose flour, cinnamon, baking soda, salt, vegetable oil, the oat mixture and the remaining 1/4 cup (50 mL) buttermilk; stir to combine well.

Prepare a griddle by spraying it with vegetable oil cooking spray. Heat the griddle over medium heat. When it is hot enough that a drop of water scatters over its surface, drop the batter by half-filled 1/4-cup (50-mL) measures onto it. Cook the pancakes for 1 to 2 minutes on each side or until they are golden and cooked through. Serve the pancakes with the flavoured yogurt.

PER PANCAKE NUTRITIONAL INFORMATION: Calories: 88, Protein: 3 g, Fat: 3 g, Saturated Fat: less than 1 g, Carbohydrate: 14 g, Dietary Fibre: 1 g

rhubarb blueberry crumble

This dessert takes phytos to the max! Blueberries, with their anthocyanins and protection against cognitive decline, may be called the new brain food. And rhubarb is no phytochemical slouch either, with its cholesterol-lowering compounds.

MAKES 6 TO 8 SERVINGS

TOPPING

3/4 cup (175 mL) oats (not instant)

1/4 cup (50 mL) brown sugar

3 tablespoons (45 mL) wheat germ

3 tablespoons (45 mL) all-purpose flour

2 tablespoons (25 mL) chopped pecans

1 teaspoon (5 mL) cinnamon

1/4 cup (50 mL) soft margarine

FILLING

2 1/2 cups (625 mL) rhubarb, sliced into 1/2-inch (1-cm) pieces

2 1/2 cups (625 mL) fresh or frozen blueberries

1/3 cup (75 mL) brown sugar

1 1/2 tablespoons (20 mL) cornstarch

1/2 teaspoon (2 mL) cinnamon

Preheat oven to 350°F (180°C).

To make the topping, in a bowl combine the oats, sugar, wheat germ, flour, pecans and cinnamon; mix well. Work in margarine with a fork or your fingertips until the margarine is distributed and all the dry ingredients are moistened.

To make the filling, in a 6-cup (1.5-L) baking dish, toss together rhubarb, blueberries, sugar, cornstarch and cinnamon. Sprinkle topping evenly over fruit.

Bake for 35 to 40 minutes or until fruit is soft and the topping is golden brown.

PER 8-SERVINGS NUTRITIONAL INFORMATION: Calories: 190, Protein: 3 g, Fat: 7 g, Saturated Fat: 1 g, Carbohydrate: 28 g, Dietary Fibre: 3 g

legumes

... measure up to more than a
"hill of beans"

As the comedian Rodney Dangerfield so often lamented, "I don't get no respect." And neither do members of the legume, or pulse, family—at least they haven't in the recent past, anyway. Legumes, or pulses, which include peas, beans, lentils and chickpeas, and traditionally thought of as peasant food, were often excluded from chic menus. As culinary horizons have broadened in the past few decades, ethnic dishes like pasta and beans or curried lentils have achieved a more fashionable status. And the pleasure of legumes and pulses, which have been eaten for many thousands of years in other cultures, are being rediscovered. As their palate-pleasing possibilities are once more being revealed, scientific research is demonstrating that when it comes to nutrition, few foods measure up to a hill of beans.

But before discussing the benefits legumes and pulses provide, let's get the terminology straight: Legumes are any plant species that have seed pods that split when ripe. Green beans, fresh peas, lentils, kidney beans and soybeans are all part of this family. Even peanuts, which are most often thought of as a nut, are members of the legumes. Pulses, from a Latin word that means thick soup, are the edible seeds of leguminous vegetables. Not all legumes, however, are considered pulses. Alfalfa, for example, is a legume but not a pulse, as it's the foliage, or leaves, that is used for animal feed. The same goes for clover, also a member of the legume family.

do yourself a favour—get beaned

Pulses have been a staple the world over, as they are an inexpensive source of protein. In many cultures, meat and other animal-protein foods were reserved for special occasions, and even then, portions were often meagre. As some cultures became more affluent, animal foods became more common—a sure sign of success—and pasta with beans gave way to pasta with giant-sized meatballs. With this shift from a diet rich in legumes to one rich in animal fat came a host of diet-related illnesses. One way to stem the tide of disease, according to accumulating research, is to elevate pulses' status. Not only are they loaded with protein but they're also a powerhouse of valuable nutrients such as fibre (both soluble and insoluble), B vitamins, calcium, copper, iron, magnesium, phosphorus, potassium and zinc. And pulses contain a pretty impressive list of phytochemicals to boot.

But back to the matter of protein. Because pulses may lack certain amino acids—the building blocks of protein—the thinking has been that these foods need to be consumed at the same time as certain other foods to provide a "complete" protein. Eating beans with grains, which contain important amino acids (methionine and tryptophan) missing in the beans, is one example of what is called complementing proteins. Combining beans with rice or peanut butter and bread was thought to be a necessary nutritional choice. But science now shows that if there's a mix of amino acids throughout the day, then having complementary proteins at the same meal isn't necessary. All the same, it can be pretty tasty. A garlicky hummus spread on whole grain pita, or a bowl of pasta fagiole—pasta and bean soup—can be yummy. For children and teens, though, complementing proteins is still recommended because of their daily nutritional requirements.

While legumes may be on more menus because they are low in saturated fat and packed with fibre, there's another noteworthy reason to include them. For people who may have kidney problems, overloading on animal proteins may further compromise their kidneys. For this reason, those who are at risk for kidney disease should consume only moderate amounts of animal protein.

So who's at risk for kidney disease? Research shows that those with type 2 diabetes are at a much greater risk than those with normal blood sugar regulation. In fact, there's speculation that by the time diabetes is diagnosed in many cases, the kidneys may already be working at a less than optimal condition. And considering the epidemic of type 2 diabetes that's expected with our ever "expanding" population (due to lack of exercise and poor eating habits), it might be time to leave the carne out of the chili every so often.

take your pulse—your heart will love you

Putting pulses on the menu on a regular basis can be economical. And not just for your budget. The bean counters looking at health-care costs would be astounded at the financial savings to be made if we became a nation of pulse eaters—although it's difficult to place a dollar value on the quality of life free of cardiovascular disease.

In a study of more than 9,600 Americans, over nearly 20 years, researchers evaluated the frequency of consuming legumes and the likelihood of becoming a victim of coronary heart disease. The research, published in the *Archives of Internal Medicine* in 2001, found that people who included beans, peas, peanuts and peanut butter on their menu four or more times per week had a 22 percent lower risk of the disease compared with those who ate legumes less than once a week. The authors concluded that increasing legume consumption is an important strategy in lowering the risk of heart disease.

Clearly, substituting pulses for meat can help to slash the amount of saturated fat in a meal. And pulses can lower blood cholesterol too. Although scientists haven't figured out the mechanism of how they work, it seems that the combinations of amino acids in pulses may have an effect on reducing artery-clogging cholesterol. Other compounds in legumes also appear to have a cholesterol-lowering punch.

Beans, chickpeas, lentils and peas also contain an extensive range of phytochemicals. Among them are isoflavones, compounds that have both estrogen-like and anti-estrogenic effects (see Soy, page 156). These phytoestrogens may offer protection against various hormone-related cancers of the breast, uterus, ovary, prostate and colon. In affairs of the heart, isoflavones may reduce blood cholesterol levels and at the same time defend against cholesterol turning into its harmful oxidized form. (Oxidized cholesterol is more likely to lead to artery damage.) These compounds can also protect against heart attacks and stroke by decreasing the risk of blood clots while promoting vasodilation, the ability of arteries to relax.

Pulses can claim the crown as the leading source of compounds known as saponins, which are making a name for themselves because of their ability to lower blood cholesterol. Saponins are able to bind with cholesterol, meaning that less cholesterol is absorbed by the body. The pharmaceutical industry is investigating saponin-based cholesterol-lowering drugs. Until these drugs are on the shelves, a good way to up your saponins is to have a bowl of chili. And keep in mind that in animal studies, saponins have been shown to inhibit the growth of certain cancer cells, including those for colon and prostate cancer and melanoma.

Phytosterols are another groups of phytochemicals with anti-cancer action. Phytosterols are plant sterols and are related to cholesterol, which is a sterol derived from animal sources. Phytosterols naturally occur in plants such as legumes, nuts and seeds, extra virgin olive oil, soy and avocado. They pack a pretty hefty disease-fighting punch and they're a boon for lowering blood cholesterol (see Avocados, page 21).

As for the cancer-fighting abilities of phytosterols, a study from the University of Buffalo in New York, published in the December 2001 issue of the *European Journal of Cancer Prevention*, looked at some of the differences between the phytosterol-rich Asian diet and the cholesterol-rich Western diet. Animals injected with human prostate cancer cells were fed either a diet containing phytosterols or one containing cholesterol.

The Asian diet yielded some astonishing results: The phytosterol regimen appeared to reduce the growth of prostate tumours by more than 40 percent and cut the spread of cancer to other parts of the body (lymph nodes and lungs, for example) by almost 50 percent. This was the first study of its kind to look at the effect of phytosterols on both prostate cancer cell growth and metastasis (the spread of cancer cells through the body). Other research is indicating that phytosterols protect against colon, prostate and breast cancers as well.

Another prominent phytochemical found in pulses used to have a less than stellar nutritional reputation. Phytates were actually known as anti-nutrients because of their effect on other nutrients. Minerals such as iron can be bound by phytates in the gastrointestinal tract, resulting in lower absorption of minerals. But recent research shows that phytates may not be nutritional demons after all. While they may have some drawbacks when it comes to mineral absorption, in the big scheme phytates may protect against some cancers, such as colon and lung cancer, as well as reduce levels of cholesterol and triglycerides. And to top it off, phytates may do double duty by protecting cholesterol from oxidization.

The cholesterol-reducing ability of pulses is enhanced by their high soluble-fibre content (see Oats, page 107), which makes them a super selection for people with type 2 diabetes and anyone interested in waist management. And then there's the plentiful supply of insoluble dietary fibre, with its health advantages (see Grains, page 102). Legumes, and beans in particular, also supply a hefty dose of the heart-healthy B vitamin folate, providing on average more than half the current daily recommended intake per serving.

beans, beans are good for the heart, the more you eat, the more you ...

Now to a less than pleasant subject, and one that has definitely affected the popularity of pulses: flatulence, or gas. It's a common complaint, and one that has led to the composition of many ditties about the musical consequences of beans. Pulses contain high concentrations of indigestible sugars, or fibres, called oligosaccharides. These fibres are fermented in the bowel by bacteria and produce gas. For some people, the result is so unpleasant that they won't eat any pulses at all; others turn to preparations designed to reduce the amount of gas produced. While you may nod your head in agreement about these decisions to avoid the objectionable consequences of consuming pulses, there's something to be aware of: the gas produced when you eat beans is actually good for you. The benefits of gas have to do with prebiotics, which are foods that feed beneficial bacteria.

Antibiotics—"anti" meaning against and "biotics" meaning bacteria—are used to kill harmful bacteria. But not all bacteria hosted by our bodies are harmful. Some may cause illness, but others may offer a variety of benefits, such as protection against yeast infections, or better immune system function, to name just a few. When antibiotics are used to wipe out the bacteria responsible for infections, they can at the same time kill off beneficial bacteria found in the body—causing, for example, diarrhea.

Enter *probiotics*—the introduction of beneficial bacteria into the intestinal tract. Consuming yogurt containing live bacterial cultures is an example of probiotics. But these bacteria need to be fed—after all, they are living organisms. Prebiotics are foods that can stimulate the growth or activity of these friendly bacteria.

That's where pulses come in. Their oligosaccharides are the perfect fare for the beneficial bacteria in your gut. Their prebiotic effects can promote healthy colons, which ultimately may lower the odds of developing colon cancer. But that's not all. Oligosaccharides provide quite a list of perks. They have been shown to raise levels of heart-healthy HDL cholesterol, lower blood triglycerides, promote bowel regularity, enhance immune system functioning and play a helpful role in regulating blood sugar.

Other compounds found in pulses also assist with blood-sugar regulation. Alpha-amylase inhibitors slow down the rate of digestion in the gastrointestinal tract, which may have the beneficial effect of leading to a slower rise in blood sugar and insulin readings. Quick rises in blood sugar and insulin levels are linked to a host of ill effects.

And here's another important point to consider: people who regularly eat pulses suffer less from abdominal rumblings than those who eat them only occasionally.

use your bean

There's no doubt about it. If you haven't been a legume lover so far, then it's time to strike up an acquaintance. Their versatility in cooking has made legumes a worldwide favourite. They partner wonderfully with seasonings from every cuisine and can be part of any course. Zesty dips, hearty soups, salads tossed with a variety of ingredients from greens to meat, fish and poultry, pastas, main course stews and even cakes can all be made with assorted beans, peas and lentils.

And contrary to popular belief, you don't have to spend the day in the kitchen if you want pulses on the menu. Lentils and split peas, unlike their kissing cousins, beans, do not need to be soaked in water before being cooked. Dried chickpeas and assorted beans do require presoaking, but canned chickpeas and beans can make pulses a fast food. Canned products are super pantry items to keep on hand. Though some people don't like the texture of canned beans—some varieties may be too mushy —brands vary in quality, so do some taste testing to find the brand you prefer.

Cooking dried pulses also allows you to control the sodium content, which can be higher in canned products. To reduce the amount of sodium in canned pulses, rinse them well. Draining and rinsing also reduces the amount of indigestible sugars, making canned varieties a super choice for beginner bean eaters, who might be more likely to experience flatulence.

Use canned beans and legumes puréed in dips and added whole to soups, pasta sauces, salads and vegetable stews for speedy preparation. And if you're looking for even faster preparation, try bean flakes, which can be found in natural food stores. Use bean flakes right out of the container to thicken a hot soup or stew, or reconstitute the flakes with water to use as a purée. They can also be used as a flour substitute.

If you're cooking beans from scratch, be sure to cook extra and freeze them in convenient portions rather than in one big lump: You can bet that a huge block of beans in the freezer will remain there until well past its prime. Divvy up the beans into practical smaller portions, including some in the amounts called for in your favourite recipes.

Here are a few tips on buying, storing and preparing beans.

sorting the beans—a pulse primer

Deciding which pulse to take is not an easy task these days. There are literally hundreds to choose from. But knowing when to use which bean, pea or lentil can mean the difference between ending up with a bowl of mush and an elegantly composed salad.

While supermarkets carry the familiar standbys, ethnic markets, specialty stores and mail-order sources are the place to find more unusual choices. As with other plant products such as vegetables, fruits and grains, consumers can choose between heirloom varieties, which have been around for centuries, and newer hybrids. Don't be surprised to find that some legumes go by different names, depending on who's selling and who's buying. Different cultures may have their own name for a particular legume, or spellings may vary, adding to the confusion.

azuki beans

Popular in Asian cuisine, these little red beans (also known as adzuki beans) are used in red bean paste. Because of their somewhat sweet flavour, azuki beans are often found in desserts and confectionery items. Available dried, they can be cooked to serve in salads and grain dishes. There is also a black variety.

black beans

Also known as turtle beans, these black, oval beans have a strong, earthy flavour and a cream-coloured interior. Black beans are a staple in spicy southwestern American and Latin American dishes. Soups, refried beans, burritos and salads with a kick are where you'll find them. They are not the same as the fermented black beans used in Asian cuisine.

black-eyed peas

Called cowpeas and black-eyed beans because of the single black spot on their white skin. Traditional southern U.S. cooking uses these peas in preparations such as hopping John, a New Year's combo of black-eyed peas and rice said to bring good luck for the coming year. Besides serving them with rice, try black-eyed peas in salads.

chickpeas

A.k.a. garbanzo beans and ceci, these round, beige beans have soared in popularity over the past few years. Hummus, a Middle Eastern dip, can be found ready-made in supermarkets across the country. Falafel, another popular dish originating from the same part of the world, is made from ground chickpeas and spices shaped into balls and fried. Chickpeas are also used throughout Europe and the Far East. In India, they are ground into a flour and used in breads. Chickpeas tend to retain their shape when cooked and are delicious additions to salads, soups, pasta sauces and stews.

cranberry beans

Borlotti is another name for these oval beans that have splashes of wine or pink on their cream-coloured skins. When they're cooked, the beans become a solid colour. Wonderful in casseroles, soups and stews. Seasonally, they are available fresh in ethnic markets.

fava beans

Dried favas, also known as broad beans, look like a brownish large lima bean. Fresh young favas, the first of the harvest, resemble small fresh green lima beans and are used in many cuisines, especially those of the Mediterranean. They need only to be shelled from their pods. The larger beans are dried and the tough skin must be removed after soaking. These types, after cooking, yield a purée and are super in hearty soups (see Fava Bean Purée with Bitter Greens, page 146).

lentils

This broad category includes pulses of all colours that, when cooked, yield a variety of textures. Red ones turn golden and don't retain their shape unless cooked whole with an acid ingredient or salt right at the start of cooking. Split red lentils never retain their shape, so should be used only in soups and purées—they also cook in a flash. Green and brown lentils require much more cooking time to lose their shape and turn into a purée—opt for them in salads, casseroles or veggie patties. The Cadillac of lentils are Le Puy, a more expensive type known for their superior flavour. They're traditionally imported from France but are now also grown in Manitoba and Saskatchewan. Use them in salads and in main courses.

lima beans

Small and large, both are available fresh, frozen, canned and dried. Fordhooks or butter beans are the large, flat ones, while baby is the name for the smaller, milder variety. Known for their buttery flavour, lima beans are frequently used in soups and stews. Succotash, a combination made with fresh corn and limas, is a traditional native American dish.

mung beans

The most common mung bean product in North American markets is known simply as bean sprouts. In India, hulled mung beans, yellow in colour, are known as moong dal. Bean thread noodles, an Asian specialty also known as cellophane or glass noodles, are made from mung bean flour. Look for mung beans in natural or specialty food shops.

split peas

Fresh peas with their skin removed and then dried are called split peas. (They split in half when there's no skin to hold the two halves together.) Green or yellow, both are popular choices for soup, with the green being more common in North America. They do not require presoaking and are a fast pulse to cook from scratch. As a purée seasoned with assorted spices, split peas can be a tasty spread for bread.

pinto beans

A little smaller than kidney beans, these beans are beige with brown flecks but turn pinkish when cooked. Commonly used in Mexican dishes, pintos are the bean used in authentic chili con carne.

red kidney beans

These kidney-shaped beans can be purchased in two hues of red. Both are popular in Mexican dishes and have taken over from the pinto as the bean to use in chili. They marry well with spices such as chili powder and cumin—add some tomatoes and rice for a tasty dish. These are also delicious in soups and as part of a bean combo in a mixed bean salad.

white beans

The different names and varieties of white beans can be confusing indeed: navy beans, pea beans, Great Northern beans, marrow beans, cannellini and flageolets are just a few of the members of this family. White beans end up in a huge array of preparations, including New England baked beans, minestrone soup made with cannellini beans, and cassoulet, the French creation containing flageolets. Use them in any number of ways—in salads, soups and in hearty casseroles, and as the base for dips.

bean buys

Supermarkets carry an assortment of packaged dried legumes, but for more unusual varieties, seek out natural or specialty food stores. Check packages and bulk bins for insects before purchasing, as any plant product can harbour these pests. Avoid packages with broken or shrivelled contents, as these are indicators of older products. Brighter colours also give a hint of age, so avoid those that appear faded. For even cooking times, avoid packages that contain an assortment of different sizes of the same bean or pea. To store at home, transfer to well-sealed containers to keep any critters at bay. And for the best quality, use pulses within a year of purchase. The older a pulse, the longer it may take to cook, so don't mix old purchases with new ones, or the cooked product will be uneven in texture.

pulse preps

Before preparing your choice of dried pulse, it's best to sort through them to discard any broken pieces or foreign matter. Many a pebble and twig has found its way into a batch of pulses. Spread the pulses out on a baking sheet or a flat surface for the best

---

TAKE A SOAK

Whichever soaking method you choose, drain all the soaking water at the end and use fresh water for cooking. The best water-to-pulse ratio is to use three or four parts water to one part pulse.

Overnight Soaking Method

After sorting and rinsing, place dried beans in a large saucepan or bowl. Cover generously with water. Let stand 8 hours or overnight. If you need to leave the beans for a longer time, to prevent spoilage, change the soaking water.

Quick-Soak Method

After sorting and rinsing, place dried beans in a large saucepan or bowl. Cover generously with water. Bring water and beans to a boil and cook 2 minutes. Remove from heat, cover, and let stand 1 hour.

---

view. After picking out the unwanted debris, place them in a strainer or colander inside a large bowl. Fill the bowl with water and swirl the pulses around. Discard the ones that rise to the top. They're older and will be tougher after cooking. Drain and repeat the process.

Other than lentils and peas, all dried pulses should be soaked before cooking. They'll soften up while they absorb the water that was lost during the drying process. And soaking not only shortens cooking times but also helps to cut down on the amount of indigestible sugars that pulses contain. While these may be good for you, only so much gas production is tolerable. Rinsing the legumes well after soaking cuts down the gas-producing sugars even more. Soaking can be done overnight or using a quick-soak method. (See Take a Soak, page 142.) Just be sure to use plenty of water.

Now you're ready to start cooking. For the best results, do not add salt until the pulses are almost tender. Salt at the initial stage can toughen them, and increases the cooking time. Acidic ingredients such as vinegar and tomatoes can have the same result, so they too should not be added until the pulses are tender. To avoid a mushy dish, simmer rather than boil the pulses, and don't stir them too often or too hard. Boiling and stirring lead to burst skins and what many people find a less than pleasing texture. For smoother results, skim off any scum that arises at the start of cooking. A couple of skims will do the trick. Keep an eye on the liquid level during cooking; the beans should always be covered by a couple of inches of water. Add more water as necessary, as too little can result in a dry, tough consistency.

COOKED YIELD

Skimp on the water during the soak and you'll come up short on your yield. Some types of pulses may also vary slightly in their yield.

1 pound (500 g) or about 2 cups (500 mL) of dry beans = 5 to 6 cups (1.25 to 1.5 L) of cooked beans

1 pound (500 g) or about 2 cups (500 mL) of chickpeas = about 4 cups (1.5 L) of cooked chickpeas

1 pound (500 g) or about 2 cups (500 mL) of uncooked split peas = 4 cups (1 L) of cooked peas

1 pound (500 g) or about 2 1/4 cups (550 mL) of uncooked lentils = 6 cups (1.5 L) of cooked lentils

---

recipes

roasted garlic hummus

Besides being packed with both insoluble and soluble fibre, chickpeas contain saponins, which have cholesterol-lowering and anti-cancer effects—all in one delicious dip. Because the garlic is roasted, this purée is a milder version of the original. Serve with whole grain pita triangles or vegetable crudités.

To roast garlic, preheat oven to 400°F (200°C). Slice 1/8 inch (3 mm) off the top of the head of garlic. Place on a double thickness of foil. Drizzle 1 teaspoon (5 mL) olive oil over garlic and wrap in foil to seal. Roast for 1 hour or until garlic is soft and forms a paste when a clove is squeezed. Unwrap to let cool. When cool enough to handle, squeeze garlic out from skins.

MAKES 10 TO 12 SERVINGS (3 CUPS/750 ML)

6 large cloves roasted garlic

2 (19-ounce/540-mL) cans chickpeas, rinsed and drained (or 4 cups/1 L cooked)

1/2 cup (125 mL) fresh lemon juice

3 tablespoons (45 mL) tahini (sesame seed paste)

3 tablespoons (45 mL) light mayonnaise

1/2–1 teaspoon (2–5 mL) ground cumin

Salt and freshly ground pepper, to taste

Paprika, for garnish (optional)

In a food processor, combine garlic, chickpeas, lemon juice, tahini, mayonnaise and cumin; blend to a smooth consistency. Season with salt and pepper. Add more cumin, if desired. Transfer to a serving bowl and sprinkle with paprika, if using.

PER 1/4-CUP (50-ML) SERVING NUTRITIONAL INFORMATION: Calories: 128, Protein: 6 g, Fat: 5 g, Saturated Fat: 1 g, Carbohydrate: 17 g, Dietary Fibre: 5 g

fava bean purée with bitter greens

This heart-healthy combo can't be beat. It contains plenty of cholesterol-lowering fibre along with folic acid and vitamin E.

MAKES 8 APPETIZER SERVINGS

2 cups (500 mL) dried fava beans

3 tablespoons (45 mL) extra virgin olive oil

Salt and freshly ground pepper, to taste

1 pound (500 g) bitter greens (such as chicory, dandelion greens, rapini or beet greens), washed and trimmed

Soak fava beans in water overnight. Drain and peel beans, discarding the skins.

Place beans in a medium, heavy saucepan; cover with water. Over medium-high heat, bring water to a boil; reduce heat and simmer, covered, for about 1 hour. During the last 15 minutes of cooking, stir regularly. Beans should be a smooth consistency when done. Add more water if necessary. Season with salt and pepper. Beat in 2 tablespoons (25 mL) of the olive oil.

While the beans are cooking, cook greens in boiling water until tender. Drain well and toss with remaining 1 tablespoon (15 mL) olive oil. Season to taste with salt.

Serve fava bean purée on a platter with cooked greens alongside.

PER SERVING NUTRITIONAL INFORMATION: Calories: 113, Protein: 5 g, Fat: 6 g, Saturated Fat: 1 g, Carbohydrate: 11 g, Dietary Fibre: 5 g

butternut squash and lentil soup

A change of pace—lentil soup with a hint of curry. And what a range of antioxidants provided by these ingredients, from the fruity olive oil, onions and garlic right through to the lentils and carotenoid-rich vegetables. This soup is perfect for the freezer.

MAKES 6 TO 8 SERVINGS

2 teaspoons (10 mL) extra virgin olive oil

1 cup (250 mL) chopped onions

1 large clove garlic, minced

3 cups (750 mL) chopped butternut squash (about 1 1/2 pounds/750 g before peeling and seeding)

1/2 cup (125 mL) chopped carrots

1/2 cup (125 mL) chopped celery

2 medium tomatoes, chopped

1 cup (250 mL) brown or green lentils, picked over and rinsed

2 tablespoons (25 mL) fresh lemon juice

1 tablespoon (15 mL) mild curry paste

1 bay leaf

6 cups (1.5 L) sodium-reduced vegetable or chicken broth

Salt and freshly ground pepper, to taste

Heat oil in a large saucepan over medium-low heat. Add onions and garlic; sauté until onions are soft, about 8 minutes. Add squash, carrots and celery; sauté another 10 minutes. Add tomatoes, lentils, lemon juice, curry, bay leaf and broth. Bring to a boil, reduce heat and simmer, uncovered and stirring occasionally, until vegetables and lentils are tender, 55 to 60 minutes. Discard bay leaf. Thin soup with additional broth, if desired. Season with salt and pepper. Serve immediately.

PER 8-SERVINGS NUTRITIONAL INFORMATION: Calories: 164, Protein: 10 g, Fat: 2 g, Saturated Fat: 1 g, Carbohydrate: 30 g, Dietary Fibre: 11 g

split pea soup with cumin and caramelized onions

Adding the caramelized onions and cumin just before serving provides a fabulous flavour boost. Freezing any leftover soup doesn't diminish the onion hit. Add the phytochemical content of the onions and cumin to that of split peas and you've got a real mix of compounds that protect against various cancers.

MAKES 8 TO 10 SERVINGS

1 tablespoon (15 mL) + 2 teaspoons (10 mL) extra virgin olive oil

3 cloves garlic, minced

2 carrots, chopped

2 stalks celery, chopped

3 cups (750 mL) dried split peas, picked over and rinsed

10 cups (2.5 L) sodium-reduced vegetable or chicken broth

1 bay leaf

3 cups (750 mL) chopped onions

3/4 teaspoon (4 mL) cumin seeds

Salt and freshly ground pepper, to taste

Heat 2 teaspoons (10 mL) of the oil in a large saucepan over medium-low heat. Add garlic, carrots and celery; sauté until soft, about 10 minutes. Stir in split peas, broth and bay leaf. Bring to a boil, reduce heat and simmer, uncovered and stirring occasionally, until peas are tender, 55 to 60 minutes. Discard bay leaf.

While soup is cooking, prepare onions. In a heavy skillet, heat remaining 1 tablespoon (15 mL) oil over medium-high heat. Add onions and cumin seeds; sauté until onions begin to brown. Reduce heat to medium and continue to cook, stirring, until onions are golden brown, 10 to 15 minutes.

In a blender, purée soup in batches until just smooth and transfer to a bowl. Stir in onion mixture and season with salt and pepper. Serve immediately.

PER 10-SERVINGS NUTRITIONAL INFORMATION: Calories: 265, Protein: 17 g, Fat: 3 g, Saturated Fat: less than 1 g, Carbohydrate: 44 g, Dietary Fibre: 17 g

lentil salad with feta and herbs

Perfect for lunch or, with all its colours, as a buffet offering. The lentils, olive oil, veggies and herbs are all rich sources of compounds that fight cancer. The lentils contain, besides a host of vitamins and minerals, phytosterols, which lower cholesterol readings while providing anti-cancer action.

MAKES 6 SERVINGS

1 1/2 cups (375 mL) lentils

2 tablespoons (25 mL) extra virgin olive oil

2 tablespoons (25 mL) red wine vinegar

1 clove garlic, minced

2 medium tomatoes, diced

1 red or yellow pepper, diced

1/2 cup (125 mL) chopped red onions

1/4 cup (50 mL) chopped fresh mint

1/4 cup (50 mL) chopped fresh parsley

4 ounces (125 g) feta cheese, crumbled

Salt and freshly ground pepper, to taste

Cook lentils in a pot of boiling water until just tender, about 20 minutes. Drain well.

In a small bowl, whisk together olive oil, vinegar and garlic.

In a large bowl, toss together lentils, tomatoes, red pepper, red onions, mint and parsley. Add dressing; toss again to coat. Stir in feta. Season with salt and pepper. Refrigerate for 1 hour to allow flavours to blend.

PER SERVING NUTRITIONAL INFORMATION: Calories: 278, Protein: 17 g, Fat: 9 g, Saturated Fat: 4 g, Carbohydrate: 33 g, Dietary Fibre: 16 g

pasta with spinach and white beans

For pasta lovers, here's an antioxidant-filled change of pace from the standard tomato sauce. Use whole wheat pasta, which, combined with the beans and spinach, provides a fibre bonanza. The ingredients also supply a pretty hefty dose of folate, the B vitamin linked to heart health and protection against colon and breast cancer.

MAKES 6 SERVINGS

12 ounces (300 g) short pasta (such as fusilli or farfalle)

2 teaspoons (10 mL) extra virgin olive oil

1 cup (250 mL) chopped onions

3 large cloves garlic, minced

1 (19-ounce/540-mL) can cannellini (white kidney beans), rinsed and drained

5 cups (1.25 L) baby spinach, picked over and washed

1/2 cup (125 mL) freshly grated Parmesan cheese

Salt and freshly ground pepper, to taste

Cook pasta in a large pot of boiling salted water until just tender; drain. Transfer pasta to a large serving bowl.

While pasta is cooking, heat oil in a large, heavy nonstick skillet over medium heat. Add onions and garlic; sauté until onions are tender, about 10 minutes. Stir in beans and spinach; cook, covered and stirring occasionally, until spinach is wilted, 5 to 7 minutes.

Toss pasta with spinach mixture, 1/4 cup (50 mL) of the Parmesan and salt and pepper. Serve immediately, sprinkled with remaining Parmesan.

PER SERVING NUTRITIONAL INFORMATION: Calories: 321, Protein: 14 g, Fat: 6 g, Saturated Fat: 2 g, Carbohydrate: 54 g, Dietary Fibre: 7 g

greek honey dill lima beans

A terrific way to convert those who say they're not bean eaters. While the indigestible fibres—called oligosaccharides—may, especially for bean novices, be associated with flatulence, they are just what a healthy colon wants to keep it disease free.

MAKES 8 TO 10 SERVINGS

2 cups (500 mL) dried large lima beans (about 12 ounces/375 g)

1 tablespoon (15 mL) extra virgin olive oil

1 large onion, finely chopped

1 (28-ounce/796-mL) can Italian plum tomatoes, coarsely chopped, with juice

2 tablespoons (25 mL) honey

3/4 cup (175 mL) chopped fresh dill

3 tablespoons (45 mL) red wine vinegar

2 tablespoons (25 mL) tomato paste

Salt and freshly ground pepper, to taste

Soak lima beans overnight or use the quick-soak method (see page 142). Drain and rinse beans well to get rid of the gas-producing indigestible sugars. Place beans in a large saucepan and cover with water by 3 inches (8 cm). Bring to a boil, reduce heat and cook, uncovered, for 45 minutes. Drain and set aside.

While beans are cooking, preheat oven to 375°F (190°C). Heat oil in a large, heavy skillet over medium heat. Add onion; sauté until onion is soft and beginning to brown, 12 to 15 minutes.

In a large bowl, stir together beans, onion, tomatoes and their juice, honey and 1/2 cup (125 mL) water. Spoon mixture into a baking dish; cover and bake for 1 1/2 hours or until the beans are tender. Stir in dill, vinegar and tomato paste. Continue baking for another 10 to 15 minutes. Season with salt and pepper.

PER 10-SERVINGS NUTRITIONAL INFORMATION: Calories: 186, Protein: 10 g, Fat: 2 g, Saturated Fat: less than 1 g, Carbohydrate: 34 g, Dietary Fibre: 9 g

chickpea mushroom burgers

For meat eaters and vegetarians alike, these are reminiscent of falafel. By substituting these for burgers made from meat, there's a double benefit—less artery-clogging saturated fat along with a hefty serving of artery-friendly soluble fibre and antioxidants.

MAKES 4 BURGERS

3 teaspoons (15 mL) vegetable oil

1 small onion, finely chopped

2 cloves garlic, minced

1 cup (250 mL) chopped mushrooms (about 4 ounces/125 g)

1 (19-ounce/540-mL) can chickpeas, rinsed and drained

2 slices bread, moistened with water and squeezed dry

1 teaspoon (5 mL) ground cumin

1/2 teaspoon (2 mL) ground coriander

1/4 teaspoon (1 mL) salt

1/4 teaspoon (1 mL) freshly ground pepper

4 pitas or crusty rolls (preferably whole grain)

Sliced tomatoes, lettuce and Spiced Tahini Dressing (page 198)

In a large nonstick skillet, heat 1 teaspoon (5 mL) of the oil over medium-high heat. Add onion and garlic; sauté until onion is softened, 3 to 4 minutes. Add mushrooms and continue to cook until moisture evaporates, another 2 to 3 minutes. Transfer mixture to a food processor. Wipe skillet to remove any of the vegetable mixture.

To the mushroom mixture, add chickpeas, bread, cumin, coriander, salt and pepper; process until finely chopped. Shape gently into 4 patties.

Add remaining 2 teaspoons (10 mL) oil to skillet and heat over medium heat. Add patties and cook for 4 to 5 minutes or until bottom is golden brown. Turn patties and cook another 4 to 5 minutes or until golden brown. Serve in pitas or rolls, topped with tomato, lettuce and Spiced Tahini Dressing.

PER BURGER NUTRITIONAL INFORMATION (WITH ROLL): Calories: 378, Protein: 13 g, Fat: 8 g, Saturated Fat: 1 g, Carbohydrate: 66 g, Dietary Fibre: 11 g

black bean chili

The goodness of chili in a flash. The range of ingredients provides a powerful phyto-chemical mix. This chili is packed with a rainbow of carotenoids and allium family members and their perks, topped off with a hit of both soluble and insoluble fibre.

MAKES 6 TO 8 SERVINGS (8 CUPS/2 L)

2 teaspoons (10 mL) extra virgin olive oil

1 cup (250 mL) chopped onions

3 large cloves garlic, finely chopped

1 green bell pepper, diced

1 cup (250 mL) 1/2-inch (1-cm) cubes zucchini (about 1 medium)

1 teaspoon (5 mL) finely chopped jalapeño pepper

2 (19-ounce/540-mL) cans black beans, rinsed and drained

1 (28-ounce/796-mL) can whole tomatoes, coarsely chopped, with juice

1 cup (250 mL) frozen corn kernels

1 tablespoon (15 mL) chili powder

1 teaspoon (5 mL) ground cumin

1 teaspoon (5 mL) dried oregano

Salt, to taste

3 tablespoons (45 mL) chopped fresh coriander, for garnish

Shredded light cheddar cheese, for garnish (optional)

Heat oil in a large, heavy pot over medium heat. Add onions and garlic; sauté 5 minutes. Add green pepper, zucchini and jalapeño pepper; sauté another 3 minutes. Add black beans, tomatoes and their juice, corn, chili powder, cumin and oregano. Reduce heat to medium-low and simmer, uncovered and stirring occasionally, for 30 minutes. Season with salt. Serve garnished with coriander and light cheddar, if using.

PER 8-SERVINGS NUTRITIONAL INFORMATION: Calories: 169, Protein: 10 g, Fat: 3 g, Saturated Fat: 1 g, Carbohydrate: 29 g, Dietary Fibre: 9 g

tex-mex skillet corn bread

A hearty dish with a top-notch phyto rating. One reason that beans are stick-to-the-ribs fare is their effect on blood sugar. Legumes and their soluble fibre promote a more gradual rise in blood sugar and a slower decrease, leaving you feeling fuller for longer. Serve with a mixed salad.

MAKES 4 TO 6 SERVINGS

BEAN FILLING

2 teaspoons (10 mL) extra virgin olive oil

2 teaspoons (10 mL) ground cumin

1 medium onion, finely diced

2 cloves garlic, minced

1 green bell pepper, diced

1 red bell pepper, diced

1 tablespoon (15 mL) finely chopped jalapeño pepper

1 (19-ounce/540-mL) can red kidney beans, rinsed and drained

2 cups (500 mL) canned tomatoes, coarsely chopped, with juice

Salt and freshly ground black pepper, to taste

2 tablespoons (25 mL) chopped fresh coriander

1/2 cup (125 mL) shredded light Monterey Jack cheese

CORN BREAD TOPPING

1 cup (250 mL) yellow cornmeal (preferably stone-ground)

3/4 cup (175 mL) all-purpose flour

2 tablespoons (25 mL) sugar

2 teaspoons (10 mL) baking powder

1 teaspoon (5 mL) salt

1 cup (250 mL) buttermilk

2 egg whites, lightly beaten

2 tablespoons (25 mL) vegetable oil

1 1/2 cups (375 mL) fresh or frozen corn kernels

Preheat oven to 400°F (200°C).

To prepare the bean filling, heat oil in a large ovenproof nonstick or cast-iron skillet over medium heat. Stir in cumin. Add onion and garlic; sauté until onion is soft, about 5 minutes. Add green, red and jalapeño peppers; sauté another 3 minutes. Stir in kidney beans and tomatoes with their juice. Cook for 1 minute more. Remove from heat. Season with salt and black pepper. Stir in coriander. Spread cheese over bean filling.

To prepare corn bread topping, in a medium bowl, combine cornmeal, flour, sugar, baking powder and salt. Mix well. Measure buttermilk in a large measuring cup. Add egg whites and oil; mix well.

Add buttermilk mixture and corn to flour mixture; stir until just moistened. Batter will be lumpy. Spread batter as evenly as possible over bean filling in skillet.

Bake for 25 to 30 minutes or until top is golden and firm and a knife inserted in centre of topping comes out clean. Let stand for 5 minutes before serving.

PER 6-SERVINGS NUTRITIONAL INFORMATION: Calories: 383, Protein: 15 g, Fat: 9 g, Saturated Fat: 1 g, Carbohydrate: 64 g, Dietary Fibre: 10 g

soy

... on heart disease, cancer, bone health, menopause and kidney function

Soyfoods have exploded onto the Western marketplace in recent years. In Asia, soy has long been a staple, but in North America, for a long time the only soy product generally used was soybean oil. A few decades ago, we began to see tofu and a few other soy products in natural food stores and ethnic markets. But back then, the mere mention of tofu was enough to elicit a common response from most people: Yuck!

So introducing tofu to people's diets took some sneaky manoeuvring. I know. I tried serving it disguised in a dip at family functions and to my kids' friends (always making sure beforehand that there were no concerns about food allergies). And the response was always, "It's delicious! What's in it?" (See my recipe for Spinach Tofu Dip, page 170.) For many people, tofu was their first real taste of soy.

Since then, many factors have changed what's on our plates. Our increasingly multicultural society provides abundant opportunities for us to sample a variety of cuisines in which soy is an integral ingredient. An increasing interest in vegetarianism has also propelled soy into the mainstream. Tofu is now joined on supermarket shelves by veggie burgers, soy nuts, soy milk and the like.

soy good

Since soy was introduced into our diets, there's been mounting research pointing to its countless health benefits. Soyfoods are the focus of research dealing with the beneficial or preventive effects of food on heart disease, certain cancers, bone health, menopausal symptoms and kidney function.

Soy is derived from the small, oval, beige soybean. Being a member of the legume family, it is high in protein, making it a nutritious alternative for those seeking meatless meals. Soy differs from most of its legume relatives in its higher fat content. Thirty-seven percent of the calories in soybeans comes from fat. But of those fat calories, 61 percent is of the polyunsaturated variety, 24 percent is monounsaturated and only 15 percent is saturated.

But soy's fatty acid profile is a very small part of the bean's contribution to preventing cardiovascular disease. Soy protein, along with its phytochemical mix, which includes compounds known as isoflavones, has been extensively studied by scientists investigating heart disease risks. One area of study is soy's lowering effects on elevated blood cholesterol. These isoflavones are thought to act as phytoestrogens and have various effects on health (see Flaxseed, page 183). The amount of these estrogen-like substances in various soyfoods depends on how the product was processed. As research continues on these compounds, food labels in the future may well list the isoflavone content of the product. With all the studies evaluating soy, it's not surprising that isoflavone supplements have become brisk sellers. But contrary to what manufacturers might like consumers to believe, it appears that consuming soy's isoflavones on their own doesn't benefit cholesterol readings. And there may even be harmful effects to taking these phytochemicals on their own. (See page 159).

A meta-analysis—a comprehensive review of previous studies—of soy's effect on cholesterol readings showed that out of 38 investigations, 34 found that soy lowered cholesterol, with an average decrease of almost 13 percent in artery-clogging LDL cholesterol and a slight increase in the beneficial HDL cholesterol.

But it's not as simple as that. Studies evaluating the effects of soy protein with varying levels of isoflavones have yielded conflicting results. An investigation from the University of Toronto, published in the *American Journal of Clinical Nutrition* in June 2002, suggests that soy protein lowers blood cholesterol levels regardless of whether it has a low or high isoflavone content. The research included both post-menopausal women and men with high blood cholesterol. In the male subjects only, the soy diets also led to a lowering of blood pressure readings. The women didn't lose out, though: higher levels of a protein in the blood linked to better immune system functioning were seen in the female subjects.

But although isoflavones may not actually result in any change in cholesterol readings, we shouldn't discount their effect on blood cholesterol. The isoflavones appear to act as antioxidants, protecting the cholesterol from turning into its more damaging form.

As with so many other plant foods, the benefits may be derived not from just a few different compounds but rather from a complex brew of a wide array of substances working together. Besides isoflavones, other phytochemicals that may play a role in disease prevention include saponins, phytic acid lignans and phytosterols, so opting for isoflavone supplements as a substitute for soy simply doesn't make much sense. In addition, when there's soy on the menu—such as in a tofu stir-fry—chances are that there will be less saturated-fat-containing meat in the meal, a double cholesterol-lowering whammy.

A lot of the hoopla about soy has to do with its possible anti-cancer action, especially with hormone-related cancers. Again, at the centre of this research are the isoflavones, two in particular: genistein and daidzein. Soy and its role in breast cancer is a hot topic, and a very controversial one as well.

The research is contradictory because these plant compounds with estrogen-like action may act differently in various individuals depending on their hormonal status. In premenopausal women, soy phytoestrogens such as genistein seem to have an anti-estrogen action, causing a decreased effect of naturally occurring estrogen, which in turn may offer protection against breast cancer. It's thought that at this stage in a woman's life soy may protect against the initiation of breast cancer cells.

In the absence of estrogen or when estrogen levels are low, as in post-menopausal women, phytoestrogens may act in a very different manner. Instead of an anti-estrogen effect, they may instead have estrogenic-like effects. That's why soy products are sought after as a possible therapy to help reduce menopausal symptoms.

Accumulating evidence suggests that consuming soy from the time of puberty may result in the greatest amount of protection against breast cancer. A study from the University of Southern California, published in September 2002, examined the soy intake of Asian-American women with breast cancer and compared them with a group of similar women without the disease. The researchers looked at soy intake during both adolescence and adulthood and found that women who consumed high amounts of soy at a young age were the least likely to develop breast cancer. Other studies are backing up these findings. It appears that exposure to isoflavones at a young age may arm breast tissue with weaponry to fight cancer-causing agents. It may be too late to start eating soy later in life as a cancer-prevention strategy. There is also concern that, for some women, consuming a high amount of isoflavones, either as a supplement or in soyfoods, may promote the growth of certain types of breast cancer cells—estrogen-receptor-positive cells in particular.

Another unknown is whether soy isoflavones interfere with the action of breast cancer chemotherapy. Consequently, it's suggested that women taking breast cancer drugs consult their physicians about soy consumption. Moderate rather than regular consumption of soy products may be a wise idea.

One of the studies that sent up a red flag about soy and breast cancer was published in the journal *Cancer Research* in September 1998. Scientists from Michigan State University found that genistein enhanced the growth of estrogen-dependent human breast cancer cells implanted in animals. Other research has linked the growth of breast cancer cells and genistein, but again only when the cancer cells were present before exposure to the soy compound. Still other studies have found a protective effect.

There simply are no definitive answers, and much more research is required. While awaiting the verdict on soy, women with a family history of estrogen-receptor-positive breast cancer should keep an important dietary principle in mind: eat a varied diet. Experts suggest that soy need not be banished from the menu of women with a history of this type of breast cancer, but it shouldn't be a staple either.

Isoflavone supplements are another story—and not just for women with a history of breast cancer. Scientists have expressed concern about the safety of women taking large amounts of isoflavones in supplement form. Large doses of isoflavones in the absence of the other healthful components of soy may cause adverse effects. Yet supplement makers scurry to bring these extracts to the marketplace. There's now a range of products available, including meal-replacement and energy bars and pill combinations of calcium and isoflavones. With what we know at this time, it's definitely a case of buyer beware.

The calcium-isoflavone combos have come about as a result of research into the effects of phytoestrogens on bone health. The research in this area is contradictory. In a recent investigation, almost 200 healthy post-menopausal women were placed in one of three groups—one group was fed a soy-rich diet, another group was placed on hormone-replacement therapy and a control group was given no treatment at all. At the outset of the study and then again after six months, investigators looked at a number of indicators of bone health, including bone mineral density. Although the soy diet was not as effective as hormone-replacement therapy, it did stimulate bone development and reduce calcium losses, suggesting that soy products could be effective in reducing the risk of osteoporosis in healthy post-menopausal women. The scientists did recommend, however, that further research be done before any conclusions could be made.

In light of the current research on hormone-replacement therapy and its possible adverse effects, increasing numbers of women are looking for natural solutions for menopausal symptoms. "Desperately seeking soy" is a label that can be attached to women who are trying to deal with the ravages of hot flashes. But again, there are no firm answers, and research continues. While some studies show that consuming soy may decrease the severity or the number of hot flashes, other studies come up cold, showing no difference in incidents between the soy-eating and placebo (untreated) groups. Scientists from the University of California at Davis suggest that there may be women who are more sensitive to the action of isoflavones and that this sensitivity may account for the beneficial effect of soy on hot flashes.

For men, soy may offer protective effects against prostate cancer. Scientists have found that genistein appears to induce cancer-fighting enzymes. Although a number of studies have shown that soy can inhibit the growth of prostate cancer, scientists still caution that there is not enough scientific evidence in human studies to recommend high phytoestrogen consumption.

Where soyfoods may offer significant protection is in preventing kidney disease. Deteriorating kidney function is linked to type 2 diabetes, the kind that partners with excess abdominal weight and a sedentary lifestyle. At the same time, research shows that a diet with an excess of animal protein can strain the kidneys even further. So as kidney function worsens, protein in the diet can exacerbate the problem. Soy protein, in contrast, protects kidney function, making it an ideal substitute for meat.

Eating a range of soyfoods, with their wide assortment of phytochemicals, definitely appears to be a wise idea. But the amounts you consume will depend on your particular health status and family history of disease. Unless you've been raised on soy, eat it with moderation. Introduce soy to your menus gradually—start slowly by incorporating it into recipes with familiar flavours and ingredients. Try blending soy into a fruit smoothie, or into a spicy tomato sauce or soup. Then become more adventurous and enjoy dishes such as tofu stir-fry or grilled tofu strips (see Thai Tofu Noodle Salad, page 172).

Tofu, a popular soy product, can be found in assorted varieties in the produce section of the supermarket. For those unfamiliar with its preparation, seasoned and ready-to-serve convenience products are readily available. Although some people find tofu tastes bland, when it's added to something like spaghetti sauce or spicy stir-fries, it absorbs various flavours in the dish and can be delicious. The silken type of tofu is terrific as a base for dips and as a way to "hide" tofu for the uninitiated. Combined with fresh fruit or frozen berries, honey and a dash of almond or vanilla extract, tofu can make a tasty shake (see Berry Tofu Smoothie, page 174).

Meat substitutes made from soybeans have come a long way since their initial versions a couple of decades ago. Some taste so much like meat that it's hard to discern between the two. The first tofu hot dogs available bore little resemblance to the real thing, but nowadays some varieties can rival the look and taste of authentic hot dogs. Some major-league ballparks are even selling the tofu version. But for those who shun anything that reminds them of animal sources, there are still soy products that bear no similarity.

sorting through soy selections

The selection of soyfoods in the marketplace seems to be increasing daily. The following list, adapted from the *U.S. Soyfoods Directory*, will help you sort through the possibilities. More and more of these products can be found in your local supermarket, although some may be available only in specialty or natural food stores. Asian markets are another place to look for an assortment of soyfoods. And if all else fails, you can purchase many of these products through mail-order catalogues and the Internet.

green soybeans (edamame)

These large soybeans are harvested when the beans are still green and sweet, and they can be served as a snack or a main vegetable dish. Edamame are often found in Asian and natural food stores, shelled or still in the pod. With their increasing popularity, some supermarkets are also carrying them in their freezer cases. To prepare, boil them in slightly salted water for 15 to 20 minutes. They're also a snap to make in the microwave, with cooking times dependent on quantities. (See Roasted Sesame Ginger Edamame, page 167.)

meat alternatives (meat analogs)

Meat alternatives made from soybeans contain soy protein or tofu and other ingredients mixed together to simulate various kinds of meat. These meat alternatives are sold fresh, frozen, canned and dried. Usually, they are used the same way as the foods they replace. Check labels for their nutritional value, as products and brands can vary considerably. So can the taste, so experiment with different products or brands. From veggie hot dogs to ground meat and pepperoni, some of the products available nowadays fool even the most discriminating meat lovers. (See also Soy Protein, Textured, below.)

miso

Miso is a rich, salty condiment that is a common flavouring in Japanese cooking. It is a smooth paste that is made from soybeans and a grain such as rice, plus salt and a mould culture, and then aged in cedar vats for one to three years. Miso pastes vary in colour and taste, with some having a stronger flavour than others. Be sure to keep it in the refrigerator. Use miso to season soups, sauces, dressings and marinades.

natto

Natto is made of fermented, cooked whole soybeans. Because the fermentation process breaks down the beans' complex proteins, natto is more easily digested than whole soybeans. It has a sticky, viscous coating with a cheesy texture. In Asian countries, natto traditionally is served as a topping for rice, in miso soups or with vegetables.

nondairy soy frozen dessert

Nondairy frozen desserts are made from soymilk or soy yogurt. Soy ice cream is a popular dessert made from soybeans. It's not always low in fat, so check the label.

soy cheese

Soy cheese is made from soymilk. Its creamy texture makes it an easy substitute for sour cream or cream cheese, and it can be found in a variety of flavours in natural food stores. Products made with soy cheese include soy pizza.

soy fibre (okara, soy bran, soy isolate fibre)

There are three basic types of soy fibre: okara, soy bran and soy isolate fibre. Okara is a pulp fibre by-product of soymilk. Although it contains less protein than whole soybeans, its protein is of high quality. It tastes similar to coconut and can be used in baked goods, such as granola and cookies.

Soy bran is made from the hull, or outer covering, of the soybean, which is removed during the initial processing. The hulls contain a fibrous material that can be refined for use in baking. Soy isolate fibre, also known as structured protein fibre (SPF), is soy protein isolate in a fibrous form.

soy flour

This flour is made from roasted soybeans ground into a fine powder. Three kinds are available, including natural, or full-fat, which contains the natural oils found in the soybean; defatted, which has the oils removed during processing; and lecithinated, which has had lecithin added to it.

All soy flour gives a protein boost to recipes; defatted soy flour is an even more concentrated source than full-fat soy flour. Although used mainly by the food industry, soy flour can be found in natural food stores and some supermarkets. Soy flour is gluten-free, so yeast-raised breads made with soy flour are more dense in texture. Replace one-quarter to one-third of the flour with soy flour in recipes for muffins, cakes, cookies, pancakes and quick breads.

soy grits

Soy grits are similar to soy flour except that the toasted soybeans have been cracked into coarse pieces rather than a fine powder. Soy grits can be substituted for flour in some recipes for baked goods. High in protein, soy grits can be cooked together with rice and other grains.

soy oil and products

Soy oil is the oil extracted from whole soybeans. Oil sold in the grocery store under the generic name "vegetable oil" is usually 100 percent soy oil or a blend of soy oil and other oils.

soy protein concentrate

Soy protein concentrate, available in a powdered form, comes from defatted soy flakes. It contains about 70 percent protein and retains most of the bean's dietary fibre. It's often used in shakes.

soy protein isolates (isolated soy protein)

When protein is removed from defatted flakes, the result is soy protein isolates, the most highly refined soy protein. Containing 92 percent protein, soy protein isolates possess the greatest amount of protein of all soy products. It can be found in health food stores and in some pharmacies. It's often used in shakes.

soy protein, textured

Textured soy protein (TSP)—also known as textured vegetable protein, or TVP—usually refers to products made from textured soy flour, although the term can also be applied to textured soy protein concentrates and spun soy fibre.

Textured soy flour (TSF) is made by running defatted soy flour through an extrusion cooker. It contains about 70 percent protein and retains most of the bean's dietary fibre. It's sold dried, in granular and chunk style. When hydrated, it has a chewy texture. It is often used as a meat extender. Although not widely available, it is sold in natural food stores and through mail-order catalogues.

soy sauce (tamari, shoyu, tamari, teriyaki)

Soy sauce is usually a dark brown liquid made from fermented soybeans. Soy sauces can be quite high in sodium, so look for sodium-reduced products. Be sure to check nutrition labels, as "light" soy sauce can sometimes refer to the colour and may actually contain more sodium than the more common darker varieties. Shoyu is a blend of soybeans and wheat. Tamari is made only from soybeans and is a by-product of making miso. Teriyaki sauce can be thicker than other types of soy sauce and includes other ingredients such as sugar, vinegar and spices.

soy yogurt

Soy yogurt is made from soymilk. Its creamy texture makes it an easy substitute for sour cream or cream cheese. Soy yogurt can be found in a variety of flavours in natural food stores.

soybeans, whole

As soybeans mature in the pod they ripen into a hard, dry bean. Most soybeans are yellow, but you can also find brown and black varieties. Whole soybeans—an excellent source of protein and dietary fibre—can be cooked and used in sauces, stews and soups. They are also soaked and roasted to make a popular snack food. These "soynuts" come in a variety of flavours, including chocolate-covered. High in protein and isoflavones, soynuts are similar in texture and flavour to peanuts.

soymilk, soy beverages

When soybeans are soaked, ground fine and strained, they produce a fluid called soybean milk, which can be used as a substitute for cow's milk. Read labels to make sure that such products are fortified, since regular soymilk does not contain some of the nutrients found in cow's milk, such as calcium, vitamin D or vitamin B-12.

soynut butter

Made from roasted whole soynuts, which are crushed and blended with soy oil and other ingredients, soynut butter has a slightly nutty taste and contains significantly less fat than peanut butter.

tempeh

Tempeh, a traditional Indonesian food, is a rich, chunky, tender soybean cake made by fermenting whole soybeans, sometimes mixed with another grain such as rice or millet. It has a smoky or nutty flavour. Found in Asian food stores and natural food stores, tempeh can be marinated and grilled or added to soups, casseroles or chili.

yuba

Yuba is made by lifting and drying the thin layer that forms on the surface of cooling hot soymilk. It has a high protein content and is commonly sold fresh, half-dried and dried. Dried yuba sheets (called dried bean curd, bean curd sheets or bean curd skin) and U-shaped rolls (called bamboo yuba or bean curd sticks) can be found in Asian food stores.

recipes

roasted sesame ginger edamame

Look for bags of shelled edamame in your freezer case. Whole soy beans provide a fibre hit that you don't get from soy milk and tofu. Serve as a yummy side dish or as part of a Japanese appetizer plate. Mirin is a sweet Japanese cooking wine that can be purchased at Asian and specialty food stores as well as some supermarkets.

MAKES 4 SERVINGS

1 tablespoon (15 mL) mirin

2 teaspoons (10 mL) sesame oil

2 teaspoons (10 mL) sodium-reduced soy sauce

1 teaspoon (5 mL) grated ginger

2 cups (500 mL) lightly steamed shelled edamame (green soybeans)

Salt, to taste

Preheat oven to 375°F (190°C).

In a small bowl, stir together mirin, oil, soy sauce and ginger. Drizzle mixture over soybeans and toss to coat well; season with salt. Arrange beans in a single layer in a shallow 8-inch (2-L) square baking dish.

Roast, uncovered, for 12 to 15 minutes, stirring twice, until edamame begin to brown. Serve immediately.

PER SERVING NUTRITIONAL INFORMATION: Calories: 130, Protein: 7 g, Fat: 7 g, Saturated Fat: 1 g, Carbohydrate: 10 g, Dietary Fibre: 4 g

eggplant dengaku

A popular appetizer in Japanese eateries. This version can match any that's served! Miso is like a phytochemical soup with its saponins, phytic acid, lignans and phytosterols. Heart smart and a defence against cancer—all in one yummy dish.

MAKES 4 SERVINGS

4 Asian eggplants
1/4 cup (50 mL) miso
2 tablespoons (25 mL) mirin (sweet Japanese rice wine)
2 teaspoons (10 mL) honey

Preheat oven to 425°F (230°C).

Place eggplants on a foil-lined baking sheet. Pierce eggplants several times with a fork. Bake until very soft and wrinkled, 20 to 30 minutes (depending on size of eggplants). Cool slightly. Cut baked eggplant in half lengthwise and arrange cut side up on the baking sheet.

While eggplant is baking, in a small saucepan combine miso, mirin and honey. Stir with a wooden spoon over medium heat. When the mixture begins to boil, remove from heat.

Spread miso mixture over cut sides of eggplant. Return to oven and cook 2 to 3 minutes or until the miso mixture is lightly browned, being careful that it does not burn.

PER SERVING NUTRITIONAL INFORMATION: Calories: 120, Protein: 4 g, Fat: 1 g, Saturated Fat: less than 1 g, Carbohydrate: 18 g, Dietary Fibre: 5 g

asian mushroom rolls

These rolls are a great introduction to tofu for people who don't eat it. They're also delicious when made with chicken: substitute two small cooked boneless and skinless chicken breasts cut into thin strips, and stir-fry until no longer pink inside. The rolls, low in fat, are super for entertaining—involve your guests by having them roll their own. The fat is a heart-healthy variety, making them a change of pace from many party appetizers.

MAKES 6 TO 8 APPETIZER SERVINGS (16 TO 20 ROLLS)

MARINADE

6 ounces (175 g) firm tofu, cut into matchstick-sized pieces

1 tablespoon (15 mL) dry sherry

1 tablespoon (15 mL) hoisin sauce

2 teaspoons (10 mL) sodium-reduced soy sauce

1 teaspoon (5 mL) minced garlic

1 teaspoon (5 mL) grated ginger

SAUCE

1 tablespoon (15 mL) honey

1/3 cup (75 mL) hoisin sauce

3 tablespoons (45 mL) sodium-reduced soy sauce

2 teaspoons (10 mL) vegetable oil

1 teaspoon (10 mL) minced garlic

1 teaspoon (10 mL) grated ginger

1 pound (500 g) shiitake mushrooms, thinly sliced

1/2 cup (125 mL) chopped green onions (green tops only)

16–20 large Boston lettuce leaves

Marinate the tofu: Place tofu in a medium bowl. Add sherry, hoisin sauce, soy sauce, garlic and ginger. Stir together thoroughly. Marinate 15 minutes or up to 8 hours in the refrigerator.

To make the sauce, in a small bowl, stir together honey, hoisin sauce and soy sauce; set aside.

In a wok or large skillet, heat 1 teaspoon (5 mL) of the oil over medium-high heat. Add tofu; stir-fry for 3 to 4 minutes or until tofu is beginning to brown. Remove to a clean bowl and keep warm.

Heat remaining 1 teaspoon (5 mL) oil in wok or skillet. Add garlic and ginger; stir-fry until fragrant, about 30 seconds. Add mushrooms; stir-fry until mushrooms are tender, 4 to 5 minutes. Return tofu to wok and heat through. Add 2 tablespoons (25 mL) of the honey-hoisin sauce and stir to coat. Place mushroom mixture in a large bowl; add green onions and toss to mix.

Make rolls by placing a heaping tablespoon of mushroom mixture in a lettuce leaf. Drizzle with 1 teaspoon (5 mL) honey-hoisin sauce and fold over lettuce to enclose filling.

PER ROLL NUTRITIONAL INFORMATION: Calories: 40, Protein: 2 g, Fat: 1 g, Saturated Fat: less than 1 g, Carbohydrate: 5 g, Dietary Fibre: 1 g

spinach tofu dip

This is an updated version of my first tofu adventures more than 20 years ago. And it's still a winner. Introducing soy to youngsters, especially young teen girls, and making it a menu staple may do more for battling breast cancer than starting to be a soy eater during menopause.

MAKES 6 TO 8 APPETIZER SERVINGS (ABOUT 2 1/2 CUPS/625 ML)

1 (10-ounce/300-g) package frozen chopped spinach, thawed

6 ounces (175 g) soft or silken tofu, pressed to remove water

2 shallots, quartered

1/2 cup (125 mL) plain low-fat yogurt

1/3 cup (75 mL) light mayonnaise

2 tablespoons (25 mL) chopped fresh parsley

1 tablespoon (15 mL) fresh lemon juice

4 teaspoons (20 mL) grainy mustard

Salt and freshly ground pepper, to taste

Squeeze spinach to remove excess liquid. Process all ingredients in a food processor or blender until smooth. Adjust seasonings.

PER 8-SERVINGS NUTRITIONAL INFORMATION: Calories: 69, Protein: 4 g, Fat: 5 g, Saturated Fat: 1 g, Carbohydrate: 5 g, Dietary Fibre: 1 g

mushroom and spinach miso soup

Almost every single ingredient is packed with cancer-fighting compounds. Sesame oil, garlic, ginger, spinach and miso each contributes different substances. For maximum cancer-fighting power from the garlic, allow it to stand for 10 minutes after it's minced before you cook it.

MAKES 3 TO 4 SERVINGS

2 teaspoons (10 mL) sesame oil

1 teaspoon (5 mL) vegetable oil

2 teaspoons (10 mL) minced ginger

1 clove garlic, minced

3 cups (750 mL) sliced shiitake mushrooms

4 cups (1 L) sodium-reduced vegetable broth

3 cups (750 mL) baby spinach

1/4 cup (50 mL) miso

Heat sesame oil and vegetable oil in a large saucepan over medium-low heat. Add ginger and garlic; cook, stirring, until fragrant, about 30 seconds. Add mushrooms; cook for 5 minutes or until beginning to soften. Add broth; bring to a boil. Reduce heat, add spinach and simmer 2 minutes. Stir in miso; cook 1 or 2 minutes or until miso is blended.

PER 4-SERVINGS NUTRITIONAL INFORMATION: Calories: 130, Protein: 8 g, Fat: 6 g, Saturated Fat: 1 g, Carbohydrate: 11 g, Dietary Fibre: 2 g

thai tofu noodle salad

Watch out that you don't nibble away all the tofu before you put it in this salad! Using tofu instead of meat not only slashes saturated fat totals but also provides an amino acid mix—or type of protein makeup—that's healthy for the arteries and the kidneys.

MAKES 4 SERVINGS

8 ounces (250 g) extra-firm tofu, cut into 1/2-inch (1-cm) slices

3 tablespoons (45 mL) + 2 teaspoons (10 mL) sodium-reduced soy sauce

3 tablespoons (45 mL) rice wine vinegar

2 tablespoons (25 mL) peanut butter

1 tablespoon (15 mL) sesame oil

1 tablespoon (15 mL) grated ginger

2 teaspoons (10 mL) sugar

Pinch red pepper flakes

8 ounces (250 g) spaghetti, broken in half

1 1/2 cups (375 mL) matchstick-sized carrot pieces

1 1/2 cups (375 mL) matchstick-sized cucumber pieces

1 red pepper, thinly sliced

3 tablespoons (45 mL) chopped fresh coriander

Preheat broiler or grill. Brush tofu slices with 1 teaspoon (5 mL) soy sauce. Broil or grill until tofu is golden, 3 to 4 minutes. Turn and brush with an additional teaspoon (5 mL) soy sauce. Broil another 3 to 4 minutes. Allow to cool. Cut into 1/4-inch (5-mm) strips; set aside.

In a small bowl, whisk together remaining 3 tablespoons (45 mL) soy sauce, rice wine vinegar, peanut butter, sesame oil, ginger, sugar and red pepper flakes; set aside.

Cook spaghetti in plenty of boiling water; drain and rinse under cold water. Drain again. Place in a large bowl. Add carrots, cucumber, red pepper, coriander, tofu and peanut butter mixture; toss well and serve.

PER SERVING NUTRITIONAL INFORMATION: Calories: 396, Protein: 17 g, Fat: 12 g, Saturated Fat: 2 g, Carbohydrate: 57 g, Dietary Fibre: 9 g

miso-glazed fish with bok choy

Here's a recipe containing many of the stellar players in current nutritional research: fish, greens, tomatoes and a touch of miso, or fermented soybean paste. The fish contributes a heart-healthy fat profile, while the accompaniments are packed with antioxidants. This recipe is adapted from that of Barbados chef Hans Schweitzer. He makes his with mahi mahi, but the recipe is also great with any firm, not-too-thin fish like tilapia and salmon.

MAKES 4 SERVINGS

1 cup (250 mL) sodium-reduced vegetable stock

1/2 cup (125 mL) white wine

2 tablespoons (25 mL) sodium-reduced soy sauce

2–3 tomatoes, peeled and chopped (about 1 1/2 cups/375 mL)

4 fish fillets, each 5–6 ounces (125–150 g)

Freshly ground pepper, to taste

1 tablespoon (15 mL) miso

1 teaspoon (5 mL) grated ginger

1 teaspoon (5 mL) minced garlic

3 cups (750 mL) sliced bok choy

Chopped fresh coriander, for garnish (optional)

Preheat oven to 350°F (180°C).

In a medium saucepan, bring stock, wine, soy sauce and tomatoes to a boil; simmer 5 minutes.

In the meantime, season fish with pepper. Mix together miso, ginger and garlic. Rub over fish.

Pour tomato mixture into an 8-inch (2-L) square baking dish. Place bok choy over the sauce; place fish on bok choy.

Bake for 20 to 25 minutes or until fish is just cooked through. Serve fish over bok choy and sauce, garnished with fresh coriander, if using.

PER SERVING NUTRITIONAL INFORMATION (WITH MAHI MAHI): Calories: 161, Protein: 30 g, Fat: 3 g, Saturated Fat: 1 g, Carbohydrate: 7 g, Dietary Fibre: 3 g

berry tofu smoothie

Here's a delicious smoothie for even those who aren't tofu lovers. For a flax boost, add 1 or 2 tablespoons (15 or 25 mL) ground flaxseed. The calcium-isoflavone combo (the calcium from the milk and isoflavones, or phytoestrogens, from the tofu and soymilk) may offer some perks for healthy bones. Both types of berries supply cancer-fighting compounds, while the blueberries are vying for the title of "new brain food champ."

MAKES 3 SERVINGS

1 cup (250 mL) frozen unsweetened raspberries

1 cup (250 mL) frozen unsweetened blueberries

1/2 cup (125 mL) 1% milk or fortified soy milk

1/2 cup (125 mL) soft tofu

1/2 cup (125 mL) plain low-fat yogurt

1/2 cup (125 mL) orange juice

1/4 cup (50 mL) honey

1/2 teaspoon (5 mL) vanilla extract

Blend all ingredients until smooth.

PER SERVING NUTRITIONAL INFORMATION: Calories: 213, Protein: 7 g, Fat: 2 g, Saturated Fat: 1 g, Carbohydrate: 45 g, Dietary Fibre: 4 g

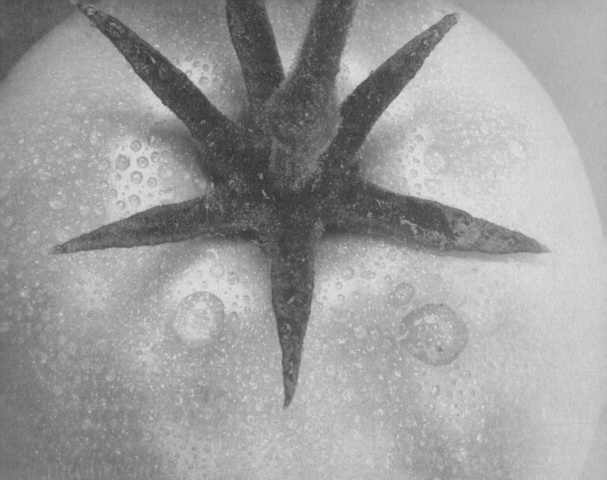

nuts and seeds

... offer a powerhouse of protection
against heart disease, stroke, cancer
and even hearing loss

Nuts have gotten a bad rap over the past few decades. Once fat was declared public enemy number one, most weight-conscious people outlawed fat-rich nuts from their diets. Now it's clear that the "no-nut-sayers" were too hasty in their condemnation. According to accumulating scientific research, these small nuggets offer a powerhouse of protection against a host of ailments, including heart disease, stroke, certain cancers and even hearing loss. They're virtually a defence against disease from head to toe.

Of course, the virtues of nuts have been known for some time. Before the war on fat began years ago, menus designed to reduce blood cholesterol regularly included nuts and seeds. Walnuts and sunflower seeds, because of their polyunsaturated fats, were munched on by the cholesterol-conscious every day. And lower blood cholesterol was the result!

fat follies

Another critical component of the cholesterol-lowering strategy was to cut the amount of artery-clogging saturated fats in people's diets. At some point, nutrition policy makers decided that the directives on fat—increase one fat (unsaturated) while decreasing another (saturated)—was just too complicated, and so they devised a very simple strategy: eat less fat overall and we would all decrease our intake of unhealthy fats. This, in turn, would provide a solution to the problem of increasing girth throughout the population—after all, with fat tallying in at double the calories per gram of carbohydrate and protein, eating less fat would surely lead to the consumption of fewer calories.

Well, the reasoning was faulty and the approach backfired. During the war on fat, the consumption of peanuts in the U.S. fell from around 375 million pounds in 1989 to 275 million in 1995. Waist watchers switched from fat-laden peanuts to pretzels and other assorted fat-free fare, munching their way to higher body weights. Snacks that were packed with a host of disease-fighting compounds—like nuts—were replaced by foods almost devoid of nutrients. Pretzels, for instance, are made from refined flour and provide little else than carbohydrates. Yet they were ranked well ahead of peanuts, which are packed with fibre—at 2 grams per ounce (30 grams)—and a variety of nutrients, including vitamin E, folate, potassium, magnesium and zinc. And then there's the peanut's assortment of phytochemicals such as phytosterols, flavonoids and resveratrol, the compound that also makes wine a heart-healthy hero. Besides offering an astonishing array of nutritional goods, peanuts can turn an Asian noodle dish into a delectable treat.

Peanut butter also became verboten. As any serial dieter knows, forbidden foods tend to bring out the worst of nutritional behaviours—avoidance and then bingeing.

Through my years of practice as a dietitian, I have had many clients who would sheepishly admit to polishing off a jar of peanut butter in one sitting but only after having sworn off eating peanuts for life. (Swearing off anything forever simply magnifies its irresistibility factor.) My peanut-butter-loving clients were always caught off guard by my surprise solution to their addiction: eat a spoonful of peanut butter at every meal for seven days. After that week, and unfailingly, they were shocked to realize they hadn't gained any weight and that they could eat peanut butter in controlled portions. The lesson is a well-worn one but worth repeating: you can enjoy peanut butter (or whatever your passion) every day but only in moderation. A host of studies on peanuts and their effect on weight control have backed me up on this.

The *absolute* folly of simplifying a complex subject like nutrition—all fat is bad— has recently become clear. Just as supermarket shelves bulge with fat-free goodies, so do waistlines. All the while, scientific evidence of the benefits of nuts and seeds continues to emerge. Being fat smart instead of fat phobic just makes sense.

Slashing the fat from your food and opting for fat-free substitutes will not only shortchange you on nutrition but it can also leave you with bland-tasting fare. Essential fats, those that our bodies don't manufacture, perform a variety of functions in the diet, including boosting the absorption of fat-soluble vitamins and disease-fighting compounds such as lycopene and lutein. Fat also carries the flavour in food. So make your fat count—choose the healthiest types and make them work in your favour to banish boring dishes.

Here's a fat primer for sorting through the choices:

- *Monounsaturated Fat:* Liquid at room temperature and found in olive and canola oils and a variety of nuts and seeds. This fat appears to slightly lower LDL cholesterol.
- *Polyunsaturated Fat:* Liquid at room temperature and found in assorted nuts and seeds along with oils such as corn, safflower, soybean and sunflower. They can lower LDL cholesterol and, when consumed in large amounts, lower HDL readings too.
- *Saturated Fat:* Solid at room temperature and found in animal products, certain vegetable oils such as coconut and palm and in products containing hydrogenated vegetable oils. These fats are thought to have an even greater effect on raising blood cholesterol than dietary cholesterol.
- *Trans Fat:* Produced during the process of hydrogenation, in which liquid oils are hardened, these fats act like saturated ones because they raise LDL levels—but they also lower the beneficial HDL cholesterol. To lower your trans fat intake, read package labels on processed foods. Trans fats are found in foods containing hydrogenated vegetable oils, such as commercial baked goods, cookies, crackers,

french fries and snack foods. Fried selections from fast-food eateries are usually loaded with these fats. To avoid trans fat in your spread, look for soft tub margarines that are non-hydrogenated. Hard margarines contain not only significant amounts of saturated fat but plenty of trans fat as well.

get thee to a nuthouse

In the early 1990s, studies linking nut consumption to possible protection against disease started to trickle in. Research from Loma Linda University, published in the journal *Archives of Internal Medicine* in 1992, found that more than 30,000 Seventh-Day Adventists who ate nuts frequently had significantly less risk of heart disease. More research in 1996 on almost 35,000 post-menopausal women in the Iowa Women's Health Study also pointed to the perks of nuts and seeds. Vitamin E from nuts and other food sources, not supplements, seemed to offer protection against dying from heart disease.

Then, in 1998, the Nurses' Health Study, an ongoing investigation out of Harvard University, also showed that "going nuts" was a good idea—in limited amounts, that is. (Being a couch potato in front of the TV munching on bowls of salted nuts is not what the research supports.) In the group of 86,000 female nurses, subjects who consumed 1 ounce (about 1/4 cup, or 50 mL) of nuts five or more times a week had 35 percent less risk of heart disease than those women who rarely ate them. Although nuts are high in fat, they contain mostly monounsaturated and polyunsaturated, which appear to offer the disease protection. In a comparison of studies, nuts appear to have as great an effect, or greater, than some cholesterol-lowering medications.

But the health advantages of nuts are even more widespread. In the ongoing Physicians' Health Study, also out of Harvard, more than 21,000 healthy men between the ages of 40 and 84 were tracked for an average of 17 years each. The subjects were categorized according to how frequently they ate nuts. The research, published in *Archives of Internal Medicine* in 2002, found that those who consumed nuts two or more times per week had a 47 percent reduced risk of sudden death from cardiac arrest compared with those who rarely or never consumed nuts. It appears that a substance found in nuts stabilizes heart rhythms after an attack.

the nuts and bolts behind the benefits

Scientists are trying to identify which compounds in nuts specifically guard against disease. Is it nuts' fatty acid profile that reduces blood cholesterol? Or is it the heart-healthy omega-3 fatty acids found in some nuts, including walnuts? What role does the protein in nuts play? What about the mineral magnesium, vitamin E or the phytosterols (plant sterols that can lower blood cholesterol and protect against cancer)? Lesser-known substances such as ellagic acid might also be players to consider. Could the answer lie in an assortment of compounds and their interactions?

Here's an example of how complex the puzzle is. Compared with animal-based protein sources like meat, nut proteins tend to contain higher amounts of the amino acid arginine. This compound not only appears to lower blood cholesterol but also seems to be a major player in keeping the endothelium, the lining of the arteries, functioning well. Lower blood cholesterol and healthier-functioning arteries are a double whammy against the risk of a heart attack. Among the best nut sources of arginine are peanuts, almonds, hazelnuts and walnuts.

Nuts and seeds have become a hotbed of research, with clinical trials evaluating countless benefits ranging from the cholesterol-lowering effects described to stroke and cancer prevention to easier waist management for those who eat—rather than abstain from—nuts.

Eating to control weight sounds like a nutty idea, but studies confirm that drastically slashing the fat, or eliminating it altogether in the battle of the bulge, often backfires. Too little dietary fat results in too little flavour. Dressing a veggie and noodle salad with an Asian dressing that contains a small amount of peanut butter and sesame can make losing weight a more pleasurable endeavour. Having a few spoonfuls of mixed nuts with a piece of fruit to bridge the gap between meals can tame the appetite much more than having the fruit alone.

when losers are winners

Researchers at Harvard Medical School and Brigham and Women's Hospital, in Boston, evaluated the long-term success of a higher-fat Mediterranean-style diet over a low-fat one. More than 100 overweight men and women were assigned to either of two weight-loss diets containing the same number of calories—a low-fat diet or a "Mediterranean-style" diet with higher monounsaturated fat. The outcome? Those on the higher-fat regimen, which included an assortment of nuts and seeds as well as avocados and olive oil, were on the winning—or rather, losing—team. The high-fat group lost an average of 11 pounds each, while the low-fat group lost an average of 6 pounds each. The reason? Almost three times as many people were able to stick to a higher-fat diet during the 18-month study.

The low-fat dieters also experienced a higher dropout rate. More than 80 percent of the subjects on the low-fat diet dropped out of the study, compared with less than half (46 percent) of the subjects on the higher-fat, Mediterranean-style diet. Those on the higher-fat diet also scored a higher nutrition rating.

One of the major reasons for these surprising results is that the higher-fat dieters could enjoy a variety of tasty options, many of which have traditionally been on a dieter's "forbidden list." Using the fattier options, but in limited quantities, helped to make vegetables and grain dishes more palate pleasing. Eating copious amounts of unadorned veggies has led to the demise of all too many a weight-loss program.

Feeling hungry all the time is a sure-fire prescription for abandoning weight-management goals. In a quest to find which snacks leave people more satisfied, scientists at Purdue University assessed the effect of foods on eating frequency and caloric intake. The results, published in the *International Journal of Obesity* in 2000, revealed that when participants snacked on peanuts or peanut butter, they weren't hungry again for about two and a half hours. However, after munching on high-carbohydrate snack choices such as rice cakes, hunger returned within half an hour. And even though the peanuts and peanut butter were not low-calorie fare, the subjects adjusted their caloric intake naturally and didn't add extra calories to their daily diets. Also, when their fat intake was analyzed, it was found that the peanut eaters had consumed a healthier fat profile—more mono- and polyunsaturated fat and less saturated fat.

One of the Purdue researchers then looked at the effect of eating peanuts daily on body weight and caloric intake. In the study (published in the same journal in August 2002), participants were placed on three different diets. Each diet involved consuming 500 calories worth of peanuts a day. The first diet, called a "free-feeding" diet, included the peanut portion each day but otherwise the subjects could eat however they wanted. In the second, the "addition" diet, the participants were told to add peanuts to their usual diet and to eat the way they did before. In the third, the "substitution" diet, the 500-calories of peanuts replaced 500 calories of other food. All the subjects followed all three diets at different times. Subjects on both the free-feeding and addition diets remarked that they felt full and could not eat all the food they typically consumed. They simply ate less, even though they were not instructed to do so. And even when they did consume more calories than they burned, their weight gain was less than expected. The speculation is that whole peanuts are not efficiently absorbed. Research on almonds points to this theory as well. A study from King's College in London, England, showed that the cell walls of almonds may play a role in the body's absorption of the fat in the nut. Chewing disrupted only some of the cell walls, leaving intact part of the almond. This may prevent all of the fat from being released for digestion and then absorption.

As research accumulates, keep in mind that in many of the studies in which nuts and seeds have shown the greatest advantages to health, they have usually been used as a substitute for—and not in addition to—highly saturated or trans fat choices such as meat, baked goods and fried snack foods. Handfuls of nuts throughout the day without making healthy substitutions elsewhere could definitely pack on the pounds.

"nuts to you"

Enjoy a variety of nuts, as each has its own nutritional contributions. For example, walnuts are high in omega-3 fatty acids while Brazil nuts are a leader on the selenium front. Here's some info to improve your nut knowledge.

almonds

Almonds, revered for centuries, were once a prized ingredient in breads served to the pharaohs of Egypt, and the Romans showered newlyweds with almonds as a fertility charm. Thought to originate in China and Central Asia, almonds are now grown throughout the Mediterranean, the Middle East and in the U.S. Their culinary uses are wide ranging. Besides being sold in-shell, shelled, blanched, slivered, chopped, roasted, sweetened and salted, they're the foundation of the popular confectionery marzipan.

Accumulating research on almonds demonstrates that their value to health can easily match their taste appeal. A study published in the American Heart Association's journal, *Circulation*, in August 2002 showed that almonds significantly lowered "bad," or LDL, cholesterol levels in people with elevated cholesterol. The researchers were also interested in how many almonds were needed to do the job. During the course of the three-month study, the 27 participants, all with high cholesterol, followed three different diets. For one month, each participant ate a full dose of almonds (average 74 grams, just over 2 ounces), which represented almost one-quarter of their total daily caloric intake. For the next month they took a half dose of almonds (average 37 grams, or 1 ounce), described as a "handful" of almonds. In the last month, each day they ate a low-saturated-fat whole wheat muffin containing the same amount of calories and polyunsaturated and saturated fats as the daily dose of almonds. The result: muffins provided more calories from starch whereas the almonds supplied monounsaturated fat. And the monounsaturated fat fared very well indeed. Artery-clogging LDL levels fell by an average of 9.4 percent with the full portion of almonds and 4.4 percent with the half portion. For the most benefit, almonds should be eaten in their natural state or "dry roasted" without added oils or salts, and with their skins.

At a scientific conference sponsored by the Federation of American Societies for Experimental Biology, held in New Orleans in 2002, researchers presented the very latest findings on almonds:

- The nutrients in almonds work together as a package—the whole kernel—to produce a greater health-promoting effect than their individual nutrients consumed alone.
- Almonds may be as effective as oats at lowering LDL cholesterol. An analysis of a number of studies consistently shows that eating almonds lowers total and LDL cholesterol by 4 and 5 percent, respectively. This cholesterol-lowering power is similar to that of oats and oat bran.
- Almonds reduce inflammation and improve blood flow, yet another indication of how they may protect against heart disease.
- Almonds and their skins are high in antioxidants—vitamin E and polyphenols— that provide powerful protection against heart disease and certain cancers and may improve immune function. When the different components were tested together to evaluate their antioxidant capacity, they performed at a greater rate than they did individually. The lesson: eat the whole nut!

brazil nuts

The area around the Amazon rainforest in South America is where these enormous nuts are grown. And like the size of these seeds, the Brazil nut tree is also massive— more than 150 feet (or 40 metres) tall, with a trunk diameter of nearly 7 feet (or 2.5 metres). About 20 to 30 nuts are found in each of the melon-shaped pods, which drop from the trees and are cracked open with a machete. As you can imagine, Brazil nut trees are avoided by locals on windy days. The first reference to nutritional benefits date back to 1569, when thousands of Brazil nuts were collected by a Spanish colonial officer to feed his starving troops. And nourish they did—Brazil nuts are chock full of such nutrients as essential fats, calcium, phosphorus, potassium and B vitamins.

Its claim to fame these days is the amount of the mineral selenium it contains. The selenium content of a food depends on the amount of the mineral found in the soil it's grown in. The selenium-rich soil of the rainforest makes Brazil nuts a top-notch source of the mineral.

Selenium has been consistently linked to a reduced risk of certain cancers, with a particularly strong association with prostate cancer. Researchers at Stanford University Medical Center, in California, investigated whether levels of selenium in the blood were related to the risk of developing prostate cancer. They assessed selenium levels of men with and without prostate cancer and found that in those with low readings of the mineral, there was a four- to fivefold increased risk of the disease. They also found, as have other researchers, that blood levels of selenium decrease with age, making the nutrient one that older men should eat more of.

Trials are evaluating the role of selenium in cancer prevention and treatment in men at different stages of disease development, from high-risk men who may have premalignant tissue to those with prostate cancer. But American researchers may have uncovered how selenium works in fighting cancer. Selenomethionine, a component of selenium, activates a gene that appears to suppress tumours. The gene may lead to the death of abnormal cells—what is called apoptosis. But the selenium doesn't appear to work alone. The researchers point out that healthy eating is also part of the package.

Taking a multivitamin and mineral formulation containing selenium and eating selenium-rich food choices may be a wise idea, but taking excessive amounts of selenium is not. Check out the total dosage contained in each supplement. Selenium toxicity, with its symptoms of fatigue, irritability, nervous system abnormalities, hair and nail brittleness, gastrointestinal disturbances and skin rash, can occur. As a result, a tolerable upper intake of 400 micrograms per day of selenium has been set by government agencies.

cashews

Cashews originated in Brazil but are now also grown in India and Mozambique. The cashew fruit consists of two distinct parts: a pear-shaped fruit called a cashew apple and the brownish nut. Although the apple is used to make juices, syrups, preserves, wine and liquors, cashew trees are grown mainly for the nuts. As for the cashew's nutritional value, its fatty acid content is similar to that of nuts like almonds, and is predominantly monounsaturated fat, making it a smart heart-healthy choice. It may also provide plenty of vitamin E and selenium, although the amount of selenium depends on where the tree is grown. Currently there isn't a great deal of information on the selenium content of cashews from places other than Brazil.

flaxseeds

Flaxseeds may be little but they pack a potent mix of disease-fighting compounds. These small brown seeds have been the focus of many studies, ranging from their

> **TIPS FOR TOASTING**
> Toasting nuts and seeds really perks up their flavour. Spread them in a single layer on an ungreased baking sheet. Place in 350°F (180°C) oven and bake 5 to 10 minutes or until nuts or seeds are slightly brown; stir once or twice until lightly toasted. Remove from pan to cool.
>
> Buying raw nuts and seeds and roasting them at home allows you to control the kinds of oils used and the amount of sodium added. Toss nuts or seeds in beaten egg whites and then in the seasonings of your choice, and bake at 300°F (150°C) for about 15 minutes. The egg white makes the spices or herbs adhere to the nuts and seeds. (See Glazed Spicy Almonds, page 196.)

effects on heart disease and diabetes to cancer risk and auto-immune and inflammatory diseases. When ground, flaxseeds are endowed with more than their share of health-promoting components.

Flaxseeds are loaded not only with fibre but also with omega-3 fatty acids and phytochemicals called lignans that may offer an assortment of health benefits. Although flaxseed oil does contain the beneficial types of fat that are found in the seeds, it has no fibre and no lignans and so none of the advantages they may provide. In fact, one has to wonder how the manufacturers of some products labelled "high lignan oils" have produced these oils when the lignans are contained in the ground meal only. It's a case of buyer beware.

It's also buyer beware when it comes to the quality of various flax oil products. The advantageous omega-3 fatty acid alpha-linolenic acid (ALA) is very unstable, meaning that it can become rancid if not handled properly. When it's in its natural environment, inside the flaxseed, the oil is taken care of, so to speak. Take it out of the seed and its shelf life can be very short. Flaxseed oil should be refrigerated and not used in dishes that are heated, because heating can produce compounds that may be harmful to human health. Capsules containing the oil have grown in popularity as the benefits of omega-3 fatty acids and ALA have become known. But you can't always tell if a capsule contains rancid oil. Consuming rancid oils over time can pose health hazards. And contrary to popular belief, capsules of oil do provide calories.

Whole flaxseeds are perfect packaging for the fatty acids. In fact, the seeds, available from bulk and natural food stores, can be safely stored for up to a year. Once ground, flax should be stored in an airtight, opaque container in the refrigerator for up to 30 days. Grinding your own seeds is certainly more economical than buying ground flaxseed in vacuum-packed containers. If you're using it regularly, a coffee grinder, which is perfect for grinding the seeds, is a worthwhile investment. Although the whole seeds give foods a crunchy texture, the goodness they contain may pass through the body, as the seeds may not be entirely digested. Grinding the seeds into a meal assures that you're not missing flax's perks.

NUTRITION FACTS PER TABLESPOON (15 ML) OF FLAXSEED

	Calories (grams)	Total fat (grams)	ALA (grams)	Protein (grams)	Fibre
Whole seed	50	4.5	2.5	2.2	3.3
Ground flax	36	3.3	1.8	1.6	2.3

Source: The Flax Council of Canada.

Ground flaxseed, with its more than 3 grams of fibre per tablespoon (15 mL), is not only a boon to those who suffer from bowel irregularity or conditions such as irritable bowel syndrome. Consuming ground flaxseed can also lead to a more gradual rise in blood sugar and therefore help to avoid the high levels that can occur with a rapid rise. Blood cholesterol readings also show an improvement. In a study from the University of Toronto, where much of the research on flax has been carried out, young, healthy people who consumed 50 grams of flax each day, in the form of a muffin, experienced a 30 percent increase in bowel movements per week and an 8 percent drop in their artery-clogging LDL-cholesterol levels. In other University of Toronto research on healthy young women, flaxseed fared even better, lowering total cholesterol by 9 percent and LDL cholesterol by 18 percent. Blood sugar readings after meals decreased by a significant 27 percent.

If you consider that flax's fibre lowers blood cholesterol and its omega-3 fatty acids lower blood triglycerides, it's clear that flaxseed can have a pretty potent effect on the risk of heart disease and stroke. But the effects of ALA may be farther reaching, especially when combined with the action of lignans.

Researchers are assessing the effects of the ALAs in flaxseed on auto-immune diseases such as lupus. At the University of Western Ontario, scientists found that in the treatment of kidney disease associated with lupus, just 30 grams of flaxseed a day benefited kidney function as well as decreasing inflammation associated with the disease. Other disorders in which flaxseed may be of benefit include rheumatoid arthritis, psoriasis and multiple sclerosis. A new area of research is the ability of flaxseed to reduce inflammation, which has potential in the treatment or prevention of cancer and artery disease. Inflamed cells may be more likely to become cancerous ones. And it's thought that inflammation of the arteries might increase the likelihood of plaque formation, leading to artery disease.

Flaxseed is one of the richest sources of lignans, a phytochemical that is a type of phytoestrogen. These compounds can interfere with how estrogen works in the body, in some cases acting in an estrogen-like manner and in others countering estrogen's effects. Lignans are also found in unrefined grains such as barley, buckwheat, millet and oats, as well as legumes and vegetables such as broccoli, carrots and spinach. But none of these foods can beat flaxseed, which has up to 800 times more lignans than any other plant source.

Lignans may also act as an antioxidant. Much research is looking at these substances and their effect on various types of cancer as well as on heart disease and stroke. They are thought to protect against hormone-sensitive cancers such as those of the breast, endometrium and prostate by interfering with the metabolism of sex hormones.

- Baked goods
  You can substitute flax for fat in your recipes, using 3 tablespoons (45 mL) ground flaxseed for each tablespoon (15 mL) of margarine, butter or cooking oil. Using flax, though, will cause baked goods to brown more quickly.
- Cereal
  Sprinkle ground flaxseed onto your morning cereal for a nutty taste.
- Cottage cheese
  Mix together flaxseed, fruit and cottage cheese.
- Soups
  If you're looking for a way to disguise ground flax, stir it into thick soups like lentil or bean varieties.
- Salads and salad dressings
  Sprinkle flaxseed over salads or mix into your salad dressing for a flax punch.
- Pasta sauces
  Stir flaxseed into pasta sauces just before serving.
- As a filler
  Use flaxseed in burgers, meatloaf and fish or vegetable patties as a filler.
- Yogurt
  Stir flaxseed into yogurt for a nutrition-packed snack.
- Pancakes
  Whether pancakes are made from scratch or a mix, ground flaxseed is a terrific addition.

University of Toronto scientists, headed by Dr. Lilian Thompson, carried out a small but significant study that may provide promising direction in the battle against breast cancer. The research, presented at the San Antonio Breast Cancer Symposium in December 2000, looked at a small group of post-menopausal women with estrogen-receptor-positive breast cancer. Women with newly diagnosed tumours who consumed just 2 tablespoons (25 mL) a day of ground flaxseed had a significant reduction in tumour growth when compared with a placebo group. According to the researchers, the effect of the flax on the cancerous cells was comparable to that seen using chemotherapy—and without the side effects. These same researchers are now assessing the effects of flaxseed on women with dense breast tissue found during mammography. This high-density tissue is associated with a greater risk of breast cancer. Another study found that ground flaxseed reduced symptoms such as breast pain, swelling and lumpiness that can occur with menstruation.

But researchers caution moderation in consuming flaxseed during pregnancy until more is known. In animal studies, large amounts of flaxseed consumed during pregnancy were associated with lighter prostate glands in male offspring. On the other hand, consuming flaxseed while breastfeeding may lower the risk of breast cancer in the baby's future. In animal studies, exposure to phytoestrogens at an early age may result in the mammary gland developing in such a way that it can fend off cancer-causing agents. This is the speculation behind the lower incidence of breast cancer seen in countries like Japan that have diets high in soyfoods, with their high phytoestrogen content. Eaten right through childhood, soyfoods may be partially behind the decreased risk in these countries.

A last cautionary note, from the University of Toronto researchers, is that there is no data on the effects of consuming foods like flaxseed in conjunction with pharmaceutical agents like tamoxifen. They may interfere with each other's action, possibly making the medication ineffective, so stay tuned for further research.

hazelnuts

Also known as filberts, people either love these or hate them. If you are a hazelnut lover, the news on the nutritional front is good. Like cashews and almonds, they contain predominantly monounsaturated fat and provide a significant amount of vitamin E. And per ounce (30 grams), they provide 3 grams of fibre and about half the potassium of bananas.

macadamias

The macadamia is the baby of the edible-nut world. Its commercial cultivation dates only from 1858. In 1882, it was introduced to Hawaii, which is now one of the principal production areas, together with Australia and New Zealand. The fruit consists of a fleshy husk that covers a hard, durable shell protecting the spherical seed, or nut—a nut that many love but, because it's one of the priciest around, tend to savour.

Macadamias aren't just a pleasure to eat. In research conducted at the University of Hawaii on men and women between the ages of 18 and 53, blood cholesterol levels were significantly reduced when the participants consumed a monounsaturated-fat diet based on macadamia nuts, rather than the typical American diet laden with saturated fat.

peanuts

In spite of their name, peanuts are a legume, not a member of the nut family (see Legumes, page 133). One way they differ from lentils and chickpeas is that, like the soybean, peanuts do contain fat, but of the healthy variety.

Peanuts are sometimes referred to as "ground nuts," since they grow underground and not on trees as true nuts do. Said to have originated in Brazil or Peru, the peanut made its way to Africa with Portuguese explorers before landing in the U.S., where it became a favourite. Inexpensive, and thought to be a source of protein, it was readily consumed by soldiers during the Civil War.

Peanuts and peanut butter are a popular option for vegetarians because they have more protein than any other legume or nut. Just 1 ounce (30 grams) of peanuts also provides 2 grams of fibre and 25 percent of your daily need of vitamin E. Besides packing a pretty good folate punch, peanuts contribute minerals such as magnesium, copper, phosphorus, potassium and zinc.

Peanuts and peanut products scored high marks as a heart-healthy food in research from Penn State University. In the study, which was published in the *American Journal of Clinical Nutrition*, several blood-cholesterol-lowering diets were compared with the typical American diet. One diet was low fat, as recommended by the American Heart Association, while the other three, high in monounsaturated fat, contained olive oil, peanut oil or peanuts and peanut butter as the predominant fat. To assess the total effect of the diet on heart disease risk, factors such as total cholesterol, HDL-cholesterol and triglyceride levels were all taken into account.

The olive oil diet offered the most protection, reducing the risk of heart disease by about 25 percent. The peanuts and peanut butter regimen was a close second, with a reduction of 21 percent. Next came peanut oil, at 16 percent. The low-fat diet did lower the likelihood of developing heart disease, but it had the lowest score of the four blood-cholesterol-lowering regimens, at 12 percent. The three diets that were high in monounsaturated fat were also linked to lower blood triglyceride readings, an emerging risk factor in the development of cardiovascular disease. Low-fat diets may boost triglyceride levels in some people.

Peanuts are a rich source of phytosterols. These compounds, with their anti-cancer (see page 136) and heart-healthy profiles, are beginning to appear in "designer food products," including some margarines and salad dressings touted as reducing blood cholesterol. But although we know the disease-fighting benefits of these compounds when they're naturally found in nuts, we do not know whether they benefit us when

HOLD THE MOULD
Discard mouldy peanuts—those that are discoloured, shrivelled or both—as they can be a source of aflatoxin, a type of mycotoxin (see "A Pitcher's Guide" sidebar, page 000). Commercial peanut butters are checked for aflatoxins, but homemade ones can be a source. Be sure to store them in the fridge.

they are isolated and injected into another food product. We can only speculate at this point. As always, be wary of the promotional claims made by food manufacturers.

A discussion about peanuts would not be complete without a cautionary note. The incidence of peanut allergy is on the rise. Research on the alarming increase has led to some recommendations by scientists and health professionals that may stem the tide. Studies show that mothers who consumed peanuts more than once a week during pregnancy were more likely to have a peanut-allergic child than mothers who consumed peanuts less than once a week. In addition, allergy-prone children who were fed peanuts at an earlier age were more likely to develop peanut allergies. Introducing peanuts at a later age may save a child from developing this potentially deadly allergy.

pecans

The pecan, an American-grown tree nut, is a member of the hickory family and was an important food in the diet of the native tribes of the central and southern United States. The nuts were also a favourite of two famous Americans, George Washington, who was said to frequently carry them in his pockets, and Thomas Jefferson, who was an avid cultivator of pecan trees.

Pecans grow wild across the U.S., although nuts from wild trees have a harder shell than cultivated varieties, with their paper-thin ones. A much-loved ingredient in pies and confectionery items (especially with chocolate and caramel), pecans are among the highest in fat and lowest in protein of all the nuts. But there is a very healthy side to them as well.

No matter where they're grown, pecans are packed with vitamin E, according to research from the University of Georgia. And like other nuts, they contain more than one kind of vitamin E. Supplements tend to contain only one type of vitamin E, alpha tocopherol, but research is pointing towards the benefits of consuming a range of different tocopherols, like the gamma and delta varieties, the mix that is naturally found in food. Gamma tocopherol is being investigated, and is showing promising results in providing benefits for intestinal health and protection from prostate cancer.

Vitamin E has also been highlighted in two studies investigating the link between nutrition and Alzheimer's disease. The research, published in the *Journal of the American Medical Association* in June 2002, points to the benefits of consuming antioxidants such as vitamin E and vitamin C from food, not from supplements, to reduce the risk of Alzheimer's disease.

In one study, the eating habits of more than 800 Chicago residents aged 65 and older who had no initial symptoms of mental decline were tracked for an average of four years. At the end of the study, the group eating the most foods high in the antioxidant vitamin E had a 70 percent lower risk of developing Alzheimer's than the group who ate few foods high in vitamin E. Supplements containing vitamin E were not linked to a lower likelihood of mental decline. An interesting note: those who carried a gene known to increase Alzheimer's risk did not see any benefit from consuming foods rich in vitamin E.

In another investigation, 5,395 people aged 55 and older in the Netherlands were followed for an average of six years. As with the American study, those with high dietary intakes of vitamins E and C were less likely to be afflicted with Alzheimer's, regardless of whether they had the gene variation. These results were most pronounced in smokers, although benefits from antioxidant-rich foods were seen for non-smokers and past smokers as well.

Pecans also protect artery health with their abundance of phytosterols and their blood-cholesterol-lowering fatty acid profile. They also supply fibre, about 3 grams per ounce (30 grams), along with more than 19 vitamins and minerals, including vitamin A, folic acid and calcium.

pine nuts

Found in pine cones around the world, pine nuts are used in cooking throughout the Mediterranean, the Middle East, Asia and China. Although the pine tree is a familiar sight in North America, until recently its nut was not a common part of our diets.

Pine nuts used to be found only in ethnic markets, but with the increased popularity of Mediterranean cuisine, fare like pesto sauce—made from pine nuts and basil—has become familiar. Now, these delicious nuts can be found even in mainstream supermarkets. Like macadamia nuts, they are pricey and so they are often used in very small amounts in cooking. Of the two main varieties, the Italian pine nut, torpedo-shaped and with a light, delicate flavour, is more expensive than the stronger-flavoured Chinese pine nut.

Pine nuts are among the higher-protein nuts and provide plenty of fibre and vitamin E. Fat-wise, they supply the monounsaturated variety. Be certain to refrigerate or freeze pine nuts to prevent their turning rancid.

pistachios

When I was a kid, you could always tell if someone was eating pistachios by the colour of their hands. Nowadays, red pistachios can still be purchased, but naturally tan ones are the more common variety. So why are some pistachios red? The first pistachios available to consumers were imported from the Middle East. North American importers dyed the shells red, both to disguise staining from antiquated harvesting methods and to make pistachios stand out among other nuts in vending machines.

If you find controlling portions of nuts to be a tough task, then pistachios are for you. A 1-ounce (30-gram) serving equals 47 pistachios—more nuts per serving than any other nut. And if you eat them out of the shell, it can take even longer to munch your way through that ounce. They provide appreciable amounts of potassium and 5 grams of protein per ounce. Along with vitamin E, they're especially rich in phytosterols.

A study out of UCLA School of Medicine found that, in people with moderately elevated cholesterol, pistachios decreased total cholesterol levels while increasing HDL readings—providing benefit in two ways.

pumpkin seeds

Pumpkin seeds were a special treat for my kids to eat when they were younger. In the autumn, we would choose the perfect pumpkin and, before carving a scary face, scoop out the insides, rinse off the seeds and roast them. And delicious they were, even more so because of the effort and care that went into every step of their preparation.

These small seeds, also known as pepitas, are much more than just the windfall from carving a jack-o'-lantern. They provide protein, fibre and an assortment of minerals such as iron, magnesium and phosphorus. Their fatty acid profile, along with their content of the amino acid arginine, also makes pumpkin seeds a heart-smart choice.

In Europe, pumpkin seeds have been at the centre of much research as part of the treatment for benign prostate disease, and the results appear to be promising. But these tasty little seeds are not for men alone. They contain a whole mix of carotenoids, including lutein, beta carotene and various types of cryptoxanthin.

sesame seeds

Perhaps because of their size, sesame seeds are most often used in Western cooking as a garnish on crackers and baked goods. But in the Middle East, sesame seeds are ground into a paste known as tahini, a condiment for all kinds of salads and dips. They're also the principal ingredient of a specialty of the region, halvah. Both the seeds and the oil predominate in Asian cuisine.

Despite their size, these tiny little seeds are packed with an abundance of flavour and an ability to thwart disease—and the oil they yield is just as potent. Research performed at Howard University, in Washington, D.C., and published in *Pharmacological Research* in June 2002, assessed the cancer-preventive effects of a number of compounds, including sesamol (a lignan found in sesame oil), sesame oil itself, resveratrol (the phytochemical found in grapes, red wine and peanuts) and sunflower oil. The scientists compared their ability to protect against certain cells and found that all four had profound effects on suppressing cancer growth. The sesame oil was the most potent, followed by sesamol and then resveratrol. And the sesamol and resveratrol actually killed off cancer cells.

In Japan, where high blood pressure is not an uncommon problem, researchers examined the effects of sesamin, from sesame oil, and vitamin E on high blood pressure and the risk of stroke in rats. The rats were fed four different diets, one rich in vitamin E, one rich in sesamin, one containing both vitamin E and sesamin, and a control diet containing neither compound. During the investigation, the scientists increased the rats' risk of stroke. (Don't ask! It involves a cranial window and a helium-neon laser...) They then measured blood pressure and the likelihood of blood clot formation. All three of the vitamin, sesamin and combination diets suppressed any rise in blood pressure when compared with the control diet.

sunflower seeds

This is yet another small seed that packs a mighty wallop against a range of diseases. According to the U.S. Department of Agriculture Nutrient Database, sunflower seeds are the best whole-food source of vitamin E. A 1-ounce (30-gram) serving of sunflower seeds contains a whopping 76 percent of the daily recommended intake of this vitamin.

Sunflower and other seeds are a terrific option for people with allergies to tree nuts and peanuts. Seed eaters can reap many of the potential benefits of nuts—a healthy

NUTRIENT COMPARISON OF NUTS AND SEEDS (PER 1-OUNCE/30-G SERVING)

	Folate (mcg)	Vitamin E (mg)	Selenium (mcg)	Iron (mg)	Zinc (mg)
Almonds	8.22	7.42	2.24	1.22	0.95
Hazelnuts	32.04	4.31	1.13	1.33	0.70
Pecans	6.24	1.04	1.70	0.72	1.28
Sesame seeds	27.41	0.64	1.62	4.12	2.20
Sunflower kernels	64.46	11.34	16.87	1.92	1.43
Walnuts	27.78	0.83	1.30	0.83	0.88

Source: U.S. Department of Agriculture (USDA) Nutrient Data Laboratory.

fatty acid profile; a rich source of antioxidants, including selenium and copper; fibre; a range of B vitamins, like folate and vitamin B-6; and the minerals manganese, iron and zinc. The protein they contain provides the amino acid arginine and its advantages for heart health. Add to that a potent phytochemical mix, including lignans, and the sunflower seed definitely makes a super nut substitute.

In fact, a new product called SunButter, which has sunflower seeds as its main ingredient, is a delicious alternative to peanut butter. For parents looking for a peanut butter substitute now that many schools have become peanut-free, it's something to cheer about—past formulations of sunflower seed spreads weren't the most palatable.

walnuts

The walnut dates back thousands of years. Jean-Luc Toussaint, in his *Walnut Cookbook*, writes, "The walnut appears in Greek mythology in the story of Carya, with whom the god Dionysus fell in love. When she died, Dionysus transformed her into a walnut tree. The goddess Artemis carried the news to Carya's father and commanded that a temple be built in her memory. Its columns, sculpted in wood in the form of young women, were called caryatides, or nymphs of the walnut tree." Although the walnut and its oil have been known since ancient times, the tree was said to have disappeared in parts of northern Europe during the glacial period but was then reintroduced by barbarian invaders and by Greco-Roman conquerors. In 1867, walnuts were first commercially grown in the U.S., which now supplies two-thirds of the world market. Most of these are grown in California, where 37 species of walnut tree can be found.

Walnuts were the first nut, back in the 1970s, to wear a heart-healthy halo. Their polyunsaturated fat was recognized even then for its cholesterol-lowering potential. However, the importance of the specific type of polyunsaturated fat found in walnuts had not yet been established in scientific circles. Omega-3 polyunsaturated fatty acids, the same fats that predominate in coldwater fish, have only recently received the nutritional accolades they deserve. In fact, until the Canadian and U.S. governments released new nutritional recommendations in September 2002, there had never been an established suggested daily intake for omega-3 fatty acids. The new recommendations, called Dietary Reference Intakes, or DRIs, differ from the old recommendations in that they look at not only how much of a nutrient should be consumed but also the optimal intake to prevent chronic diseases that afflict our society.

The guidelines called for consuming two types of polyunsaturated fatty acids, alpha-linolenic acid (an omega-3 fatty acid that's also found in flaxseed) and linoleic acid (an omega-6 fatty acid)—neither of which is made by the body. For alpha-linolenic acid, the recommended intake is 1.6 and 1.1 grams per day for men and women, respectively. The good news about walnuts is that just 1 ounce (30 grams) contains 2.5 grams of alpha-linolenic acid—more than enough to meet the recommendation. (For other sources, see Top-Scoring Omega-3 Foods, below.)

TOP-SCORING OMEGA-3 FOODS

Fish Sources

Mackerel, Atlantic 2.6 g
Trout, lake 2.0 g
Herring, Atlantic 1.7 g
Sturgeon, Atlantic 1.5 g
Tuna, albacore 1.5 g
Salmon, Atlantic 1.4 g
Bluefish 1.2 g
Bass, striped 0.8 g
Halibut, Pacific 0.5 g

Plant Sources

Flaxseed 18.0 g
Walnuts, English 6.8 g
Soybeans, green, raw 3.2 g
Soybeans, dry 1.6 g
Spinach, raw 0.9 g
Wheat germ 0.7 g
Purslane 0.4 g
Kale, raw 0.2 g

One of the first studies pointing to the health advantages of walnuts was published in 1993 in the *New England Journal of Medicine.* The study, conducted at Loma Linda University, showed an average drop of 12 percent in total cholesterol blood levels and 16 percent in LDL-cholesterol levels when subjects were fed walnuts as part of their diet. But they certainly had to consume a lot of walnuts—3 ounces a day. The researchers used the large amount to see if walnuts really had an effect.

In April 2000, another landmark walnut study was published, in the *Annals of Internal Medicine.* This one, conducted in Barcelona, had men and women with high cholesterol incorporate walnuts into a healthy Mediterranean diet. This time they ate only a handful of nuts, as a substitute for some of the healthful monounsaturated fat in the diet. The participants' harmful LDL cholesterol dropped by almost 6 percent and their heart disease risk by 11 percent—beyond what would be expected from the Mediterranean diet alone. Just think of the effect walnuts could have on a typical North American diet, which is often loaded with artery-clogging saturated and trans fats.

A number of other clinical trials have all seen cholesterol levels reduced when walnuts were substituted for other fats in the diet. But walnuts have other nutritional advantages to offer. In laboratory research, when tested with ellagic acid, a powerful antioxidant, walnuts' polyphenols performed well in preventing the oxidation of LDL cholesterol. And this study didn't take into account the nuts' plentiful supply of vitamin E, a well-performing antioxidant.

recipes

glazed spicy almonds

Wonderful as a nibble for entertaining or toting along as a tasty snack, this recipe is adapted from that of the California Almond Board. Almonds are packed with heart-healthy perks. Not only do they lower LDL-cholesterol readings but they also have anti-inflammatory action, which appears to benefit arteries.

MAKES 12 SERVINGS

2 cups (500 mL) raw almonds (about 8 ounces/250 g)

1 large egg white

1 tablespoon (15 mL) chopped fresh rosemary

2 teaspoons (10 mL) brown sugar

1 teaspoon (5 mL) ground coriander

3/4 teaspoon (4 mL) salt

1/2 teaspoon (2 mL) cayenne pepper

Preheat oven to 300°F (150°C).

Place almonds on a baking sheet and roast for 12 to 15 minutes or until golden. Allow to cool for 2 minutes.

In a medium bowl, lightly beat egg white until foamy. Add warm nuts, rosemary, sugar, coriander, salt and cayenne pepper; toss to coat evenly.

Line the baking sheet with parchment paper and spread nuts in a single layer. Return to oven and roast for 15 to 20 minutes for a deep golden glaze.

PER SERVING NUTRITIONAL INFORMATION: Calories: 145, Protein: 5 g, Fat: 12 g, Saturated Fat: 1 g, Carbohydrate: 5 g, Dietary Fibre: 3 g

tahini and date dip

An Israeli dessert version of a peanut butter and jam combo from Jerusalem chef Moshe Basson. Use fresh fruit slices—bananas are super—or warm pita bread for dipping. Date syrup can be purchased at Middle Eastern grocery stores.

MAKES 4 SERVINGS

1/4 cup (50 mL) tahini (sesame seed paste)
2 tablespoons (25 mL) date syrup

Spread tahini evenly over a plate. Drizzle date syrup in a circle about 1 inch (2.5 cm) from the edge of the plate. Repeat twice more, making smaller circles inside each other and moving closer towards the centre. To slightly blend the date mixture with the tahini—and for decorative effect—draw a toothpick through the spread as if dividing it into quarters and then divide each quarter in half.

PER SERVING NUTRITIONAL INFORMATION: Calories: 103, Protein: 5 g, Fat: 8 g, Saturated Fat: less than 1 g, Carbohydrate: 8 g, Dietary Fibre: 2 g

walnut bean dip

Serve this orange-scented dip, adapted from the Califoria Walnut Commission, with crudités.

MAKES 6 TO 8 SERVINGS (2 CUPS/500 ML)

1/3 cup (75 mL) toasted walnut pieces
2 tablespoons (25 mL) walnut or extra virgin olive oil
1 (19-ounce/540-mL) can cannellini (white kidney beans), rinsed and drained
1 clove garlic, minced
1/4 cup (50 mL) orange juice
1 teaspoon (5 mL) orange zest
2 tablespoons (25 mL) coarsely chopped fresh parsley
Salt and freshly ground pepper, to taste

In a food processor, blend walnuts, oil, beans and garlic. Add orange juice and zest; process until smooth. Stir in parsley and season with salt and pepper.

PER 8-SERVINGS NUTRITIONAL INFORMATION: Calories: 117, Protein: 4 g, Fat: 7 g, Saturated Fat: 1 g, Carbohydrate: 11 g, Dietary Fibre: 3 g

spiced tahini dressing

The phytochemical sesamin, found in sesame seeds, has been shown to be a boon for maintaining healthy blood pressure readings. Serve this dressing with Chickpea Mushroom Burgers (page 152) or as a spread on sandwiches.

MAKES 4 SERVINGS (ABOUT 2/3 CUP/150 ML)

1/4 cup (50 mL) each tahini (sesame seed paste) and plain low-fat yogurt

2 tablespoons (25 mL) chopped fresh coriander

2 teaspoons (10 mL) fresh lemon juice

1/2 teaspoon (2 mL) each ground cumin and ground coriander

1–2 teaspoons (5–10 mL) water

Salt and freshly ground pepper, to taste

In a bowl whisk together tahini, yogurt, fresh coriander, lemon juice, cumin and ground coriander; thin to desired consistency with water. Season with salt and pepper.

PER 2-TABLESPOON (25-ML) SERVING NUTRITIONAL INFORMATION: Calories: 67, Protein: 3 g, Fat: 6 g, Saturated Fat: 1 g, Carbohydrate: 2 g, Dietary Fibre: 1 g

enlightened eater's™ trail mix

Both pumpkin seeds and pecans contain cholesterol-lowering fats. Pumpkin seeds have the added bonus of a variety of carotenoids, such as lutein, beta carotene and cryptoxanthin.

MAKES 12 SERVINGS

1 cup (250 mL) each toasted pumpkin seeds and toasted pecan halves

1/2 cup (125 mL) each dried cranberries and diced dried papaya

Mix together and serve.

PER 1/4-CUP (50-ML) SERVING NUTRITIONAL INFORMATION: Calories: 150, Protein: 4 g, Fat: 11 g, Saturated Fat: 2 g, Carbohydrate: 10 g, Dietary Fibre: 2 g

asian peanut salad rolls

These vegetable-filled rolls provide an Asian taste without all the fat of typical spring rolls. Rice-paper rounds can be purchased at specialty and Asian stores. Have extra rice papers on hand in case any tear during the preparation. And by including peanuts instead of meat or poultry in these rolls, you'll do your heart a double favour—less cholesterol-boosting saturated fat and more cholesterol-lowering unsaturated fat.

MAKES 12 ROLLS, SERVING 4 TO 6

12 (6-inch/15-cm) rice-paper rounds

10–12 lettuce leaves (preferably Boston or butter)

1/3 cup (75 mL) shredded carrots

1/3 cup (75 mL) fresh coriander leaves

1/3 cup (75 mL) chopped green onions (green tops only)

1/3 cup (75 mL) coarsely chopped unsalted dry-roasted peanuts

1/4 cup (50 mL) fresh mint leaves

2 tablespoons (25 mL) hoisin sauce

Place two paper towels on a work surface. Fill a shallow pan or pie plate with warm water. Soak two rice-paper rounds in water until they are pliable, about 30 seconds. Remove rice-paper rounds, allowing water to drip back into pan. Place each on a paper towel.

Put one piece of lettuce on bottom half of each soaked rice paper, leaving a 1-inch (2.5-cm) border along the edge. Tear lettuce if necessary to make it fit. Spread 1 teaspoon (5 mL) of the shredded carrot over lettuce. Repeat with 1 teaspoon (5 mL) each of the coriander, green onions and peanuts. Place two or three mint leaves on top. Drizzle with 1/2 teaspoon (2 mL) of the hoisin sauce.

Fold sides of rice-paper sheets over filling and roll up jelly-roll fashion. Gently press seam to seal; place, seam side down, on a plate and cover with a dampened tea towel. Repeat with the remaining rice-paper rounds and ingredients. (May be made up to 6 hours ahead. Cover dampened tea towels with plastic wrap and refrigerate.)

PER ROLL NUTRITIONAL INFORMATION: Calories: 50, Protein: 1 g, Fat: 2 g, Saturated Fat: less than 1 g, Carbohydrate: 7 g, Dietary Fibre: 1 g

banana flax bread

Banana and flax make a great combo. Here they are in an updated version of an old favourite from *The Enlightened Eater*. Flaxseeds have it all in one little package—soluble fibre with its blood sugar and cholesterol-lowering perks, omega-3 fatty acids with their myriad advantages from head to toe, and lignans and their anti-cancer action.

MAKES 18 SLICES

1 1/2 cups (375 mL) whole wheat flour

2 teaspoons (10 mL) baking powder

1/2 teaspoon (2 mL) cinnamon

1/4 teaspoon (1 mL) baking soda

1/4 teaspoon (1 mL) salt

Pinch nutmeg

1/2 cup (125 mL) sugar

1/3 cup (75 mL) ground flaxseed

3 tablespoons (45 mL) wheat germ

2 eggs

1 cup (250 mL) mashed ripe bananas

1/4 cup (50 mL) vegetable oil

1/3 cup (75 mL) carob or chocolate chips

Preheat oven to 350°F (180°C). Lightly grease and flour a 9- x 5-inch (2-L) loaf pan.

In a large bowl sift together flour, baking powder, cinnamon, baking soda, salt and nutmeg. Stir in sugar, flaxseed and wheat germ.

Beat eggs, bananas and oil together in a medium bowl. Pour into the centre of the dry ingredients and stir only until the mixture is moistened. Stir in the carob chips. Pour batter into the loaf pan.

Bake for 50 to 60 minutes or until a toothpick inserted into centre comes out clean. Cool for 10 minutes, then remove from the pan. Cool completely on a wire rack.

PER SLICE NUTRITIONAL INFORMATION: Calories: 129, Protein: 3 g, Fat: 5 g, Saturated Fat: 1 g, Carbohydrate: 19 g, Dietary Fibre: 3 g

date nut bread with pistachios

Adapted from that of the California Pistachio Commission, this recipe is sure to become a regular in your household. Vitamin E, phytosterols and a healthy fat profile—no wonder research shows that the pistachio is a nut your heart will love.

MAKES 18 SLICES

1 cup (250 mL) boiling water

1 cup (250 mL) dates, chopped

3/4 cup (200 mL) all-purpose flour

1/2 cup (125 mL) whole wheat flour

1/2 cup (125 mL) natural pistachios, coarsely chopped

1/2 cup (125 mL) sugar

1 teaspoon (5 mL) baking powder

1 teaspoon (5 mL) baking soda

1/4 teaspoon (1 mL) salt

2 eggs, beaten

2 tablespoons (25 mL) soft margarine, melted

1 teaspoon (5 mL) grated orange zest

1 teaspoon (5 mL) vanilla

Preheat oven to 350°F (180°C). Grease a 9- x 5-inch (2-L) loaf pan.

In a small bowl, pour boiling water over dates; let soak until cool (do not drain).

In a large bowl, stir together all-purpose flour, whole wheat flour, pistachios, sugar, baking powder, baking soda and salt. In a separate bowl, combine dates with their soaking water, eggs, margarine, orange zest and vanilla. Stir wet ingredients into flour mixture; mix only until moistened. Spoon into the loaf pan.

Bake for 45 to 50 minutes or until a toothpick inserted near centre comes out clean. Cool for 10 minutes, then remove from the pan. Cool completely on a wire rack.

PER SLICE NUTRITIONAL INFORMATION: Calories: 119, Protein: 3 g, Fat: 4 g, Saturated Fat: 1 g, Carbohydrate: 20 g, Dietary Fibre: 2 g

almond meringue cookies

These melt in your mouth. A perfect accompaniment to a fruit sorbet. And while you're enjoying them, keep in mind that almonds—including their skins—are loaded with a variety of antioxidants, some of which may improve immune system function.

MAKES 6 TO 7 DOZEN COOKIES

4 egg whites

1 tablespoon (15 mL) white vinegar

Pinch salt

3/4 cup (175 mL) sugar

1/4 cup (50 mL) finely chopped almonds

1 teaspoon (5 mL) almond extract

Preheat oven to 325°F (160°C). Line a cookie sheet with parchment paper.

In a large bowl, beat egg whites until foamy. Beat in vinegar and salt. Slowly add sugar, 2 tablespoons (25 mL) at a time, continuing to beat until stiff peaks form. Fold in almonds and almond extract.

Drop batter by teaspoonfuls on cookie sheet. Bake for 25 minutes or until golden. Let cool for 1 minute before removing from pan. Transfer to a wire rack and allow to cool.

PER COOKIE NUTRITIONAL INFORMATION: Calories: 10, Protein: less than 1 g, Fat: less than 1 g, Saturated Fat: 0 g, Carbohydrate: 2 g, Dietary Fibre: 0 g

berry almond tart

For almond lovers, here is a dessert that is irresistible! It's perfect for entertaining, and your guests won't have any idea that it's not laden with fat.

MAKES 8 TO 10 SERVINGS

ALMOND CREAM

1/2 cup (125 mL) natural almonds

1/3 cup (75 mL) sugar

3 tablespoons (45 mL) soft margarine

Pinch salt

1 large egg

1 tablespoon (15 mL) rum

1 teaspoon (5 mL) almond extract

4 sheets phyllo pastry, thawed

3 cups (750 mL) whole berries (or hulled and halved strawberries)

2 tablespoons (25 mL) apricot jam

Preheat oven to 375°F (190°C). Prepare a 10- or 11-inch (25- or 27-cm) tart pan with removable bottom by spraying with vegetable oil cooking spray.

To make almond cream, in a food processor pulse almonds with 2 tablespoons (25 mL) of the sugar until finely ground. Add margarine, remaining 3 tablespoons (45 mL) sugar and salt; process until fluffy, about 3 minutes. In a small bowl, whisk together egg, rum and almond extract; gradually add to almond cream, processing until well combined, about 3 minutes.

Place one sheet of phyllo pastry in the tart pan and press into sides of the pan. Keep remaining phyllo sheets covered with a damp towel to prevent drying. Flute edges by folding and pressing the overhang into the sides of the pan. Spray sheet with vegetable oil cooking spray. Repeat with each sheet of phyllo, criss-crossing so the bottom and sides are an even thickness. Spray each layer. Spread almond cream evenly over phyllo. Bake for 15 minutes or until top is golden. Remove from oven and cool on a wire rack. Top tart with berries. Melt jam in a small saucepan over medium-low heat, about 5 minutes. Brush over berries.

PER 10-SERVINGS NUTRITIONAL INFORMATION: Calories: 150, Protein: 3 g, Fat: 8 g, Saturated Fat: 1 g, Carbohydrate: 18 g, Dietary Fibre: 2 g

herbs, spices and oils

... and their effect on cancer have
spurred a flurry of research

Fresh herbs and spices have long been used as a seasoning in cuisines around the world. The vibrant assortment now available has only recently become an essential part of North American cooking as the trend towards slashing the fat from foods left many a dish boring and tasteless. Fresh herbs and spices are often used as a rescue attempt to liven up flavourless fare. And with the familiarity with assorted seasonings came the desire to explore the culinary flavours of the world even further. Today's kitchen spice racks bear little resemblance to those of years gone by. Bottles of "Italian Mix" have been replaced by single bottles of different types of oregano and thyme. Or fresh herbs may be in the refrigerator or in a pot on the windowsill. Formerly exotic spices such as cumin, coriander and turmeric have also been added to cooks' repertoires. In many cases, fresh herbs or more exotic spices are reserved for special occasions such as dinner parties. For everyday fare, many people simply don't bother with a garnish of fresh cilantro. But they should: fresh herbs and spices contribute a wealth of assorted phytochemicals.

Various cultures seemed to know more about the value of seasonings well before scientists. Research now shows that many spices and herbs possess significant anti-microbial action. Simply put, they protected against foodborne illness at a time when storing food was not as easy as opening a refrigerator door.

For example, in India, spices such as turmeric and cumin have been used since ancient times to preserve foods because of their antiseptic and disinfectant properties. Scientists at the University College of Science, in Calcutta, screened 35 Indian spices for anti-microbial activities and found that a substantial number could wipe out microbes, including cloves, cinnamon, chili peppers, horseradish, cumin, tamarind, pomegranate seeds, nutmeg, garlic and onion. Other research has found similar effects with thyme, oregano and allspice. But that's not to say that you can abandon safe food-handling techniques in favour of spicy fare. (See Food Safety Savvy, page 30.)

Recently, herbs and spices and their effect on cancer have spurred a flurry of research. Among the common seasonings cancer investigators are probing are black pepper, chili peppers, thyme, turmeric, oregano and verbena. What's coming to light is that the ways in which the phytochemicals work with these seasonings are as varied as their flavours. At almost every stage of the cancer process, there may be phytochemicals from assorted seasonings that have a positive effect. And the range of compounds contained in herbs and spices is staggering—from phytoestrogens to antioxidants and anti-inflammatory agents to substances that detoxify cancer-causing agents.

The list of diseases that herbs and spices have a beneficial effect on continues to grow rapidly—among them are heart disease and stroke, macular degeneration (an all too common cause of blindness in the elderly) and protection against stomach ulcers. The potential wonders of spices seem endless. Here are just a few recent findings:

- Turmeric

  Research from the University of South Carolina School of Medicine links turmeric's anti-inflammatory action to protection against precancerous changes in the colon. It has also been shown to kill leukemia cells in the laboratory. The compound in the spice thought to have these anti-cancer effects is curcumin.

- Parsley, sage, rosemary and thyme

  These herbs are more than a Simon and Garfunkel song. Along with mint, they contain a variety of compounds, including limonene, which are being investigated for its possible role in preventing breast and liver cancers.

- Hot peppers

  A research piece published in the September 2002 issue of the *Journal of the National Cancer Institute* was entitled "More Than Spice: Capsaicin in Hot Chili Peppers Makes Tumor Cells Commit Suicide." Among the cancers being examined is colon cancer. Capsaicin is also linked to slightly boosted metabolic rates.

- Ginger

  Ginger is being investigated for its effects on a number of cancers, including leukemia and ovarian cancer. Ginger tea is an age-old remedy for nausea, a property that scientists are now investigating.

- Fenugreek

  This spice may offer protection against stomach ulcers and may decrease the rate of blood clotting, offering a potential defence against heart attack and stroke. Some of the other seasonings that can affect blood clotting are anise, capsicum, cloves, parsley and turmeric—a fact that anyone on blood-thinning medication, such as warfarin, should take note of.

The question is, how much of these seasonings do you need in order to enjoy their beneficial effects—or, for that matter, how much can you eat? The answers are not clear cut. In some cases, scientists may isolate the active ingredient and then use it in large, or what's called pharmacologic, doses to fight disease. But some research shows that if herbs and spices are used in normal amounts in a phytochemical-rich diet, there are greater benefits to be reaped.

According to Dr. Charles Elson, a scientist from the University of Wisconsin, eating a variety of these substances together offers a more powerful punch against disease than consuming just one at a time. He has been investigating one class of phytochemicals called isoprenoids, of which there are more than 22,000 individual kinds.

Elson's group looked at one group of isoprenoids called beta-ionone and its effect in mice on an extremely aggressive form of the deadly cancer melanoma. The isoprenoids were found to suppress an enzyme that the cancer cells require in order to multiply. Researchers specifically looked for substances able to suppress cancer growth when consumed at the low concentrations that might be part of a normal day's intake of seasonings. And when two different isoprenoids were consumed, the impact was substantially greater than when only one was eaten.

To obtain beta-ionone, choose anise, citrus peel, ginger, mint, parsley and thyme to season your food. Other foods rich in this isoprenoid are apples, apricots, berries, cantaloupe, cherries, grapes (and wine), peaches, pineapples, plums, tomatoes, broccoli, carrots, corn, endive and sweet potatoes. But don't forget about the other thousands of isoprenoids. A well-seasoned mix of plant foods such as fruits, vegetables, grains and the like might just be the prescription for good health.

Here's another perk: using an assortment of herbs and spices makes it easier to moderate your salt intake. The subject of salt has been debated for many years, and it seems that the verdict is finally in. An excess of sodium not only is linked to high blood pressure but may also contribute to osteoporosis. High sodium intake has been shown to cause calcium loss through the urine, possibly leading to bone thinning.

In boosting your intake of herbs and spices, be adventurous. If your use of these seasonings is somewhat limited, try out new recipes that will help your palate adjust to the variety of flavours. And when it comes to fresh herbs, keep them handy and be generous. Instead of using just a parsley sprig as a garnish, add lots of the fresh

---

DASHING WITH LESS SALT

These tips from the DASH program—Dietary Approaches to Stop Hypertension (see DASH Your Way To Better Health, page 47)—give some simple ways to reduce your sodium intake:

- Use reduced-sodium or no-salt-added products, such as no-salt-added canned vegetables or dry cereals that have no added salt.
- Be "spicy" instead of "salty." In cooking, flavour foods with a variety of herbs, spices, wines, lemon, lime and vinegars.
- Avoid the salt shaker on the table, or replace it with a herb substitute.
- Eat more whole, unprocessed foods. Choose fewer processed, canned and convenience foods.
- Choose lower-sodium versions of condiments like soy sauce and teriyaki sauce.
- Read food labels to become aware of high-sodium foods and to select the lowest-sodium varieties.
- Limit cured foods (such as bacon and ham) and foods packed in brine (such as pickles, pickled vegetables and sauerkraut).
- Choose fruits or vegetables instead of salty snack foods.

chopped herb. The same goes for basil. And don't save these garnishes solely for guests. They may certainly look nice but their beauty is much more than "skin deep."

olive oil

Throughout the ages, the olive tree has been valued for several attributes—its branches are an ancient and universal symbol of peace, while its oil is used not only in food preparation but also in religious rituals. The wisdom of traditional food patterns that used olive oil as the predominant oil in cooking is now backed by scientific research, which has shed light on olive oil's myriad nutritional benefits. Perhaps for this reason, as well as its flavour, the oil is in vogue as never before. A fragrant, peppery extra virgin oil drizzled over sliced tomatoes and basil or on a garlic-laden hummus is now more palate-pleasing than it might have been 15 years ago when tasteless oils were the more common choice.

Not too long ago in North America, if you wanted to buy olive oil, there were only a few choices available. But over the past decade, the marketplace has exploded with all manner of offerings with a wide range of tastes and prices. Labels on bottles read "Extra virgin olive oil," "Virgin olive oil," "Olive oil," "Light olive oil" and "Extra light olive oil." In stores carrying a wider variety of olive oils, the labels on extra virgin oils may go even further, listing the place of origin and even the kinds of olives used to make the oil. The characteristics of an extra virgin olive oil—aroma, colour and taste —are, like wine's, dependent on a number of factors, such as the variety and ripeness of the olives used.

Sorting through the labels can be extremely confusing. What is the distinction between "extra light" and "extra virgin"? And are there nutritional differences? Understanding the classifications of the various oils can help to clear the murky waters.

The classification of olive oil is the same worldwide and is governed by the International Olive Oil Council, which sets global standards no matter where the oil originates.

- *Virgin* olive oil is simply the oily juice pressed from the olive fruit. It is unrefined; in other words, it has not been subjected to any treatments other than washing, decantation (to get rid of sediment), centrifugation and filtration. The acidity of the oil, which can be affected by the quality of the olives and the harvesting techniques, determines the classification and whether any refining is needed. (An oil that is above the acidity guidelines or that is very acidic and off in colour, aroma or taste needs to be refined; see *Lampante* oils below.) The term *virgin* refers to oils that are slightly more acidic than the more expensive extra virgin ones, containing no more than 3 grams free oleic acid per 100 grams of oil.

- *Extra virgin* oils, which are the least acidic, have a maximum acid level of 1 gram of free oleic acid per 100 grams of oil. They vary in taste depending on the variety of olive used to make them. (There may come a day when olive oil lovers buy an oil for the type of olive used much in the same way that wine connoisseurs opt for a particular grape.)
- *Lampante* oils are those that do not meet taste, appearance or aromatic criteria or that have high acid levels. These are not considered acceptable to be sold as is and therefore must be refined. (Before modern processing technology was available, the lower-quality oils were used as lamp fuel, thus the name lampante.) Along with lampante oils, which need to be refined, are "pomace" oils, in which solvents have been used on the olives to extract the oil. A percentage of virgin oil is then added to the refined product to yield what is simply called "olive oil."
- *Extra light* and *light* olive oils are the most highly refined of all. Despite their name, these are no lower in calories and fat than the non-light, or more colourful and fragrant varieties. Unlike refined olive oil, extra light and light have no virgin olive oil added to them. Consumers on both sides of the Atlantic have been led to believe that "light" products may bestow more health benefits. For instance, Italian consumers are bombarded with advertisements that equate the less-aromatic and lighter-coloured seed oils with slender silhouettes. All of this is misleading: Light olive oils are, simply, refined oils without the taste or beneficial phytonutrients of the olive.

All vegetable oils, whether olive, corn or canola, pack the same caloric and fat wallop of 115 calories per tablespoon (15 mL). But a flavourful and fruity extra virgin oil can make reducing fat consumption a much more pleasurable endeavour. Because you don't need as much to get the flavour, just a little of a flavour-packed extra virgin oil can go a long way. Spoonfuls of the light varieties, on the other hand, will add fat and calories with very little taste.

No matter whether processed or not, olive oil is a monounsaturated oil. Besides containing a heart-healthy fat profile, the unrefined, or extra virgin, oils contain an impressive array of compounds with disease-fighting actions. The list of such substances in extra virgin oil is exceedingly long and packed with complex names, among them phenolic antioxidants, simple phenols (hydroxytyrosol, tyrosol), aldehydic secoiridoids, flavonoids and lignans (acetoxypinoresinol, pinoresinol).

New methods of chemical analysis that can determine amounts of various phytochemicals in foods have allowed scientists to delve into olive oil's secrets. A team from the National Cancer Institute, in Genoa, Italy, headed by Dr. Attilio Giacosa has published a number of papers in prestigious scientific journals such as *Lancet,*

Oncology and the *European Journal of Cancer* on just these micro-components of extra virgin olive oil. One paper concluded that future studies evaluating cancer risk should take into account both the nature and the source of the olive oil consumed. Oils rich in antioxidants seem to provide considerable protection against coronary heart disease, colon, breast and skin cancers, and even the ravages of aging. But all of the extra virgin varieties contain a variety of phytochemicals and phytonutrients, including vitamin E, carotenoids and lignans. And there are phytochemicals that, among other things, provide colour to the oil, including beta carotene and lycopene.

Olive oil also lends its weaponry to enhancing the healthful qualities of other phytochemical-rich foods. Eating a food rich in a specific phytochemical, for instance, doesn't always mean that its antioxidant power will be unleashed. At the Northern Ireland Centre for Diet and Health, scientists assessed the antioxidant activity in the blood when tomatoes and tomato products, rich in the antioxidant lycopene, were consumed with either extra virgin olive oil or sunflower oil. As lycopene is fat soluble, it's best absorbed when eaten with a little fat. Both types of oil were found to boost lycopene absorption, *but only the extra virgin olive oil boosted the antioxidant activity in the blood.*

It seems that a splash of extra virgin olive oil over a garlicky tomato sauce is more than just a match made in culinary heaven. Other research has found that the absorption of lycopene, as well as other carotenoids, is higher when it is consumed with olive oil rather than other refined vegetable oils such as corn oil.

But even the fruitiest olive oil, if not treated with TLC, won't provide the same taste or nutrition perks as one properly stored and used. Light and heat are enemies of olive oil, as they may destroy some of the phytochemical content and shorten the shelf life of the fatty acids contained. That's why some manufacturers package it in dark glass or cans. To preserve the fruity components and give your olive oil a longer shelf life, store it in the cupboard (away from the stove) rather than out on the counter.

When cooking with olive oil—or sesame oil—add it at the *end* of the cooking time, because heat can cause the aromatic compounds to evaporate into the air, leaving you with less flavour in your cooked food. For example, use a minimal amount of oil to sauté your garlic for a tomato sauce. When the sauce is finished, add a splash of the fruity oil. Your kitchen won't smell as good, but the taste hit you'll get will more than compensate. Use the same method when grilling fish and vegetables. Using the oil in this way will allow you to get the maximum taste from the minimum amount of oil— a super way to save on calories and to make an expensive oil go further.

recipes

zesty charmoula sauce

Not only is this sauce packed with a range of phytochemicals, provided by the herbs, garlic, spices and olive oil, but it makes eating other phyto-rich foods, even simple steamed vegetables, very pleasurable indeed. It's exceptional in Savoury Moroccan Vegetable Soup (page 74). Freeze any leftovers in ice cube trays for a quick garnish. Be sure to add it when the cooking is all done, because cooking makes the sauce less flavourful.

MAKES 12 SERVINGS (ABOUT 3/4 CUP/175 ML)

2 cloves garlic, minced

1/4 cup (50 mL) finely chopped fresh coriander

1/4 cup (50 mL) finely chopped fresh parsley

1/4 cup (50 mL) extra virgin olive oil

1/4 cup (50 mL) fresh lemon juice

2 teaspoons (10 mL) grated ginger

2 teaspoons (10 mL) paprika

1/2 teaspoon (2 mL) ground cumin

1/2 teaspoon (2 mL) salt

1/4 teaspoon (1 mL) freshly ground black pepper

Pinch cayenne pepper

In a small bowl, combine all ingredients until well blended.

PER 1-TABLESPOON (15-ML) SERVING NUTRITIONAL INFORMATION: Calories: 41, Protein: less than 1 g, Fat: 4 g, Saturated Fat: 1 g, Carbohydrate: 1 g, Dietary Fibre: less than 1 g

nutty fattouch salad

This flavourful herb salad, inspired by Israeli chef Avi Steinitz Style of the Dan Hotels, will have them begging you to make it regularly. It is also wonderful as a bed for grilled fish. Za'atar, a blend of dried hyssop, sumac and sesame seeds, is available at Middle Eastern grocers. Together with a good-quality olive oil, it's a wonderful topping for flatbreads and pitas. Herbs are packed with antioxidants, but they're all too often eaten just as a garnish and in small amounts. Combined with nuts, and their cholesterol-lowering action, this dish is definitely a heart-smart choice.

MAKES 4 SERVINGS

1 large tomato, diced

1 red pepper, diced

3 cups (750 mL) coarsely chopped assorted fresh herbs (parsley, chives, coriander, dill, mint)

2 tablespoons (25 mL) coarsely chopped toasted assorted nuts (walnuts, pecans, pine nuts)

1 tablespoon (15 mL) za'atar

2 tablespoons (25 mL) extra virgin olive oil

2 tablespoons (25 mL) fresh lemon juice

Salt and freshly ground pepper, to taste

2–3 small pitas (6 ounces/175 g), toasted, cooled and broken into large pieces

In a large bowl toss together tomato, red pepper, herbs, nuts and za'atar. Drizzle with oil and lemon juice; toss again. Season with salt and pepper. Place the equivalent of one pita on each plate and ladle salad mixture over the pitas. Alternatively, toss the pita pieces with the vegetables and herbs.

PER SERVING NUTRITIONAL INFORMATION: Calories: 234, Protein: 7 g, Fat: 10 g, Saturated Fat: 1 g, Carbohydrate: 31 g, Dietary Fibre: 5 g

herb and cherry tomato linguine

A summertime treat, especially if you have a herb garden. The quick cooking of the cherry tomatoes helps to increase the absorption in the body of the heart-healthy and cancer-fighting lycopene. Olive oil not only adds taste but also enhances the lycopene absorption.

MAKES 4 TO 6 SERVINGS

3/4 pound (375 g) dry linguine (preferably whole wheat)

2 tablespoons (25 mL) extra virgin olive oil

4 cloves garlic, chopped

4 cups (1 L) ripe cherry tomatoes

Salt and freshly ground pepper, to taste

3/4 cup (175 mL) chopped assorted fresh herbs (parsley, basil, oregano, mint)

1/3 cup (75 mL) freshly grated Parmesan

Cook pasta in a large pot of boiling salted water until just tender; drain.

Meanwhile, in a large skillet, heat 1 tablespoon (15 mL) of the oil over medium-low heat. Add garlic and cook, stirring, until soft and fragrant, 4 to 5 minutes, taking care that garlic does not brown. Increase heat to high and add cherry tomatoes. Sauté until about one-third of tomatoes begin to pop. Remove from heat and season with salt and pepper. Add pasta and toss. Toss in fresh herbs and remaining tablespoon (15 mL) oil; adjust seasoning. Serve sprinkled with freshly grated Parmesan.

PER 6-SERVINGS NUTRITIONAL INFORMATION: Calories: 282, Protein: 12 g, Fat: 8 g, Saturated Fat: 2 g, Carbohydrate: 46 g, Dietary Fibre: 8 g

fettuccine with portobello mushrooms, red onions and roasted peppers

Adapted from Toronto chef David Gaunt, whose specialty is making fabulous fare out of simple but top-quality ingredients. This recipe is a super example of how to boost your intake of phyto-rich herbs. Why go for just a sprinkling when a generous serving provides so much phytochemical goodness?

MAKES 4 SERVINGS

3 cloves garlic

4 teaspoons (20 mL) + 1 teaspoon (5 mL) extra virgin olive oil

2 tablespoons (25 mL) balsamic vinegar

1/4 cup (50 mL) mixed chopped fresh basil and parsley

Salt and freshly ground pepper, to taste

4 portobello mushrooms (10–12 ounces/325–375 g), stems removed

1 red onion, cut into 1/4-inch (5-mm) rings

1/2 pound (250 g) fresh egg fettuccine

2 red peppers, roasted, peeled and cut into strips

2 tablespoons (25 mL) chopped good-quality black olives

1/3 cup (50 mL) freshly grated Parmigiano-Reggiano cheese

Sliver 2 cloves garlic; set aside. Chop remaining 1 clove garlic.

In a shallow dish, whisk together chopped garlic, 1 teaspoon (5 mL) of the olive oil, 1 tablespoon (15 mL) of the balsamic vinegar and 1 tablespoon (15 mL) of the basil and parsley; season with salt and pepper. Add mushrooms, turning to coat. Allow to marinate for 15 minutes.

Meanwhile, preheat grill. Preheat oven to 350°F (180°C).

Remove mushrooms from marinade, reserving marinade, and grill until slightly charred on each side. Put mushrooms in a small baking dish; drizzle with reserved marinade and remaining 1 tablespoon (15 mL) balsamic vinegar. Bake for 10 minutes. Allow to cool for a few minutes. Slice mushrooms, reserving cooking liquid. Set aside.

Grill onions until slightly charred on each side. Set aside. (Above vegetables may be prepared in advance.)

Cook pasta in a large pot of boiling water until just tender; drain.

Meanwhile, in a large skillet, heat 2 teaspoons (10 mL) of the oil over medium heat; add slivered garlic and cook, stirring, for 2 minutes, taking care that garlic does not brown. Increase heat to high; add mushrooms, onion, red peppers, olives and mushroom cooking liquid. Sauté until heated through. Remove from heat.

Add pasta, remaining basil and parsley, remaining 2 teaspoons (10 mL) olive oil, salt and pepper; toss well. Serve sprinkled with freshly grated Parmigiano-Reggiano.

PER SERVING NUTRITIONAL INFORMATION: Calories: 372, Protein: 12 g, Fat: 12 g, Saturated Fat: 2 g, Carbohydrate: 55 g, Dietary Fibre: 4 g

pasta with goat cheese and tomatoes

Enjoy this no-cook pasta sauce when summer tomatoes are at their best. Including both the peel and seeds boosts the total fibre count and retains the tomatoes' anti-blood clotting action.

MAKES 8 SERVINGS

8–10 plum tomatoes (about 1 1/2 pounds/750 g)
1/2 cup (125 mL) loosely packed basil leaves, coarsely chopped
3 tablespoons (45 mL) sliced black olives
2 tablespoons (25 mL) extra virgin olive oil
2 tablespoons (25 mL) balsamic vinegar
3 ounces (90 g) crumbled low-fat goat cheese
3/4 pound (375 g) short pasta (such as fusilli or penne)
Salt and freshly ground pepper, to taste

In a food processor, coarsely chop tomatoes; place in a large bowl. Stir in basil, olives, oil, vinegar and goat cheese. Set aside.

Cook pasta in a large pot of boiling salted water; drain. Toss pasta with tomato mixture. Season with salt and pepper.

PER SERVING NUTRITIONAL INFORMATION: Calories: 230, Protein: 8 g, Fat: 6 g, Saturated Fat: 2 g, Carbohydrate: 36 g, Dietary Fibre: 2 g

enlightened sweet potato and green pea samosas

Enjoy the taste of samosas without all the fat that's typically used when they're deep-fried. Turmeric, cumin, onion and ginger make a flavourful mix that contains powerful compounds that have been shown to battle various cancers.

Make extra samosas and freeze them, unbaked, in a single layer on a baking sheet and then pack into a container, separating the layers with wax paper. Bake them right out of the freezer, increasing the baking time by 10 to 15 minutes. Serve with mango chutney. The turmeric-scented filling is also super on its own as a side dish.

MAKES 30 PASTRIES

FILLING

2 teaspoons (10 mL) vegetable oil

2 teaspoons (10 mL) ground cumin

1/2 teaspoon (2 mL) turmeric

1 cup (250 mL) chopped onions

3 cloves garlic, minced

1 tablespoon (15 mL) grated ginger

1/8 teaspoon (0.5 mL) red pepper flakes

2 medium sweet potatoes (about 1 pound/500 g), peeled and cut into 1/4-inch (5-mm) dice

1 1/2 cups (375 mL) green peas

1/4 cup (50 mL) chopped fresh coriander

Salt and freshly ground pepper, to taste

10 sheets phyllo pastry, thawed

To prepare filling, heat oil in a large skillet over medium heat. Add cumin and turmeric; heat, stirring occasionally, until fragrant, about 30 seconds, being careful not to burn the spices. Add onions, garlic, ginger and red pepper flakes; cook, stirring, until soft, 5 to 8 minutes.

Reduce heat to medium-low. Stir in sweet potatoes, a pinch of salt and 1/2 cup (125 mL) water. Simmer, stirring occasionally, for 15 minutes. Stir in green peas; cook another 10 minutes or until sweet potatoes are tender. Remove from heat and stir in coriander. Season with salt and pepper. Let cool.

Preheat oven to 375°F (190°C). Prepare a baking sheet by spraying with vegetable oil cooking spray.

Place one sheet of phyllo pastry on a work surface. Keep remaining phyllo covered with a damp towel to prevent drying. Spray sheet with vegetable oil cooking spray. Top with a second sheet and spray with vegetable oil cooking spray. Cut into lengthwise strips about 2 1/2 inches (6 cm) wide.

Place a scanty tablespoon (15 mL) of the vegetable mixture at one end of each phyllo strip. Fold up one corner to form a triangle. Continue folding and making a triangle shape. Place on baking sheet, seam side down. Repeat with remaining pastry and vegetable mixture. Spray the triangles well with vegetable oil cooking spray. Bake for 15 to 20 minutes or until golden and crispy. Watch carefully that they do not burn. Serve warm.

Reheat refrigerated samosas at 375°F (190°C) for 25 to 30 minutes.

PER SAMOSA NUTRITIONAL INFORMATION: Calories: 39, Protein: 1 g, Fat: 1 g, Saturated Fat: less than 1 g, Carbohydrate: 7 g, Dietary Fibre: 1 g

asian salmon rolls

Omega-3 fatty acids combined with antioxidants—just what your heart desires! If you like, substitute shredded cooked chicken for the fish in these yummy appetizer rolls. These are best served on the same day as they're made.

MAKES ABOUT 36 ROLLS

4 (10-inch/25-cm) flour tortillas

1/2 cup (125 mL) hoisin sauce

8–10 lettuce leaves (preferably Boston or butter)

2 1/2 cups flaked cooked salmon (12–14 ounces/375–450 g)

1/2 cup (125 mL) coriander leaves

1/4 cup (50 mL) chopped green onions (green tops only)

Lay one flour tortilla on a work surface. Spread 2 tablespoons (50 mL) hoisin sauce evenly on tortilla, leaving a 1-inch (2.5-cm) border at edge farthest from you and 1/2-inch (1-cm) border around other edges. Arrange lettuce leaves side by side over hoisin. Cover lettuce with one-quarter of the salmon. Spread one-quarter of the coriander over the salmon and top with one-quarter of the green onions. Starting at the bottom, roll tortilla up tightly. Wrap rolled tortilla tightly in plastic wrap. Repeat with remaining three tortillas and refrigerate for at least 1 hour.

Unwrap tortillas and, using a sharp knife, cut each tortilla into 1-inch (2.5-cm) slices. Place on a platter and serve.

PER 1-INCH (2.5-CM) PIECE NUTRITIONAL INFORMATION: Calories: 52, Protein: 3 g, Fat: 1 g, Saturated Fat: less than 1 g, Carbohydrate: 6 g, Dietary Fibre: less than 1 g

chicken, olive and arugula sandwiches

Why buy a sandwich for lunch when you can dine on a delicious one like this? This one shows that the garnishes make the sandwich. And garnishes can also substantially elevate the phytopower of your sandwich. The olives, containing all the goodness of olive oil, and the dark leafy greens promote healthy arteries and good vision—all in one mighty tasty sandwich. When eating out, make note of tempting combos so you can add zest to your own sandwiches.

MAKES 4 SERVINGS

10 Kalamata olives, pitted and finely chopped

1/4 cup (50 mL) light mayonnaise

1 teaspoon (5 mL) extra virgin olive oil

1 teaspoon (5 mL) balsamic vinegar

4 crusty whole grain rolls, split in half

4 grilled skinless boneless chicken breasts

1 bunch arugula, washed and trimmed

Stir together olives, mayonnaise, olive oil and balsamic vinegar. Spread 1 tablespoon (15 mL) of the olive mixture on bottom half of each roll. Top with chicken and arugula. Top with second half of the roll.

PER SERVING NUTRITIONAL INFORMATION: Calories: 360, Protein: 32 g, Fat: 11 g, Saturated Fat: 3 g, Carbohydrate: 31 g, Dietary Fibre: 4 g

tea, red wine and chocolate

... can assist in cancer prevention and a lower risk of heart attack and stroke

Coffee or tea—which to choose? For some people, the choice of beverage is almost a sacred rite, particularly first thing in the morning, while for others, a big, hot mug of either, and at any time, will do. As the results of scientific investigations come to light, it appears that opting for tea leaves over coffee beans is the healthier choice. Yet for many years, coffee has been a hot media topic while tea has been left out in the cold. Given tea's attributes, it's time the media started warming up to the leaf brew. Numerous studies have found tea to be brimming with phytochemicals such as flavonoids that help combat heart disease and stroke, certain cancers and osteoporosis.

But there's tea, and then there's tea! The teas at the centre of much scientific scrutiny—green, black and oolong—come from the same plant, *Camillia sinensis*. Differences among these types of tea are due to the different processing techniques. The firing, or steaming and drying, of the leaves immediately after picking yields green tea. That brew is the beverage of choice in Asia and the Middle East, although its popularity is rapidly climbing in North America. Green tea is produced by steaming fresh leaves at high temperatures, which also results in tea with the highest level of polyphenols. Black tea, which is traditionally found in Western teacups, is exposed to oxygen before it is fired, resulting in a darker colour and an aroma distinct from that of green tea. The oolong varieties are partially oxidized, making them stronger than green tea yet milder than the black.

Unlike black, green and oolong teas, herbal teas are not really teas at all. Brews such as chamomile and mint are infusions of herbs, or tisanes. Although herbal teas likely contain an assortment of phytochemicals, the studies on tea reported in scientific journals don't pertain to them.

Much of tea's possible health attributes appear to arise from the antioxidant effects of the polyphenols flavonoids and their kissing cousins, flavonols. These substances are the same as those found in the beverage with a heart-healthy halo, red wine. The French Paradox (the theory that red wine protects against heart disease, even when accompanied by a diet of fat-laden foods) is mainly about the flavonoids found in red wine. To date, tea—so rich in flavonoids—just doesn't have the same hype.

tea leaves—predictions of a healthier future

The Zutphen Elderly Study, published in the journal *Lancet* in 1993, was one of the first studies to look at flavonoid intake and the risk of heart disease. Dutch scientists assessed the flavonoid intake of more than 800 men between the ages of 65 and 84 who were free of heart disease and tracked them for the next five years. The men who consumed the least amount of flavonoids were the ones most likely to develop and die from heart disease. Of the various foods evaluated, the major source of flavonoids was tea, at 61 percent. Some of these same researchers were involved in a 15-year study, another part of the Zutphen Elderly Study, that looked at flavonoids and the risk of stroke in a group of more than 500 men aged 50 to 69. Again, it was found that the men who suffered strokes had low flavonoid intakes. In those whose flavonoid intake appeared to offer protection, 70 percent of their intake was obtained by drinking more than five cups of black tea daily over an extended period.

In 2001, the researchers published their evaluation of the various flavonoids examined in the Zutphen Elderly Study. The results were intriguing. One flavonoid, catechin, seemed to reduce the risk of heart disease but not stroke; it appears that another flavonoid was at work decreasing the stroke risk. So before you purchase that flavonoid supplement, keep in mind that the healthy mix found in food may not be contained in the pill. Lending evidence to this is yet another Dutch tea study, the Rotterdam study, published in the *American Journal of Clinical Nutrition* in 2002. Researchers found that the greater the flavonoid intake, the lower the risk of a fatal heart attack.

American scientists investigated 1,900 patients who were in hospital after suffering a heart attack and followed them for four years. Their findings, published in the journal *Circulation* in May 2002, again showed that tea drinking was protective.

Researchers are looking more closely at just what it is in tea that may lessen the odds of dying from heart disease if arteries are clogged and hardened. But one thing's for sure: the development of clogged arteries is not an overnight process. Rather, the effects accumulate over time.

have a tea party—it's heart healthy

Boston University School of Medicine scientists investigated the effect of short- and long-term consumption of black tea on endothelial function. Endothelial function affects the arteries' ability to relax to allow blood to flow through them. Arteries that have hardened through the years because of an accumulation of plaque are much less able to accommodate good blood flow.

The researchers theorized that drinking tea would reverse the poor functioning of the endothelium in patients with proven coronary artery disease. The patients were placed on two different regimens. One included the drinking of almost a quart (or litre) of tea a day, and the other replaced the tea with water. Using ultrasound testing, the scientists examined the effects of tea versus water two hours after drinking the beverages, as well as the long-term effects of each. The good news for tea drinkers was that tea improved the blood flow. If you're not a tea "totaller," there's no time like now to convert.

Having a cup of tea may, based on this research, be very relaxing indeed—especially for your arteries if you have heart disease. After a high-fat meal, a glut of fat is released into the arteries. If they are already stiff, there's a greater chance for a heart attack. A cup of tea may lessen that risk. Stay tuned for more research in this area.

The Third International Scientific Symposium on Tea and Human Health (subtitled "The Role of Flavonoids in the Diet"), which was held in September 2002 in Washington, D.C., looked at new evidence of tea's protective effect on heart disease. Scientists examined the effect of tea on LDL-cholesterol readings when combined with a cholesterol-lowering diet. The same diet was used for all three of the test groups, but the beverages varied: subjects consumed five cups a day of either caffeinated tea, a caffeine-free placebo beverage (whose colour and flavour closely matched that of tea) or a similar placebo beverage with the same concentration of caffeine as in tea. The tea regimen led to a 10 percent lowering of the LDL cholesterol—a remarkable reduction. But researchers point out that this was just a short study; if more comprehensive ones duplicate the data, then it would make tea a pretty heavy hitter in its potential impact on cholesterol. (Not only does it appear to lower blood cholesterol but it may also protect the cholesterol that is in the bloodstream from being oxidized and turned into a more damaging form.)

A great deal of compelling research links both black and green tea to a reduced risk of various types of cancer. Some of these investigations have simply examined how much tea is consumed by a certain population and related it to the incidence of certain cancers. Other types of research, called case-controlled studies, compared the diets of people with a certain type of cancer with those of subjects free of that cancer. From around the globe, findings point to tea as lowering cancer risk. From a case-control study on stomach cancer in India to an examination of ovarian cancer in China and to one in Los Angeles where thyroid cancer was investigated in females, tea consumption has been linked to protection in all cases.

But not all the studies credit tea with having anti-cancer effects. A large study of post-menopausal women in Iowa has yielded few links between tea and cancer. But conflicting reports are not uncommon in medical research; we hear them on the news almost daily. When different studies show contradictory results, looking at some of the possible reasons why can help to clear up any confusion.

In the Iowa study, the differing results might be explained by the possibility that the absorption of phytochemical compounds varies from person to person. Some of these compounds may be absorbed at different sites in the body—some in the stomach, others in the colon. Green tea's flavonoids, compared with those of black, may be more quickly absorbed. If you then throw genetics into the mix—diverse people with diverse genes—it's easy to see why apparently similar studies don't yield the same results.

Researchers have delved further into the tea-cancer relationship by looking at the effects of drinking tea on laboratory animals and their risk for cancer, including lung and skin. At Rutgers University, both black and green tea suppressed skin tumour growth in mice exposed to ultraviolet light treatments. Interestingly, decaffeinated teas were less effective.

Similar research on laboratory animals that looked at tea and its effect on cancer-causing agents in tobacco has paved the way for human studies. Scientists from the American Health Foundation have shown that green tea, when consumed as their sole beverage, inhibits the development of lung tumours in animals injected with a potent tobacco carcinogen. In a later study, the same researchers added black tea to the mix and examined its effect on damaged DNA in lung tissue. Damaged DNA can trigger healthy cells to undergo mutation and become cancerous. The researchers found that black tea, like green, acted as an antioxidant.

Also at the Third International Scientific Symposium on Tea and Human Health, researchers presented a human study from the University of Arizona on tea and DNA damage from tobacco. In this four-month study, groups of smokers drank four cups daily of decaffeinated green tea, decaffeinated black tea or water. Researchers then looked at several indicators of oxidative stress, or DNA damage. Early results found that smokers who drank green tea showed significantly less DNA damage.

Tea appears to act at various stages of tumour development. Some cancer studies have focused on inflamed cells, which are much more likely to mutate into cancerous cells. A growing body of research shows that anti-inflammatory medications such as aspirin are linked to a lower risk of colon—and other—cancers. These medications, however, may not be well tolerated by some people. Scientists at the University of South Carolina are looking for those same anti-inflammatory properties in plant products. For the past ten years, they've tested more than 150 compounds, including many with botanical or herbal origins, as potential cancer preventives. And way up there on their list of promising candidates is green tea.

Tea is definitely a hot item—especially in its relationship to cancer. A search of the medical literature on tea reveals more than 1,050 scientific papers in which tea is mentioned along with cancer. But with so many foods already linked to cancer prevention, how does tea measure up?

Scientists from Jean Mayer Human Nutrition Research Center on Aging, at Tufts University in Boston, who have done a great deal of research on the antioxidant capacity of various plant foods, subjected tea to the ORAC test (see ORAC: A True Test of Antioxidant Power, page 13). They found a great deal of variability among the green and black commercial teas they tested. The highest-scoring teas outranked the best performers in the fruit and vegetable categories, but there were also some commercial teas with very low ORAC values.

Speculating that differing brewing techniques might be responsible for the different results, the scientists then standardized their brews. They prepared both green and black teas by placing one tea bag (1.95 grams) in 5 ounces of boiling water. In the first brewed cup, approximately 84 percent of the total antioxidant activity was extracted from the tea bag within the first 5 minutes of brewing. In the second brewed cup, an additional 13 percent of the antioxidant activity was extracted with an additional 5 minutes of brewing. The scientists concluded that, with their longer method of preparation, tea could make a significant contribution to the total daily antioxidant intake.

Research is still inconclusive as to whether other factors might decrease the antioxidant content of tea. Originally, the addition of milk to tea was believed to reduce their content, but a number of studies have found it to be of no consequence.

If all this data on tea and health isn't enough to pique your interest, consider this: tea, particularly the green variety, may truly have an edge when it comes to managing weight. Japanese research on mice assessed the effect of green tea powder on body weight along with food intake and found that consumption of green tea went hand in hand with lower body weight and food intake.

Human research also looks promising. Swiss scientists investigated whether a green-tea extract could increase metabolic rates, or calorie-burning capacity, along with fat breakdown. They speculated that the effect would be due to the combination of green tea's caffeine and the particular flavonoids in green tea, called catechins. Study subjects were given a green-tea extract containing phytochemicals and caffeine, a caffeine-only beverage or a placebo at breakfast, lunch and dinner. Their metabolic rates were then measured over a 24-hour period. Caffeine was included as one of the test regimens because there is speculation that the caffeine is responsible for the higher calorie-burning capacities. But the clear winner in boosting metabolic rates was the green tea. It also increased the breakdown of fatty tissue. The researchers then went on to identify how green tea affects the stimulation of metabolic rates and found that it was the phytochemicals in tea that were responsible.

Increased metabolism translates to higher energy levels, but there are a few considerations to keep in mind. First, the research doesn't mean that you can forget healthy eating, abandon exercise and just sip green tea. The effect isn't that substantial. Second, for some people the boost in metabolism at the wrong time of day could lead to sleepless nights. So if you start adding green tea to your daily menu, be aware of when you drink it and how it affects your sleep pattern. And because the effect was due

NOT A STRANGE BREW

Making a good cup of tea isn't rocket science, but there are some tips that can make for more pleasurable tea drinking. The following are some pointers from the Tea Council of Canada.

For the perfect cup of hot tea

Keep in mind that only boiling water will bring out the maximum flavour from the tea leaf.

Start with fresh-drawn cold water and bring it to a rolling boil.

Warm the teapot by filling it with boiling water and allowing it to sit for five minutes. This will help keep your tea hot longer.

Use one tea bag for every two cups of tea desired. Be sure to choose a quality blend!

When the water is boiling, empty the teapot, take the warmed teapot to the kettle and pour the water over the tea bags. Cover and let steep for 3 to 5 minutes. Remove the tea bags and enjoy.

For fresh-brewed iced tea

A rule of thumb when preparing fresh-brewed iced tea is to double the strength of hot tea, since it will be poured over ice.

Put 6 tea bags in a 4-cup (1-L) heatproof pitcher. Pour 1 1/4 cups (300 mL) of freshly boiled water over tea bags and steep for 5 minutes. Remove tea bags. Fill pitcher with fresh cold water.

Pour tea over ice in serving glasses. Garnish and sweeten to taste.

Store iced tea in the refrigerator.

---

to the polyphenols rather than the caffeine, even decaffeinated green tea could leave you tossing and turning at night.

On the matter of caffeine, although it's found in both coffee and tea (as well as other beverages such as cola soft drinks), the amount in coffee can be significantly more than in tea. The caffeine content, though, depends upon how each is prepared. Drip coffee, for example, contains 140 milligrams of caffeine in a 5-ounce (150-mL) cup, while instant has just 60 milligrams. The same amount of tea provides only 30 milligrams if brewed for one minute and 45 milligrams for a five-minute steep. Decaffeinated varieties of both coffee and tea are almost caffeine free.

Caffeine's effect varies from person to person. Not only are there individual variations but reactions to its stimulant effect are also influenced by a person's weight and body size. This explains why for one person, a cup of coffee in the late afternoon can lead to a sleepless night whereas for another, an after-dinner double espresso can be a bed-time soother.

Besides being linked to irritability and sleeplessness, caffeinated beverages may, in some people, lead to irregular heart rhythms such as tachycardia (rapid heart rate). Tea, on the other hand, is often thought of as a calming beverage, but caffeine counts can quickly add up for those who sip tea all day long. Using both regular and decaf tea may be preferable for caffeine-sensitive tea drinkers.

Your choice of teas and how you consume them can have a major influence on how many calories you consume in a day. Ordering tea or coffee used to be uncomplicated ("With milk, lemon or black?"), but a visit to any of the increasingly popular specialty coffee and tea shops shows how much things have changed. Plain tea and coffee are calorie free, but the calories, fat and caffeine contained in some specialty drinks, especially considering the variety of sizes available, give new meaning to the expression "tea for two." Some of the new frozen and blended teas, often served with whipped cream, can supply almost 800 calories and 16 grams of fat in the biggest serving. Go for a hot chai latte and the calories could exceed 400. If you decide to accompany that with a commercially prepared low-fat muffin, check out the nutrition information first. Some contain more than 400 calories apiece. Together with your beverage, they could total almost half a day's calorie quota—just for your tea break.

Iced tea, an old standby, can be both refreshing and nutritious. Research shows that iced varieties are all flavonoid packed. But if they're served up in the typical Canadian fashion—presweetened with sugar—frequent consumption can pack a mighty caloric wallop. In the U.S., iced tea is almost always served the same way as hot tea or coffee—unsweetened. Try American-style homemade brews, prepared with smaller amounts of sweetening agents—they won't add heft to your waistline. (See Not a Strange Brew, page 227.)

There are assorted new tea products on the shelves that can be a boon to waist watchers. Some of the spice-scented or flavoured black teas are quite satisfying when food cravings hit. And, unlike regular teas, which go well with scones, cookies, bread and more, flavoured teas don't match up with food as well and are often best on their own.

Pure tea comes in an enormous variety of tastes and aromas. When you get beyond the three basics—black, green and oolong—there are roughly 3,000 varieties to choose from. And then there are blends of all those. Among the black teas, there's a choice of Assam, Darjeeling, Nilgiri or Sikkim from India, Ceylon from Sri Lanka, Keemun, Lapsang Souchong, Yunnan from China or the old favourite, Earl Grey. Gunpowder, Dragon Well, Jasmine, Sencha Bancha, Hojicha, Genmaicha and Spider Leg are a few of the green teas available. And if that's not enough choice for you, oolong tea can be purchased as Formosa Oolong, Ti Kuan Yin, Tai Guan-Yin or Black Dragon (the literal translation of the word "oolong").

With so many options, tea shouldn't be confined to your cup. Use brewed tea as a base for dressings or for poaching both savoury and sweet items such as chicken, fish or fruit. Or try tea loose as a dry rub on meat before grilling or roasting.

One last scientific note about tea. The process of cooking meat has been linked to the production of potentially cancer-causing substances called heterocyclic amines. However, a number of studies reveal that both green and black tea may inhibit the formation of abnormal cells linked to cooked meat. Since marinating meat has been connected to lesser amounts of the cancerous compounds being produced, be creative and try a tea marinade next time you want to serve grilled beef or poultry.

red wine: a toast to your health

Toasting to your health while sipping a glass of wine could be a smart nutrition choice. There certainly is an accumulating list of benefits associated with consuming alcoholic beverages, and red wine in particular. But it's important to sort through the facts and make choices best suited to your own health, particularly if you have "girth control" issues.

One myth to dispel immediately is that red wine is somewhat like an artery cleaner, allowing you to down the fattiest of meals, have a red wine chaser and all will be well. All too many people have been left with the impression that even if they're overweight and sedentary, if they're at risk for heart disease, the best step they could make is to simply add a glass of red wine to their daily menu. Wine's benefits are best reaped when its consumption is part of a healthy lifestyle.

Much of this misconception results from the reporting of the French Paradox in the early 1990s. In France, a country where a diet of pâté, high-fat cheese and plenty of wine is the norm, the rate of heart disease was half that reported in North America. The news spread like wildfire and red wine sales soared. Is there really a paradox here?

A logical, but not necessarily welcome, explanation was put forth by Dr. Marion Nestle, a professor of nutrition at New York University and author of the book *Food Politics*. She looked at dietary recommendations and eating styles in the U.S. and France over a number of years to determine whether wine lovers were right in their claim that a glut of fat could be consumed as long as it was washed down by a goblet of burgundy.

Food-supply data from the U.S. and France were compared with heart disease rates. What Nestle found was not good news for those who wanted to dine solely on pâté and baguette.

Americans had been eating a high-fat diet with a lower nutritional score for 40 to 50 years. Alarmingly, fat consumption, especially higher amounts of saturated fat, clocked in at about 40 percent of total calories. In France in 1961, on the other hand, the fat intake was only 28 percent of total calories. By 1965, fat was on the rise, at 30 percent, and it continued to climb. By 1988, France's fat consumption had reached the American level of 39 percent.

But while the French have always indulged in rich sauces and other fat-laden fare, the portions of high-fat foods had traditionally been small. Fresh fruit and vegetables, along with a variety of breads, provided most of the calories. Data shows that in the past few years the French have been indulging in more meat, dairy products, eggs and table fats, and they're opting for less in the way of breads, cereals, fruits and vegetables.

Since coronary heart disease is a progressive disease, arteries don't immediately become clogged by a fatty diet. It takes 20 to 30 years for the effects of fat-laden eating patterns to show up in heart disease rates. Dr. Nestle suggested that the two countries' differences in rates was simply a time lag and that France's rates of heart disease would soon catch up to America's. Another point to consider is that the French use a different method of reporting deaths from heart disease, resulting in fewer being reported. Scientists speculate that this could account for a difference of up to 20 percent.

Even with a time-lag consideration, scientific research is pointing to significant health benefits in moderate alcohol—and in particular red wine—consumption. While red wine may not act as an artery cleaner, it does contain, like the abundant fruits and vegetables in the Mediterranean diet, a variety of phytochemicals. Since the reporting of the French Paradox, scientists have been intrigued about how red wine confers health benefits. It seems that with each passing month, there are more and more answers.

What we do know is that in moderation all alcohol—be it wine, beer, spirits or liqueurs—may boost levels of beneficial HDL cholesterol as well as prevent platelet aggregation, the likelihood of clots forming and then sticking to the artery walls. But red wine's phytochemicals take the effect much further. Resveratrol (see Grapes, page 27) and assorted other polyphenols not only make the blood cells less sticky and less likely to form clots but they also have a positive effect on the lining of the artery wall, or the endothelial function, keeping the blood flowing through.

And then there's the antioxidant functions of red wine's polyphenols and their possible effect on preventing cholesterol from being oxidized, making it therefore less likely to be deposited in the arteries.

All in all, this is great news for drinkers of red wine. But when it comes to alcohol consumption, we should take a few lessons from Mediterranean cultures. In this region, people tend to drink alcohol not on its own but rather as an accompaniment to a meal. Placed in the Mediterranean context, drinking wine is part of a healthy lifestyle that includes active living and nutritious food.

Harvard University's ongoing Nurses' Health Study of 80,000 women supports the concept of wine being part of a team—not a player on its own. The scientists found that the strongest protective effect of *moderate* alcohol intake was observed in women who had the highest intake of the B vitamin folate. A diet rich in fruits and vegetables, especially dark leafy greens such as spinach and kale, provides plenty of folate.

As for women concerned about alcohol consumption and the risk of breast cancer, research from Harvard on these same women provides some direction. While alcohol has been linked to protection against heart disease, it has also been linked to the growth of breast cancer cells in some women. The researchers examined the relationship between breast cancer, alcohol and folate. If the women who consumed more alcohol were short on folate, there was an increased likelihood of developing breast cancer. Those at a high risk for this disease (women with a close relative with breast cancer) should discuss with their physicians whether they should consume alcohol.

> **MODERATION**
> Whatever your choice of alcoholic beverage, enjoy it in moderation. That translates into
> - one drink a day for women
> - one or two drinks a day for men
>
> One drink equals 12 ounces (350 mL) of beer, 5 ounces (150 mL) of wine or 1 1/2 ounces (50 mL) of liquor.

Currently, red wine's resveratrol is at the centre of numerous investigations of its effects on various types of cancer, and it appears to have a preventive effect on skin, oral, breast, colon and prostate cancers. Research on pancreatic cancer cells, published in November 2002 in the journal *Pancreas*, showed that the resveratrol in red wine not only inhibited the growth of these cancer cells but also caused cell apoptosis (an occurrence likened to "cell suicide"). Various types of leukemia may also be susceptible to resveratrol's action. Japanese researchers assessed its impact on human acute myeloid leukemia cells in test tubes and found that it inhibited the growth of these cells as well.

too much of a good thing

Alcohol in excess doesn't offer any benefits for anyone, man or woman. It's linked to high blood pressure, stroke, osteoporosis and some cancers. And for people with high levels of triglycerides in their blood, alcohol can boost these artery-clogging fats even further.

Drinking styles can also have an effect on alcohol's disease-fighting effectiveness. Research shows that having an aperitif can do exactly what it's meant to do—stimulate the appetite. But excess alcohol may result in eating with abandon. If you're concerned about weight control, beware—research has linked higher waist measurements with alcohol intake.

Alcohol can take a higher caloric toll depending on the mixer. Many liquors may be combined with beverages that provide as many or more calories than the alcohol itself. Soft drinks such as colas, ginger ale, fruit drinks and punch—even tonic water—ring in at around 100 calories per 8 ounces (250 mL). Creamy drinks like piña coladas pack an even greater punch, with coconut milk containing more than 200 calories in a mere 4 ounces (125 mL).

Moderating alcohol intake is easier if you're aware of its dehydrating effects. Alcohol can actually make you thirsty, which may lead you to drink even more. If you consume an alcohol-free and calorie-free drink between each alcoholic one, you'll drink less alcohol overall.

Most experts agree on one point when it comes to wine and health—if you don't drink, don't start just for the health benefits. There are plenty of phytofoods to make up for red wine's offerings.

chocolate

For many people, chocolate is a guilty pleasure. And, as a British study revealed in 1995, for those who believe that eating chocolate is an indulgent activity, the pleasure is short-lived and tinged with feelings of guilt.

But chocolate wasn't always a forbidden treat. Thousands of years ago, in drink form and often spiced with chili peppers, it was worshipped by the Mayans as an idol —in the true religious sense, not in the gastronomic one. "Food of the gods" is the direct translation of Theobroma, the name given to the cacao tree by the chocolate-loving European botanist Linnaeus. It is the Theobroma from which the cacao seed or bean—the source of chocolate—is derived.

Chocolate, or rather the cacao bean, was also used as currency. And when early explorers took the cacao bean back to Europe from Central America, it became popular with the aristocracy as a hot beverage. Once the pleasure of drinking chocolate—first with the addition of cane sugar and later, milk—was revealed to the underclasses about two centuries later, there was no turning back.

In the 1600s, in Italy, chocolate was combined with nut pastes to make confections. During the eighteenth century, chocolate was used as a remedy for stomach aches. Unsweetened squares of "Baker's chocolate" were manufactured in the U.S. by a Dr. James Baker as a cure for various ailments, not as an ingredient in baking!

The first chocolate bar was produced by the Fry Chocolate Factory in Britain in the mid-1800s. But it was the Swiss—Henri Nestlé and Daniel Peter, in particular—who, 30 years later, introduced milk chocolate. Milton Hershey, an American, has been credited with bringing affordable chocolate bars to the masses in the early 1900s.

The effect of the fat found in chocolate on blood cholesterol remains somewhat controversial. There has been debate about the predominant type of saturated fatty acid in chocolate and its true effect on blood cholesterol readings. While there is no consensus in this area, research does show that pure chocolate may indeed provide some health benefits.

The cacao bean is a rich source of flavonoids, the same phytochemicals found in apples, onions and tea. But are these phytochemicals able to do their stuff when consumed in the form of chocolate bars? Researchers at Penn State University set out to determine if the flavonoids in cocoa powder and in dark chocolate affected cardiovascular disease risk factors. Among the indicators they assessed were the rate of LDL oxidation and the antioxidant capacity in the blood. Healthy subjects were fed two different diets over two periods. One was an average American diet with controlled amounts of fibre, caffeine and theobromine, one of the phytochemicals found in chocolate. The other regimen was identical but was supplemented daily with 22 grams of cocoa powder and a 16-gram bar of dark chocolate, which provided a fixed amount of phytochemicals called procyanidins. The combination of chocolate and cocoa did protect against LDL oxidation as well as lead to higher amounts of antioxidant capacity in the blood. And it did so better than the phytochemical theobromine acting on its own.

There is a possibility that chocolate and cocoa powder assist in cancer prevention (preliminary studies have begun). And they may also have anti-inflammatory effects and decrease the rate of blood clotting, which leads to a lower risk of heart attack and stroke. In a study from the University of California at Davis that examined the effect of a cocoa beverage and a caffeine-containing drink on blood-clotting indicators, cocoa consumption had an aspirin-like effect on the arteries. Aspirin has been shown to decrease the risk of blood clots because it makes platelets—part of the red blood cell—less sticky. When platelets stick together, they form blood clots, which can block arteries and cause heart attack or stroke.

It then seemed logical to pit cocoa against aspirin in its effects on platelet function. At the University of Wisconsin-Green Bay, the effect on blood clotting of a flavonol-rich cocoa beverage was investigated alone and in combination with aspirin. On separate test days, a small group of healthy adults consumed aspirin, or a cocoa beverage, or aspirin plus cocoa. In the end, the cocoa beverage acted in a similar fashion to aspirin, although its effects were less profound. Cocoa and aspirin taken together, however, seemed to have even more effect in decreasing the blood-clotting rate.

Results like these point not only to the incredible possibilities of enlightened food choices but also to the potential risks in loading up on an assortment of phytochemical-rich foods (for instance, too little blood clotting may lead to uncontrolled bleeding and the risk of hemorrhage).

chocolate imposters

When you're selecting chocolate, whether for the health perks or just the enjoyment, be aware that there are imposters lurking on the shelves. Nowadays, the variety of chocolate available is staggering. But so too is the range in quality. At one end we have products that definitely classify as "food of the gods," and at the other end we find a product that looks suspiciously like chocolate but tastes very little like the real thing. Before buying chocolate, take time to read the ingredient list on the box or label. The imposter chocolate is dominated by sugar and cholesterol-raising hydrogenated vegetable oils, and is low in—or doesn't contain any—cocoa butter, which is always the primary ingredient of real chocolate.

There is a substantial difference in taste and nutrition between true chocolate and the imposters. Many of these chocolate imposters provide the same amount of fat and calories as the real thing, 140 to 150 calories and 10 to 15 grams of fat per ounce (30 grams). But that's where the similarity ends. Products with lots of hydrogenated oils may boost LDL cholesterol while reducing levels of the protective HDL cholesterol. To add insult to injury, they may be very low in phytochemical content.

For people with chocolate allergies, there's always carob. Carob is not an imposter but is a substitute made from carob pods that grow on an evergreen tree native to the Mediterranean region. If you choose products like carob chips for the sake of nutrition, be aware that these types of products contain as many calories as chocolate. While their fat content is similar to that of real chocolate, the fat frequently used in carob chips and bars is usually one made from hydrogenated oils. As well, carob's phytochemical content is likely very different, so you won't necessarily derive the same benefits.

And for those who have been avoiding chocolate because of milk allergies or lactose intolerance, there's good news to report. Bittersweet or semisweet varieties do not necessarily contain any milk. Read labels carefully to find milk-free products. Products that contain only butterfat, with no milk solids added, should not be a problem for the lactose intolerant.

crazy for chocolate

Plenty of research is looking at the various chemical compounds contained in chocolate and their effects on brain chemistry. Mood alterations, aphrodisiac qualities and effects on premenstrual syndrome are just a few of the links being investigated.

But chocolate cravings may also be a signal of imbalanced eating. Skipping meals or eating skimpy meals through the early part of the day (breakfast and lunch) can often trigger a craving for chocolate. If you tend to overindulge when chocolate is nearby, learning how to indulge can be an invaluable lesson.

The first step is to purchase your favourite kind. For lovers of milk chocolate, opting for a dark or bittersweet truffle won't hit the spot. When was the last time you made your selection from a boxful of chocolates, found it wasn't your favourite and didn't go back for another? Instead, be discerning, and your choice will satisfy.

cocoa: the taste of chocolate without a glut of fat

Cocoa powder, which has had most of the cocoa butter—the fat that's naturally found in the cocoa bean—removed, is a super lower-fat alternative in baking. With less than 15 calories and 1 gram of fat per tablespoon (15 mL), it provides an easy way to cut down on the fat in desserts. Compare that with 140 to 150 calories and 8 to 10 grams of fat for an ounce (30 grams) of chocolate.

Make leaner brownies and cakes by substituting applesauce or puréed prunes for part of the added fat in your tried-and-true recipes. For example, if a recipe calls for 1/2 cup (725 mL) of margarine, substitute 1/4 cup (50 mL) applesauce or puréed prunes and 1/4 cup (50 mL) margarine. If you're pleased with the final product, next time reduce the fat a little more while boosting the fruit component. Then maybe throw in a few chocolate chips for a chocolate boost.

Here are some other lower-fat substitutions that can help you to enjoy cocoa-containing baked goods more often. Lowering the fat count in these ways makes room for some real chocolate in a recipe.

- Use 2 egg whites in place of 1 whole egg as a substitute for some of the eggs in a recipe. Use trial and error in adapting recipes. For example, if a recipe calls for 6 eggs, use 4 egg whites and 4 whole eggs. If you like the results, next time try the recipe using 6 egg whites and 3 whole eggs.
- Use evaporated skim milk, 2% milk or buttermilk instead of cream or sour cream.
- Add instant coffee or instant espresso powder to enhance the taste of a lower-fat chocolate dessert.

recipes

black tea rub

Here's a taste of Morocco with an added twist—tea. The spices and tea also add a super antioxidant mix. Use it to spice poultry or fish before grilling or roasting. For a stronger flavour, coat chicken or fish with a larger amount of the rub.

MAKES ENOUGH FOR ABOUT 1 POUND (500 G) OF FISH OR CHICKEN

1 tablespoon (15 mL) black tea leaves (from about 2 tea bags)

1 tablespoon (15 mL) brown sugar

1/2 teaspoon (2 mL) cinnamon

1/2 teaspoon (2 mL) ground coriander

1/4 teaspoon (1 mL) salt

1/4 teaspoon (1 mL) freshly ground pepper

In a small bowl, stir together tea leaves, sugar, cinnamon, coriander, salt and pepper. Mixture keeps, stored in a tightly closed jar, for a couple of months.

Rub on chicken or fish and allow to sit for 20 minutes. Brush with extra virgin olive oil before cooking.

PER 2-TEASPOON (10-ML) SERVING NUTRITIONAL INFORMATION: Calories: 12, Protein: less than 1 g, Fat: less than 1 g, Saturated Fat: less than 1 g, Carbohydrate: 3 g, Dietary Fibre: less than 1 g

asian tea marinade

Research shows that marinades decrease the production of potentially harmful substances formed during the grilling process. This tasty marinade, wonderful on both poultry and fish, not only offers health perks, but it's also brimming with flavour.

MAKES ENOUGH FOR 1 POUND (500 G) OF FISH OR CHICKEN

1 clove garlic, chopped

2 tablespoons (25 mL) rice vinegar

1 1/2 tablespoons (20 mL) black tea (from about 3 tea bags)

1 tablespoon (15 mL) sodium-reduced soy sauce

1 tablespoon (15 mL) sesame oil

1 tablespoon (15 mL) honey

2 teaspoons (10 mL) grated ginger

Salt and freshly ground pepper, to taste

In a small bowl, stir together garlic, vinegar, tea leaves, soy sauce, sesame oil, honey, ginger, salt and pepper until well combined. Pour over chicken or fish and marinate for at least 20 minutes, covered, in the refrigerator.

PER 1-TABLESPOON (15-ML) SERVING NUTRITIONAL INFORMATION: Calories: 20, Protein: less than 1 g, Fat: 1 g, Saturated Fat: less than 1 g, Carbohydrate: 2 g, Dietary Fibre: less than 1 g

iced mint green tea with lime

Refreshing at any time of year. And considering the preliminary research showing tea's possible protection against skin cancer, it might be more than just a thirst-quenching drink. Remember, though, since green tea can boost your metabolic rate, for some this is best served earlier in the day.

MAKES 4 TO 6 SERVINGS

4 bags green tea

2 tablespoons (25 mL) fresh mint leaves

3 cups (750 mL) boiling water

4–6 wedges fresh lime

Honey, to taste

Place tea bags and mint in a heatproof carafe. Pour boiling water over and allow to steep for at least 15 minutes or until cool. Remove tea bags and mint. Refrigerate until serving time. Pour tea over ice cubes in glasses. Squeeze in lime juice from wedge and sweeten with honey to taste.

PER 6-SERVINGS NUTRITIONAL INFORMATION (WITHOUT HONEY): Calories: 2, Protein: 0 g, Fat: 0 g, Saturated Fat: 0 g, Carbohydrate: less than 1 g, Dietary Fibre: 0 g

PER 6-SERVINGS NUTRITIONAL INFORMATION (WITH 1 TEASPOON/5 ML HONEY): Calories: 23, Protein: 0 g, Fat: 0 g, Saturated Fat: 0 g, Carbohydrate: 6 g, Dietary Fibre: 0 g

chai

Chai beverages are soaring in popularity these days. Here's a flavourful one that can help you save on calories compared with those from specialty coffee shops. And it's much cheaper, too. By including the seasonings, you're not only boosting the flavour, you're topping up the tea's antioxidant totals even further.

MAKES 4 SERVINGS

1 cinnamon stick

8 black peppercorns

5 whole cloves

1 (1-inch/2.5-cm) piece ginger root, cut into 4 slices

1/2 teaspoon (2 mL) cardamom seeds

1 tablespoon (15 mL) black tea leaves (Ceylon or Darjeeling) (from about 3 tea bags)

1 cup (250 mL) 1% milk

Honey or other sweetener, to taste

Bring 4 cups (1 L) water to a boil in a saucepan. Add cinnamon stick, peppercorns, cloves, ginger and cardamom seeds. Reduce heat, cover and simmer 10 minutes. Remove from heat. Add tea leaves and steep 10 minutes. Add milk and heat until mixture just begins to simmer—do not boil. Strain chai through cheesecloth or a fine-mesh sieve. Serve immediately, sweetened to taste.

PER SERVING NUTRITIONAL INFORMATION (WITHOUT HONEY): Calories: 25, Protein: 2 g, Fat: 1 g, Saturated Fat: less than 1 g, Carbohydrate: 3 g, Dietary Fibre: 0 g

soba noodle salad with earl grey tea vinaigrette

Deep, rich-tasting tea is the perfect ingredient to take the place of fat in salad dressings and marinades. This tea-based dressing can be used as a marinade for meat or fish, for flavouring stir-fries, as a basting sauce for grilled vegetables or as a vinaigrette for green and pasta salads. And as you look down the list of ingredients, you'll find that almost every one provides a heart-healthy or anti-cancer action—if not both!

MAKES 6 TO 8 SERVINGS

SALAD

12 ounces (375 g) soba noodles

1 cup (250 mL) diagonally sliced snow peas (about 1/4 pound/125 g)

1 cup (250 mL) carrots cut into long matchsticks

1 cup (250 mL) thinly sliced red peppers

1 cup (250 mL) thinly sliced red onions

1/4 cup (50 mL) chopped fresh basil

VINAIGRETTE

1 cup (250 mL) strong brewed Earl Grey tea

1/4 cup (50 mL) orange juice

1 teaspoon (5 mL) sugar

1 clove garlic, minced

1/4 cup (50 mL) sesame oil

2 tablespoons (25 mL) rice wine vinegar

1 tablespoon (15 mL) minced shallots

1 teaspoon (5 mL) grated ginger

1/2 teaspoon (2 mL) salt

1/2 teaspoon (2 mL) freshly ground pepper

To make the salad, cook noodles in plenty of boiling water until just tender. Drain and let cool.

Meanwhile, make the vinaigrette. Place tea, orange juice and sugar in a small saucepan or skillet and bring to a boil; reduce to about 1/4 cup (50 mL). Remove from heat and stir in garlic, sesame oil, vinegar, shallots, ginger, salt and pepper.

In a large bowl, toss together soba noodles, snow peas, carrots, red peppers, onions and basil; drizzle with warm vinaigrette and toss to combine. Taste and adjust seasoning, if necessary.

PER 8-SERVING NUTRITIONAL INFORMATION: Calories: 242, Protein: 9 g, Fat: 7 g, Saturated Fat: 1 g, Carbohydrate: 40 g, Dietary Fibre: 3 g

mulled wine

A perfect drink to have in cold weather while sitting by a roaring fire. The spices, citrus and wine all contribute to a wonderful antioxidant brew.

MAKES 4 TO 6 SERVINGS

3 cups (750 mL) dry red wine

3 thin lemon slices

6 thin orange slices

1 cinnamon stick

5 whole cloves

1 tablespoon (15 mL) sugar

1/8 teaspoon (0.5 mL) freshly grated nutmeg

In a saucepan, combine wine, lemon slices, 3 of the orange slices, cinnamon stick, cloves, sugar and nutmeg. Bring to a boil, reduce heat and simmer for 5 minutes. Strain. Serve in a mug, garnished with half an orange slice.

PER 6-SERVINGS NUTRITIONAL INFORMATION: Calories: 93, Protein: less than 1 g, Fat: 0 g, Saturated Fat: 0 g, Carbohydrate: 4 g, Dietary Fibre: 0 g

cinnamon and tea poached pears

The flavonoid combo—from the pears and the tea—makes this a heart-healthy dessert. For a perfect taste match, serve these poached pears atop low-fat vanilla frozen yogurt.

MAKES 4 SERVINGS

3 black tea bags

1/4 cup (50 mL) sugar

4 whole cloves

2 cinnamon sticks

1/2 teaspoon (2 mL) cardamom seeds

1/4 teaspoon (1 mL) allspice

4 medium pears (about 2 pounds/1 kg), peeled, cored and halved

In a medium saucepan, bring 3 cups (750 mL) water, tea bags, sugar, cloves, cinnamon, cardamom and allspice to a boil over medium-high heat. Reduce heat and simmer for 2 to 3 minutes. Discard tea bags.

Place pears in saucepan; cover, reduce heat to medium-low and simmer 10 minutes. Turn pears over; cover and simmer an additional 10 minutes or until pears are tender. Using a slotted spoon, transfer pears to a large shallow dish; set aside.

Increase heat to medium-high and boil tea mixture for 15 minutes to reduce. Strain through a sieve and discard solids. Pour tea sauce over pears. Cover and place in refrigerator to chill for at least 3 hours.

To serve, place pears in dessert goblets and pour over 3 tablespoons (45 mL) of tea sauce.

PER SERVING NUTRITIONAL INFORMATION: Calories: 140, Protein: 1 g, Fat: 1 g, Saturated Fat: 0 g, Carbohydrate: 32 g, Dietary Fibre: 4 g

chocolate almond biscotti

These treats are wonderful for dipping into a dessert wine or a hot beverage. The fact that they contain compounds that have anti-clotting effects on the blood is just an added bonus.

MAKES 40 TO 45 BISCOTTI

1/3 cup (75 mL) whole unblanched almonds

2 teaspoons (10 mL) instant coffee granules

1 tablespoon (15 mL) hot water

2 cups (500 mL) all-purpose flour

1 cup (250 mL) sugar

1/2 cup (125 mL) unsweetened cocoa powder

1 teaspoon (5 mL) baking powder

1/4 teaspoon (1 mL) salt

1/3 cup (75 mL) chocolate chips

2 each eggs and egg whites

1 tablespoon (15 mL) vegetable oil

1 teaspoon (5 mL) vanilla extract

1/2 teaspoon (2 mL) almond extract

Preheat oven to 350°F (180°C). Spread almonds on a baking sheet and toast for 10 minutes. Allow to cool.

In a small bowl, dissolve coffee in hot water; set aside.

In a large bowl, sift together flour, sugar, cocoa, baking powder and salt. Stir in almonds and chocolate chips.

In a medium bowl, stir together coffee, eggs, egg whites, oil, vanilla and almond extract until well blended. Add to flour mixture and stir to combine until almost all the dry mixture is worked in (dough will be sticky). With floured hands, turn onto a floured surface and knead until dough is smooth.

Prepare the baking sheet by spraying with vegetable oil cooking spray. Divide dough into two portions. Place on a baking sheet and shape each into a 10- by 2 1/2-inch (25- by 6-cm) log. Bake for about 30 minutes or until logs feel firm when touched.

Remove from oven and allow to cool on baking sheet on a rack for about 10 minutes. Reduce oven temperature to 275°F (140°C).

Place one log on a cutting board. Cut on a diagonal into 1/2-inch (1-cm) slices and place slices in a single layer, cut side up, on baking sheet. Repeat with second log. Bake for 15 minutes. Turn biscotti over and bake another 15 minutes or until biscotti are dry when touched. Transfer biscotti to wire racks and let cool completely. Biscotti will keep for up to one month in a tightly covered container.

PER PIECE NUTRITIONAL INFORMATION: Calories: 58, Protein: 1 g, Fat: 2 g, Saturated Fat: less than 1 g, Carbohydrate: 11 g, Dietary Fibre: 2 g

cocoa meringue kisses

For a fudgier taste, keep these in the freezer until serving. Cocoa is packed with antioxidants and is fat-free to boot.

MAKES 4 TO 4 1/2 DOZEN COOKIES

1/4 cup (50 mL) unsweetened cocoa powder

3/4 cup (175 mL) sugar

4 egg whites

1 tablespoon (15 mL) white vinegar

Pinch salt

1/4 cup (50 mL) chopped pecans

2 ounces (60 g) bittersweet or semisweet chocolate, finely chopped

1 teaspoon (5 mL) vanilla extract

Preheat oven to 325°F (160°C). Line a cookie sheet with parchment paper.

In a small bowl, mix together cocoa powder and 1/4 cup (50 mL) of the sugar; set aside.

In a large bowl, beat egg whites until foamy. Beat in vinegar and salt, then slowly beat in the remaining 1/2 cup (125 mL) sugar, 2 tablespoons (25 mL) at a time. Slowly beat in cocoa-sugar mixture until stiff peaks form. Fold in pecans, chocolate and vanilla extract. Drop by teaspoonfuls on cookie sheet. Bake for 22 to 25 minutes or until firm when touched. Let cool for 1 minute before transferring to wire racks. Allow to cool completely.

PER MERINGUE NUTRITIONAL INFORMATION: Calories: 22, Protein: less than 1 g, Fat: 1 g, Saturated Fat: less than 1 g, Carbohydrate: 4 g, Dietary Fibre: less than 1 g

chocolate angel food cake with raspberry coulis

Gorgeous enough for company—nutritious enough for every day! The combination of berries—with their top-notch antioxidant compounds—and chocolate—also rich in antioxidant power—has always been a favourite. Who knew that it was so healthy?

MAKES 12 TO 14 SERVINGS

1 cup (250 mL) cake-and-pastry flour

1/3 cup (75 mL) unsweetened Dutch-process cocoa powder

1 3/4 cups (425 mL) sugar

1 1/2 cups (375 mL) egg whites (about 12 large eggs)

1/4 teaspoon (1 mL) salt

1 1/2 teaspoons (7 mL) cream of tartar

1 teaspoon (5 mL) vanilla extract

RASPBERRY SAUCE

4 cups (1 L) frozen unsweetened raspberries

1/3 cup (75 mL) sugar

3 tablespoons (45 mL) liqueur such as almond-flavoured

Low-fat frozen yogurt and assorted berries, for garnish

Preheat oven to 375°F (190°C).

In a bowl, sift together cake-and-pastry flour, cocoa and 3/4 cup (175 mL) of the sugar.

In another large bowl, beat egg whites and salt on high speed with an electric mixer until foamy. Add cream of tartar and beat until soft peaks form. Gradually add remaining 1 cup (250 mL) sugar, 2 tablespoons (25 mL) at a time, and beat until stiff peaks form. Fold in vanilla extract. Fold in flour-cocoa mixture gently but thoroughly, scraping bottom to prevent any lumps.

Pour batter into an ungreased 10-inch (25-cm) tube pan. Run a knife through the batter to remove any air bubbles and to smooth out the top. Bake in middle of oven 35 to 40 minutes or until a tester inserted in the centre comes out dry.

Invert pan and let cake cool in the pan for 1 1/2 hours. To remove cake from pan, run a knife around the edges. Invert cake onto a plate.

Meanwhile, make raspberry sauce. Combine raspberries and sugar in a medium saucepan. Bring to a boil over medium heat; reduce heat and simmer, stirring occasionally, 3 to 4 minutes. Remove from heat and stir in liqueur. In a food processor or blender, purée mixture until smooth. Strain through a sieve into a bowl. Chill sauce, covered, for at least 30 minutes.

To assemble dessert, spoon 2 tablespoons (25 mL) of the sauce in a circle on the outer part of a dessert plate. Place a slice of cake in the centre. Top with frozen yogurt and assorted berries and serve immediately.

PER 14-SERVINGS NUTRITIONAL INFORMATION: Calories: 193, Protein: 4 g, Fat: 1 g, Saturated Fat: less than 1 g, Carbohydrate: 43 g, Dietary Fibre: 1 g

from page to plate

knowing what's good to eat doesn't necessarily

translate into healthy eating

Enlightened eating—combining luscious-tasting healthy fare with nutritional and caloric needs—shouldn't be a daunting task. We know what we should be eating: we're told over and over again by experts in every medium. But knowing what's good to eat doesn't necessarily translate into healthy eating. The growing epidemic of obesity in North America is a prime example of how our nutritional knowledge must far surpass our actual practices.

But what accounts for this disconnect? One credible theory is that we've lost our way: we no longer know *when* and *what combinations* to eat. The concepts of mealtime and, within that, meal balance are no longer approached with the same respect. Our busy lives result in too many skipped meals. We grab an energy bar or a meal replacement drink that can be quickly gobbled up or guzzled down. When there's finally time to eat, appetite regulation and nutrition sense seemingly go out the window. Our lack of ability to recognize when our bodies actually need food translates into our inability to realize when we should stop eating. Over time, the lack of appetite regulation leads to the practice of eating gargantuan portions.

portion distortion

If during the day you regularly indulge in large-sized coffee drinks and monster muffins, what are the chances you'll want to munch on an apple a couple of hours later? Portion distortion not only contributes to excess weight but it also lessens your appetite for phytofoods. And this problem of portion distortion is everywhere. In restaurants, appetizers are no longer the teasers they were meant to be. Instead, they have become meals unto themselves. (Yet many people still order entrees with their entree-size appetizers.) Single portions of pasta are now frequently served on plates the size of platters. Steak-house servings of meat may be double or triple the recommended number of ounces. And when it comes to decadent delights, many eateries have abandoned the small dessert plate and opted for the much larger dinner-plate size. (But somehow, no matter how few share the plate, it all tends to disappear —so who has room for that fruit salad?)

It's time to relearn how to recognize when your body is truly hungry. Fuelling up with balanced eats *only* when you are hungry will result in your knowing when you feel full and should stop eating. Eating at regular times is the first step in recapturing what you did automatically when you were a baby.

breaking the fast

How many times have you heard that breakfast is the most important meal of the day? Well, it's true. When it comes to recapturing appetite regulation, breakfast is the key.

Here's something to consider: Many people who are constantly battling with their weight often exclaim that they don't experience hunger—particularly in the morning —and that when they do overindulge, it has little to do with feeling hungry. Those who claim that they eat when they are glad, sad, mad or just bored are often the very same people who skip meals. But in fact, if you skip breakfast, or if your morning menu consists of just a slice of toast and coffee, you've lost touch with your need to eat (after fasting overnight, metabolic rates are slower and blood sugar readings are low). And if you don't know when your body is hungry, then you won't know when your body is satisfied. The result is that you may eat when it's convenient, not when your body needs nourishment.

Scientific research continues to provide evidence of how important it is to do more than just "smell the coffee" in the morning. In a Tufts University study, researchers examined the effect of three different breakfasts on the amount of food obese teenage boys ate in the five hours after lunch. The breakfasts, all with the same number of calories, were evaluated according to their glycemic index (GI), the measure of how fast the blood sugar is raised after eating (see page 104). Meals with a high glycemic index produce a quick rise in blood sugar and insulin readings, whereas those with a low glycemic index result in a slower increase in blood sugar and insulin levels, with levels never reaching those found after the high-GI breakfast. The high glycemic index breakfast in the study consisted of instant oatmeal plus milk, the medium glycemic one, steel-cut or large-flake oats (the longer-cooking variety) plus milk, and the low glycemic breakfast, a vegetable omelette plus fruit. The subjects were allowed to eat freely throughout the remainder of the day, according to their appetite.

Those who ate the high-GI breakfast ate 53 percent more calories than those who ate the medium-GI meal and a whopping 81 percent more than those who ate the low-GI meal.

It's important to note that eating a meal containing foods with different glycemic indexes changed the glycemic index of the entire meal. So adding a food with a very low GI, such as a protein, to a meal can change the entire picture. And that's where balance comes in. Phytofoods offer a cornucopia of goodness, but the other foods on the plate can make all the difference in providing meal balance, which leads to fewer cravings for high-calorie foods short on nutrition. For example, including a protein-rich selection such as an egg, cottage cheese, fish or even a few ounces of meat or poultry for breakfast slows the rate of blood-sugar absorption, which in turn will help tame a raging appetite. A small amount (an ounce or two, or 30 to 60 grams) of low-fat cheese, lean meat, fish or poultry or an egg is enough. You'll know that you're on the right track if you feel hungry about three to four hours after breakfast.

Besides decreasing the chances of spontaneously buying that mid-morning pastry off the coffee cart, it can also decrease those mid-afternoon cravings. Feeling satisfied after dinner is another potential benefit.

Eating a balanced breakfast can actually boost calorie burning while fuelling the body. But it doesn't stop there. That morning meal can determine energy levels, and have an impact on appetite regulation, right through the day. Craving a sweet or a snooze mid-afternoon or finding yourself nodding off after lunch? Or maybe you can't stop nibbling after your evening meal. What you had for breakfast—or more likely, what you *didn't* have—may be to blame.

Breaking the fast with a balanced meal puts you in tune with your body's fuel needs. Eating a balanced breakfast each and every day—even if you don't feel hungry—is the route to healthy appetite regulation. It may be difficult initially, but over time, as the night-time munchies disappear, eating breakfast will become a pleasant pastime rather than a forced activity. And if typical breakfast fare doesn't tempt you in the morning, go for other options—be adventurous. A bean burrito topped with cheddar or a slice of veggie pizza will provide as much energy as more traditional choices do.

While making the right selections will give you pep, a fat-laden breakfast can make you want to go back to bed. On the other hand, options that are quickly digested, such as a slice or two of toast with jam, a bowl of cereal or even a breakfast bar, can leave you hungrier an hour or two after breakfast than if you'd had nothing to eat at all. Sound complicated? It doesn't have to be. Go for a balance of whole grains, fruit or vegetables and a protein-rich option instead of just a slice of toast and coffee.

don't run on empty

Eating the right kinds of foods every four hours not only keeps you in touch with your body's need for food but can also lead to higher metabolic rates—or calorie burning —when compared with going long periods of time without fuelling up. Research shows that eating a variety of food has a "thermal effect" on our metabolism. We see the thermal effect of food at work when, if we're cold, hungry and tired, after eating we feel warmer and energized. Protein foods have a higher thermal effect and

Food	What It Looks Like
1 ounce (30 g) meat, poultry or fish	matchbox
1 ounce (30 g) cheese	four dice
3 ounces (90 g) meat, poultry or fish	deck of playing cards
1 cup (250 mL) fruit or yogurt	baseball
1/2 cup (125 mL) vegetables, pasta, rice or fruit	half a baseball or tennis ball
1 medium potato	computer mouse
1 teaspoon (5 mL) fat	tip of your thumb

carbohydrates have less. Fatty foods have almost none. But, of course, there are limits. Non-stop munching on large portions, or grazing as frequently as every one or two hours, won't send metabolic rates soaring. It will just pile on the extra calories.

Besides leading to higher metabolic rates, eating every three or four hours throughout the day results in better blood sugar regulation, lower insulin readings and reduced blood cholesterol levels.

Choosing nutritious eats, including antioxidant-rich selections such as fruits and veggies, right through the day provides other perks. Research shows that antioxidant activity lasts only a few hours, so for maximum benefit, have servings from this food group right through the day (see Top-Scoring Fruits, page 15 and Top-Scoring Vegetables, page 59).

Think of snack time as an opportunity to meet your nutrient needs while satisfying your preferences. Are you short on dairy? Have a fruit and yogurt smoothie or low-fat cheese and crackers with some fruit. Need some fibre? Pack 1 cup (250 mL) of cold whole grain cereals, dried fruit and nut mixes to munch on. Or how about 2 cups (500 mL) of air-popped or light microwave popcorn if you are in the mood for a savoury snack?

Eating smaller portions more often provides the fuel for active living. And the more active you are, the more calories you burn, once again leaving more room to eat your phytofoods.

fitness fanfare

Active living provides an assortment of perks. On the heart disease and stroke front, physical activity can have a range of beneficial effects. Regular exercise of just 30 minutes a day doesn't just help to control waist measures. It's been shown to boost

THE TRADITIONAL HEALTHY MEDITERRANEAN DIET PYRAMID

Take a page from the Mediterranean diet and use this guide as a foundation for your daily meals.

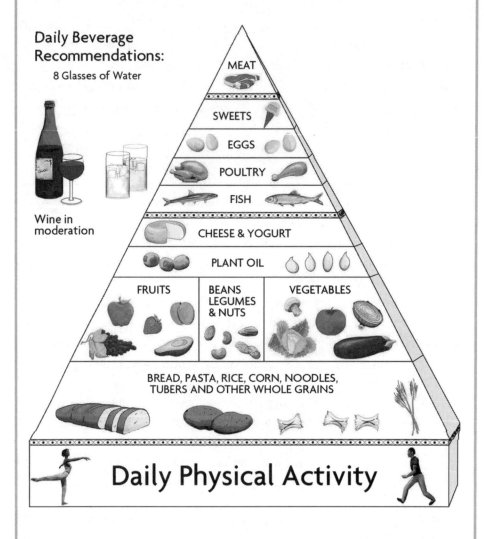

Daily Beverage Recommendations:

8 Glasses of Water

Wine in moderation

MEAT

SWEETS

EGGS

POULTRY

FISH

CHEESE & YOGURT

PLANT OIL

FRUITS

BEANS LEGUMES & NUTS

VEGETABLES

BREAD, PASTA, RICE, CORN, NOODLES, TUBERS AND OTHER WHOLE GRAINS

Daily Physical Activity

Copyright © 2002 Oldways Preservation & Exchange Trust.

levels of the protective HDL cholesterol and improve blood pressure control. Not only does it offer protection against developing type 2 diabetes, for those with the disease it also plays a vital role in regulating blood sugar. Being active is also connected to a lower risk for colon, breast and prostate cancer. Weight-bearing exercise has been shown to guard against the bone-thinning disease osteoporosis. As well, physical activity may result in better immune system function as well as providing benefit to those suffering from depression. A pretty impressive list!

Several generations ago, strenuous physical activity—laundering clothes with a washboard, carrying pails of water for a bath or simply walking a couple of hours—was a part of everyday life. Then, being active didn't have to be scheduled into a daily routine. Because our daily chores are so much less vigorous today, active living no longer just happens—it now takes some planning.

fight or flight

Physical activity is a super antidote to stress, which can certainly take a toll on your health, not to mention your appetite. When stressed, your body reacts in the same way animals do when they perceive a physical threat. The fight-or-flight response readies the animal to either confront the threat or flee. Adrenalin is released, muscles tense, blood sugar levels rise to fuel these muscles, and blood vessels constrict so that blood quickly pumps through the body. For animals, this survival mechanism arises in a life-or-death situation, but for humans, the fight-or-flight response can be triggered simply by emotions—excitement, fear or anxiety. And all too often, we sit and stew while stress hormones circulate through the bloodstream. The result, in the short term, can be a sore neck, a headache and the like. Being in a state of stress can also make eating very unappealing. And over the long term, constant stress can take a major toll on our health.

While the "fight" response may not be the best approach, "flight"—that is, physical activity—can certainly help to rid the body of the stress hormones. Exercise lowers adrenalin and blood sugar levels and results in a calmer disposition. It won't solve the stressful situation, but it will reduce the tension and anxiety, which may help you better cope with the situation. So when you're feeling stressed, walk, cycle, swim—anything that uses large muscles in a sustained way.

Try also to incorporate more activity into your daily routines. We live in a society in which people spend enormous sums for memberships in fitness clubs, yet drive around the lot at the local mall looking for the closest parking spot. Instead of joining a gym or buying expensive fitness equipment, go for a one- or two-hour—or even half-hour—brisk walk in your neighbourhood, which is one of the best ways to keep fit. When outdoor temperatures are too hot or cold, walk in your local shopping mall.

Get physically more active by assessing your regular routines and look for simple ways to burn calories and windows of opportunity within which to fit the activity.

The following are a few suggestions to help you get started:

- Take the stairs instead of the elevator.
- Take a 15-minute walk before lunch.
- When using public transit, get off the bus a few stops early and walk the last stretch.
- When shopping, find the parking spot farthest from your destination. Better yet, leave your car at home and walk to the local store.
- Put away the remote control for the television set.
- Instead of talking on the phone to a friend who lives nearby, get caught up by going for a walk.
- Go out dancing or dance at home.

supplement savvy

When it comes to supplements, keep in mind exactly what they are—additions to healthy eating, not a substitute for it. Contrary to what the advertising says, they don't make up for enlightened food choices when you're too busy to eat well. But the research does support taking a multivitamin and mineral supplement in the amounts that are recommended for daily intakes. Mega-doses (those that are many times the daily recommended intake) can mean lots of money for supplement makers, but the science simply doesn't back up their use; beta carotene supplements are a good example of this (see page 8).

go for the record

The first step in making changes to your food style and activity level is to track what you usually do each day. Food records can help to reveal where your eating problems lie and what habits should be changed. Write down everything you eat after you eat it so you won't worry too much about making the right choices. Include the "what," "when" and "how much" of everything you eat and drink. At the same time, keep an activity log as well. Besides intense activities such as running, cycling or swimming, be sure to note daily activities such as walking to work or to the store, how many times you took the stairs and raking the backyard.

Once you've begun to change the way you eat and your level of activity, continue to keep food and activity records. But now, consider writing down your choices before you eat or exercise. This will allow you a chance to think about your actions beforehand. Keep your food and activity logs convenient—on a handy size of paper that you can easily carry with you. Continue to analyze your records once a week to help you gain insight into your habits.

Use these records to identify problem areas and make positive changes. Work on one area at a time in order to make permanent changes. One good way is to go meal by meal, starting with breakfast, then moving on to lunch, and so on. Soon you will have a new set of eating habits that, like the pieces of a jigsaw puzzle, fall happily into place. The same goes for increasing activity. When you are assessing your food and activity logs and endeavouring to make changes, keep in mind that there is no room for perfectionism, criticism, blame or guilt. Changing many small aspects of your behaviour and weathering the setbacks are all part of the healthy-eating learning process. Alter one aspect at a time and you will end up with a new and improved lifestyle.

sample menus

Here are a few sample menus to get you started on a phytofood-packed eating style. Add low-fat milk and yogurt to bridge long gaps between meals as well as to meet daily nutritional quotas.

	BREAKFAST	LUNCH
DAY 1	Apple Cheese Quesadillas (page 38) Beverage	Chicken, Olive and Arugula Sandwich (page 220) Fresh fruit Beverage
DAY 2	Cottage cheese topped with fresh or frozen berries Banana Flax Bread (page 200) Tea	Cabbage, Beet and Apple Slaw (page 78) Salmon salad on whole grain bread Honey-Lime Fruit Salad (page 42) Beverage
DAY 3	Sautéed Maple Apple Slices (leftover) Lower-fat French Toast Beverage	Eggplant, Roasted Red Pepper and Goat Cheese Sandwiches (page 92) Raw vegetables Fresh Fruit
DAY 4	Boiled egg Wild Blueberry and Apple Muesli (page 34) Beverage	Couscous, Chickpea and Vegetable Salad (page 119) Leftover grilled chicken Fresh fruit
DAY 5	Pita Pizza (melted cheese, tomato sauce and veggies on a whole wheat pita) Beverage	Fish and Vegetable Chowder (page 96) Whole grain roll Orange and grapefruit sections
DAY 6	Smoked salmon, low-fat cream cheese and whole grain bagel Grapefruit half Beverage	Lentil Salad with Feta and Herbs (page 149) Whole grain roll Fresh fruit

DAY 7	Boiled egg
	Oatmeal topped with blueberries and
	   slivered almonds
	Beverage
		Split Pea Soup with Cumin and Caramelized
		   Onions (page 148)
		Turkey sandwich on whole grain bread with
		   spinach and tomato garnish
		Fresh fruit

AFTERNOON SNACK	DINNER
Enlightened Eater's™ Trail Mix (page 198)	Mushroom Soup (page 72) Pasta with Spinach and White Beans (page 150) Fresh fruit and low-fat yogourt
Glazed Spicy Almonds (page 196)	Gazpacho (page 77) Chickpea Mushroom Burgers (page 152) on whole grain pita Spiced Tahini Dressing (page 198) and vegetable garnish Sautéed Maple Apple Slices (page 41) Tea
Date Nut Bread with Pistachios (page 201) Low-fat milk	Citrus Barley Salad (page 118) Grilled chicken breast Mixed greens Fresh fruit
Air-popped popcorn	Fava Bean Purée with Bitter Greens (page 146) Grilled Salmon and Mediterranean Vegetable Salad (page 99) Roasted Amaretto Peaches (page 43) with low-fat frozen yogourt
Tahini and Date Dip (page 197)	Savoury Moroccan Vegetable Soup (page 74) Zesty Charmoula Sauce (page 212) Lemon Chicken with Dried Figs (page 40) Steamed brown rice Broccoli florets Cinnamon and Tea Poached Pears (page 244)
Dried cranberries and mixed nuts	Roasted Garlic Hummus (page 145) with vegetable crudités Grilled fish on Nutty Fattouch Salad (page 213) Rhubarb Blueberry Crumble (page 132)
Low-fat yogourt, fresh fruit and nut combo	Orange, Grapefruit and Onion Salad (page 35) Linguini with Oven-Dried Tomatoes and Garlic (page 94) Fresh Strawberries with Balsamic Vinegar (page 43)

the bottom line

science can provide miracle cures,
but it can also lead to tampering
where there should be none

Nature's brew is a heady mix of nutrients and phytochemicals that interact to thwart disease. Meeting your quota of phytofoods on a daily basis is at least part of the prescription for good health.

Or so it appears. Of course, at this point there aren't any guarantees. While scientific research is revealing that phytochemicals may prevent or delay disease, it is possible that other factors may play a role. Whatever the scenario, it's important to maximize your odds by eating well and living actively. After all, if you don't train for the game, you'll never be in the running.

As you sort through the continuing barrage of scientific research—it's enough to make your head spin—use common sense. If the promotional literature for a food product or supplement sounds too good to be true, then it likely is. Ask yourself some questions before you buy any new "miracle" food product or supplement:

- Where is the research coming from?
- What are the possible costs to my health?

Don't always believe the promotional material provided by the manufacturer—no matter how legitimate they may seem or how reliable the venue. For example, pharmacies often stock marketing brochures provided by supplement manufacturers touting the benefits of these products—no matter that science doesn't necessarily support the findings.

functional foods—boon or snake oil?

Stores shelves now contain a whole new "genre" of food products for the health-conscious consumer. Functional foods, designer foods or nutraceuticals—whatever you call them—are foods fortified, or sometimes naturally packed, with phytochemicals and phytonutrients. These foods contain components that appear to promote good health or prevent or treat disease.

Some products touted as functional foods are really just old standbys with a new label promoting their potential health benefits. Others may have a phytochemical or two added to the old mix. The problem is, many of these new food products appear in the marketplace well before science has truly evaluated a phytochemical's effectiveness.

And as scientists continue to unravel the mysteries surrounding the beneficial substances in these phytofoods, manufacturers ready themselves to bring even more products to the marketplace. But the transition from laboratory to dinnerplate is never a simple one.

Before functional foods are developed in product form for the marketplace, numerous issues must first be addressed. For example, once active components such as lycopene—tomato's red pigment—or flavonoids—from citrus fruits—are isolated from certain foods and then added to other products, will they maintain their positive effects? Do phytochemicals need their "natural companions" to do their thing? Functional foods and nutraceuticals may very well offer a great deal in the war against disease, but whether the battles will be won very much depends on how the food manufacturers use the scientific findings.

We could end up with a whole lot of potentially dysfunctional foods, things like fried snacks loaded with vitamin E, or lycopene cupcakes. Alternatively, fabulous new products with a host of benefits could be produced. In the U.S., researchers are working on a new fat substitute made from oats that could make low-fat baked goods healthier and tastier to boot.

It's up to consumers—less-than-gullible ones—to demand the goods and to force manufacturers to act responsibly. It's an area with enormous promise, but also one with potential for harm.

hands off the plants—for now

As more research comes to light on the stunning array of phytochemicals that may offer benefit to humans, it is also being revealed just how important these compounds are to the health of the plants themselves. This may not seem terribly important to you as you seek strategies for good health, but it does provide food for thought when it comes to plant breeding. Since each compound found in plant foods seems to serve a purpose in the plant, such as protection against pests or ultraviolet light, breeding "super" plants that have increased amounts of any of these compounds could have health implications, for the plants and for us. So can modifying various foods to make them more appealing. How does an odourless garlic or an onion that won't induce tears compare with those loaded with assorted sulfur compounds? What about a peanut with its allergenic protein modified?

Changing the makeup of a plant might result in its producing a different amount of a phytochemical. Does the protein makeup of peanuts have anything to do with the amount of antioxidants, like resveratrol, that it produces? If you boost the amounts of different carotenoids in produce, what happens to the other ones that are usually found in lesser quantities? It could have dire consequences. For example, we know that too much beta carotene in supplement form increases the risk of lung cancer in susceptible individuals. If we boost the beta carotene in modified foods, it could be at the expense of other nutrients, such as alpha carotene, which might counter the risk of cancer. Some years ago, when the beta carotene found in carrots, squash and other foods in the orange-yellow plant kingdom was thought to be the knight in shining armour in the battle against lung cancer, companies rushed to produce carrot juices with higher than normal beta carotene. They were premature: only a few years later, it was discovered that the true hero was alpha carotene.

Boosting disease-fighting phytonutrients isn't the only reason why manufacturers tamper with plant foods and plant genes. In time, as producers try to make their foods more palatable, plants may be bred to remove their bitter compounds. But again, at what cost? Removing the bitter flavonoids from a citrus fruit—the same flavonoid that protects the fruit from pests—may lead to the substitution of natural pesticides with manufactured ones.

Science can provide the world with miracle cures, but it can also lead to tampering where there should be none. On the other hand, sound scientific research combined with a patient public willing to wait for answers may yet lead to the secret for living a long life full of zest and vitality.

bibliography

the power of whole foods

Albanes, D., et al. Alpha-tocopherol and beta-carotene supplements and lung cancer incidence in the alpha-tocopherol, beta-carotene cancer prevention study: effects of base-line characteristics and study compliance. J Natl Cancer Inst. 1996 Nov 6;88(21):1560-70.

Drewnowski, A., Gomez-Carneros, C. Bitter taste, phytonutrients, and the consumer: a review. Am J Clin Nutr. 2000 Dec;72(6):1424–35. Review.

Kimura, N., Keys, A. Coronary heart disease in seven countries. X. Rural southern Japan. Circulation. 1970 Apr;41(4 Suppl):I101–12.

Skibola, C.F., Smith, M.T. Potential health impacts of excessive flavonoid intake. Free Radic Biol Med. 2000 Aug;29(3-4):375–83. Review.

Vainio, H. Chemoprevention of cancer: lessons to be learned from beta-carotene trials. Toxicol Lett. 2000 Mar 15;112-113:513–7. Review.

fruits

Arima H., Danno G. Isolation of antimicrobial compounds from guava (Psidium guajava L.) and their structural elucidation. Biosci Biotechnol Biochem. 2002 Aug;66(8):1727–30.

Bagchi D., Bagchi M., Stohs S., Ray S.D., Sen C.K., Preuss H.G. Cellular protection with proanthocyanidins derived from grape seeds. Ann N Y Acad Sci. 2002 May;957:260–70.

Brack M.E., et al. The citrus methoxyflavone tangeretin affects human cell-cell interactions. Adv Exp Med Biol. 2002;505:135–9.

Brown L.M., et al. Diet and nutrition as risk factors for multiple myeloma among blacks and whites in the United States. Cancer Causes Control. 2001 Feb;12(2):117–25.

Burkhardt S., Tan D.X., Manchester L.C., Hardeland R., Reiter R.J. Detection and quantification of the antioxidant melatonin in Montmorency and Balaton tart cherries (Prunus cerasus). J Agric Food Chem. 2001 Oct;49(10):4898–902.

Freedman, J., et al. Select flavonoids and whole juice from purple grapes inhibit platelet function and enhance nitric oxide release. Circulation. 2001; 103:2792–8.

Jensen, M.E., et al. Assessment of the effect of selected snack foods on the remineralization/demineralization of enamel and dentin. J Contemp Dent Pract. 2000 Aug 15;1(3):1–17.

Jimenez-Escrig A., Rincon M., Pulido R., Saura-Calixto F. Guava fruit (Psidium guajava L.) as a new source of antioxidant dietary fiber. J Agric Food Chem. 2001 Nov;49(11):5489–93.

Joseph J.A., et al. Reversals of age-related declines in neuronal signal transduction, cognitive, and motor behavioral deficits with blueberry, spinach, or strawberry dietary supplementation. J Neurosci. 1999 Sep 15;19(18):8114–21.

Liu M., Li X.Q., Weber C., Lee C.Y., Brown J., Liu R.H. Antioxidant and antiproliferative activities of raspberries. J Agric Food Chem. 2002 May 8;50(10):2926–30.

Noda Y., Kaneyuki T., Mori A., Packer L. Antioxidant activities of pomegranate fruit extract and its anthocyanidins: delphinidin, cyanidin, and pelargonidin. J Agric Food Chem. 2002 Jan 2;50(1):166–71.

Shaheen, S.O., et al. Dietary antioxidants and asthma in adults: population-based case-control study. Am J Respir Crit Care Med. 2001 Nov 15;164(10 Pt 1):1823–8.

Silalahi, J. Anticancer and health protective properties of citrus fruit components. Asia Pac J Clin Nutr. 2002;11(1):79–84. Review.

Singletary K.W., Meline, B. Effect of grape seed proanthocyanidins on colon aberrant crypts and breast tumors in a rat dual-organ tumor model. Nutr Cancer. 2001;39(2):252–8.

Tsao, Rong, et al. Antioxidant Phenolic Acids and Polyphenols in Ontario. Apples Food Research Program, Agriculture and Agri-Food Canada.

Stein, J., et al. Purple grape juice improves endothelial function and reduces the susceptibility of LDL cholesterol to oxidation in patients with coronary artery disease. Circulation 1999; 100: 1050–5.

Terris M.K., Issa M.M., Tacker J.R. Dietary supplementation with cranberry concentrate tablets may increase the risk of nephrolithiasis. Urology 2001 Jan;57(1):26–9.

Tian Q., Miller E.G., et al. Differential inhibition of human cancer cell proliferation by citrus limonoids. Nutr Cancer. 2001;40(2):180–4.

Van der Sluis, A.A., et al. Activity and concentration of polyphenolic antioxidants in apple: effect of cultivar, harvest year, and storage conditions. J Agric Food Chem. 2001 Aug;49(8):3606–13.

Waffo-Teguo, P., et al. Potential cancer-chemopreventive activities of wine stilbenoids and flavans extracted from grape (Vitis vinifera) cell cultures. Nutr Cancer. 2001;40(2):173–9.

Wang H., et al. Antioxidant and antiinflammatory activities of anthocyanins and their aglycon, cyanidin, from tart cherries. J Nat Prod. 1999 Feb;62(2):294–6.

Youdim, K.A., Joseph, J.A. A possible emerging role of phytochemicals in improving age-related neurological dysfunctions: a multiplicity of effects. Free Radic Biol Med. 2001 Mar 15;30(6):583–94.

Youdim K.A., McDonald J., Kalt W., Joseph J.A. Potential role of dietary flavonoids in reducing microvascular endothelium vulnerability to oxidative and inflammatory insults (small star, filled). J Nutr Biochem. 2002 May;13(5):282–8.

vegetables

Bonnesen, C., et al. Dietary indoles and isothiocyanates that are generated from cruciferous vegetables can both stimulate apoptosis and confer protection against DNA damage in human colon cell lines. Cancer Res. 2001 Aug 15;61(16):6120–30.

Borchers, A.T., et al. Mushrooms, tumors and immunity. Proc Soc Exp Biol Med. 221(4):281–93, 1999.

Buddington K.K., Donahoo J.B., Buddington R.K. Dietary oligofructose and insulin protect mice from enteric and systemic pathogens and tumor inducers. J Nutr. 2002 Mar;132(3):472–7.

Chen, S., et al. Prevention and treatment of breast cancer by suppressing aromatase activity and expression. Ann N Y Acad Sci. 2002 Jun;963:229–38.

Chiao, J.W., et al. Sulforaphane and its metabolite mediate growth arrest and apoptosis in human prostate cancer cells. Int J Oncol. 2002 Mar;20(3):631–6.

Dutta-Roy A.K., Crosbie L., Gordon M.J. Effects of tomato extract on human platelet aggregation in vitro. Platelets. 2001 Jun;12(4):218–27.

Dwyer, J.H., et al.Oxygenated carotenoid lutein and progression of early atherosclerosis: the Los Angeles atherosclerosis study. Circulation. 2001 Jun 19;103(24):2922–7.

Fahey, J.W., et al. Sulforaphane inhibits extracellular, intracellular, and antibiotic-resistant strains of Helicobacter pylori and prevents benzo[a]pyrene-induced stomach tumors. Proc Natl Acad Sci U S A. 2002 May 28;99(11):7610–5.

Fleischauer, A.T., Arab, L. Garlic and Cancer: A Critical Review of the Epidemiologic Literature. J Nut. 2001;131:1032S–40S.

Giovannucci, E. Tomatoes, tomato-based products, lycopene, and cancer: review of the epidemiologic literature. J Natl Cancer Inst. 1999 Feb 17;91(4):317-31. Review.

Giovannucci, E., et al. Intake of carotenoids and retinol in relation to risk of prostate cancer. J Natl Cancer Inst. 1995 Dec 6;87(23):1767–76.

—. A prospective study of tomato products, lycopene, and prostate cancer risk. J Natl Cancer Inst. 2002 Mar 6;94(5):391–8.

Gebhardt, R. Antioxidative and protective properties of extracts from leaves of the artichoke (Cynara scolymus L.) against hydroperoxide-induced oxidative stress in cultured rat hepatocytes. Toxicol Appl Pharmacol. 1997 Jun;144(2):279–86.

—. Inhibition of cholesterol biosynthesis in primary cultured rat hepatocytes by artichoke (Cynara scolymus L.) extracts. J Pharmacol Exp Ther. 1998 Sep;286(3):1122–8.

Goel, V., et al. Cholesterol lowering effects of rhubarb stalk fiber in hypercholesterolemic men. J Am Coll Nutr. 1997 Dec;16(6):600–4.

—. Effect of dietary rhubarb stalk fiber on the bioavailability of calcium in rats. Int J Food Sci Nutr. 1996 Mar;47(2):159–63.

Griffiths, G., et al. Onions—a global benefit to health. Phytother Res. 2002 Nov;16(7):603–15.

Grube, B.J., et al. White button mushrooms phytochemicals inhibit aromatase activity and breast cancer cell proliferation. J Nutr. 2001 131:3288-93.

Han, S.Y., et al. S-propyl cysteine reduces the secretion of apolipoprotein B100 and triacylglycerol by HepG2 cells. Nutrition. 2002 Jun;18(6):505–9.

Hara, H., et al. Fermentation Products of Sugar-Beet Fiber by Cecal Bacteria Lower Plasma Cholesterol Concentration in Rats. J Nutr. 1998 Apr;128(4):688–93.

Harunobu, Amagase, et al. Intake of garlic and its bioactive components supplement: recent advances on the nutritional effects associated with the use of garlic as a supplement. J Nutr. 2001;131:955S–62S.

Hertog, M.G., et al. Dietary antioxidant flavonoids and risk of coronary heart disease: the Zutphen Elderly Study. Lancet. 1993 Oct 23;342(8878):1007–11.

Ioku, K., et al. Various cooking methods and the flavonoid content in onion. J Nutr Sci Vitaminol (Tokyo). 2001 Feb;47(1):78–83.

Ishizuka, S., et al. Dietary sugar beet fiber ameliorates diarrhea as an acute gamma-radiation injury in rats. Radiat Res. 2000 Sep;154(3):261–7.

Johnson, E.J. The role of carotenoids in human health. Nutr Clin Care. 2002 Mar-Apr;5(2):56–65. Review.

Kanner, J., et al. Betalains—a new class of dietary cationized antioxidants. J Agric Food Chem. 2001 Nov;49(11):5178–85.

Knekt, P., et al. Dietary flavonoids and the risk of lung cancer and other malignant neoplasms. Am J Epidemiol. 1997 Aug 1;146(3):223–30.

—. Flavonoid intake and coronary mortality in Finland: a cohort study. BMJ. 1996 Feb 24;312(7029):478–81.

Ko, S.K., et al. Anti-platelet aggregation activity of stilbene derivatives from Rheum undulatum. Arch Pharm Res. 1999 Aug;22(4):401–3.

Kohno, H., et al. Silymarin, a naturally occurring polyphenolic antioxidant flavonoid, inhibits azoxymethane-induced colon carcinogenesis in male F344 rats. Int J Cancer. 2002 Oct 10;101(5):461–8.

Kun, Song, and John A. Milner. Heating Garlic Inhibits Its Ability to Suppress 7,12-Dimethylbenz(a)anthracene-Induced DNA Adduct Formation in Rat Mammary Tissue 1 2 3 4. J Nutr.1999;129:657–61.

—. The Influence of Heating on the Anticancer Properties of Garlic. J Nutr. 2001;131:1054S–7S.

Le Marchand, L., et al. Intake of flavonoids and lung cancer. J Natl Cancer Inst. 2000 Jan 19;92(2):154–60.

Lyle, B.J., et al. Serum carotenoids and tocopherols and incidence of age-related nuclear cataract. Am J Clin Nutr. 1999 Feb;69(2):272–7.

Malaveille, C., et al. Dietary phenolics as anti-mutagens and inhibitors of tobacco-related DNA adduction in the urothelium of smokers. Carcinogenesis 1996 Oct;17(10):2193–200.

Mares-Perlman, J.A.. Too soon for lutein supplements. Am J Clin Nutr. 1999 Oct;70(4):431–2.

Mares-Perlman, J.A., et al. The body of evidence to support a protective role for lutein and zeaxanthin in delaying chronic disease. Overview. J Nutr. 2002 Mar;132(3):518S–524S. Review.

Mitchell, S.C. Food idiosyncrasies: beetroot and asparagus. Drug Metab Dispos. 2001 Apr;29(4 Pt 2):539–43.

Nagai, T., et al. Dietary sugar beet fiber prevents the increase in aberrant crypt foci induced by gamma-irradiation in the colorectum of rats treated with an immunosuppressant. J Nutr 2000 Jul;130(7):1682–7.

Negishi, O., et al. Effects of food materials on removal of Allium-specific volatile sulfur compounds. J Agric Food Chem 2002 Jun 19;50(13):3856–61.

Noda, Y., et al. Antioxidant activity of nasunin, an anthocyanin in eggplant peels. Toxicology. 2000 Aug 7;148(2-3):119–23.

Pavlov, A., et al. Biosynthesis and radical scavenging activity of betalains during the cultivation of red beet (Beta vulgaris) hairy root cultures. Z Naturforsch [C] 2002 Jul-Aug;57(7-8):640–4.

Pereira, D.I., Gibson, G.R. Effects of consumption of probiotics and prebiotics on serum lipid levels in humans. Crit Rev Biochem Mol Biol 2002;37(4):259–81.

Perez-Garcia, F., et al. Activity of artichoke leaf extract on reactive oxygen species in human leukocytes. Free Radic Res 2000 Nov;33(5):661–5.

Rao A.V., Agarwal S. Role of antioxidant lycopene in cancer and heart disease. J Am Coll Nutr. 2000 Oct;19(5):563–9. Review.

Rissanen, T.H., et al. Low serum lycopene concentration is associated with an excess incidence of acute coronary events and stroke: the Kuopio Ischaemic Heart Disease Risk Factor Study. Br J Nutr. 2001 Jun;85(6):749–54.

Seddon, J.M., et al. Dietary carotenoids, vitamins A, C, and E, and advanced age-related macular degeneration. Eye Disease Case-Control Study Group. JAMA. 1994 Nov 9;272(18):1413–20.

Singh, R.P., Agarwal R. Flavonoid antioxidant silymarin and skin cancer. Antioxid Redox Signal 2002 Aug;4(4):655–63.

Slattery, M.L., et al. Carotenoids and colon cancer. Am J Clin Nutr. 2000 Feb;71(2):575–82.

Stoewsand, G.S. Bioactive organosulfur phytochemicals in Brassica oleracea vegetables-a review. Food Chem Toxicol. 1995 Jun;33(6):537–43. Review.

You, W.C., et al. Allium vegetables and reduced risk of stomach cancer. J Natl Cancer Inst. 1989 Jan 18;81 (2):162–4.

whole grains

Adlercreutz, H. Phyto-oestrogens and cancer. Lancet Oncol 2002 Jun;3(6):364–73.

Adom, K.K., Liu, R.H. Antioxidant activity of grains. J Agric Food Chem 2002 Oct 9;50(21):6182–7.

Anderson, J.W., and Gustafson, N. J. 1988. Hypocholesterolemic effects of oat and bean products. Am. J. Clin. Nutr. 48:749–53.

Anderson, J.W., et al. Whole grain foods and heart disease risk. J Am Coll Nutr 2000 Jun;19(3 Suppl):291S–299S.

—. Oat-bran cereal lowers serum total and LDL cholesterol in hypercholesterolemic men. Am. J. Clin. Nutr. 52:495–499, 1990.

—. 1984. Hypocholesterolemic effects of oat-bran or bean intake for hypercholesterolemic men. Am J Clin Nutr; 40: 1146–1155.

Ascherio, A., et al. A prospective study of nutritional factors and hypertension among US men. Circulation. 86:1475–1484, 1992.

Braaten, J.T., et al. High beta-glucan oat bran and oat gum reduced postprandial blood glucose and insulin in subjects with and without type 2 diabetes. Diabet. Med. 11:312–318, 1994.

Elson, C.E., et al. Isoprenoid-mediated inhibition of mevalonate synthesis: potential application to cancer. Proc Soc Exp Biol Med. 1999 Sep;221(4):294–311. Review.

Ferguson, L.R., Harris PJ. Protection against cancer by wheat bran: role of dietary fibre and phyto-chemicals. Eur J Cancer Prev. 1999 Feb;8(1):17–25. Review.

Fung, T.T., et al. Whole-grain intake and the risk of type 2 diabetes: a prospective study in men. Am J Clin Nutr. 2002 Sep;76(3):535–40.

Ghai, G., et al. Phytochemicals and their bioactivities from the seeds of Quinoa (Chenoposium quinoa) Presentation National Meeting of the American Chemical Society, 2001.

Grasten, S.M., et al. Rye bread improves bowel function and decreases the concentrations of some compounds that are putative colon cancer risk markers in middle-aged women and men. J Nutr. 2000 Sep;130(9):2215–21.

Handelman, G.J., et al. Antioxidant capacity of oat (Avena sativa L.) extracts. 1. Inhibition of low-density lipoprotein oxidation and oxygen radical absorbance capacity. J. Agric. Food Chem. 47:4888–4893, 1999.

Hu, F.B., et al. Prospective study of major dietary patterns and risk of coronary heart disease in men. Am J Clin Nutr 2000 Oct;72(4):912–21.

Jacobs, D.R. Jr., et al. Whole grain food intake elevates serum enterolactone. Br J Nutr. 2002 Aug;88(2):111–6.

—. Whole-grain intake may reduce the risk of ischemic heart disease death in postmenopausal women: the Iowa Women's Health Study. Am J Clin Nutr 1998 Aug;68(2):248–57.

Juntunen, K.S., et al. Consumption of wholemeal rye bread increases serum concentrations and urinary excretion of enterolactone compared with consumption of white wheat bread in healthy Finnish men and women. Br J Nutr.2000 Dec;84(6):839–46.

Kushi, L.H., et al. 1999. Cereals, legumes, and chronic disease risk reduction: evidence from epidemiologic studies. Am J Clin Nutr; 70(Suppl): 451S–458S.

Li, S.Q., Zhang, Q.H. Advances in the development of functional foods from buckwheat. Crit Rev Food Sci Nutr. 2001 Sep;41(6):451–64. Review.

Liu S, Manson, J.E., et al. Whole grain consumption and risk of ischemic stroke in women: A prospective study. JAMA 2000 Sep 27;284(12):1534–40.

Liu, S, et al. Dietary glycemic load and atherothrombotic risk. Curr Atheroscler Rep. 2002 Nov;4(6):454–61.

Nanqun Zhu, et al. Triterpene Saponins from Debittered Quinoa (Chenopodium quinoa) Seeds. J Agri Food Chem 2002 50:865–867.

Pereira, M.A., et al. Effect of whole grains on insulin sensitivity in overweight hyperinsulinemic adults. Am J Clin Nutr. 2002 May;75(5):848–55.

Plotnick, G.D., et al. Effect of antioxidant vitamins on the transient impairment of endothelium-dependent brachial artery vasoactivity following a single high-fat meal. JAMA. 278:1682–1686.

Qureshi, A.A., Sami S.A., Khan F.A. Effects of stabilized rice bran, its soluble and fiber fractions on blood glucose levels and serum lipid parameters in humans with diabetes mellitus Types I and II. J Nutr Biochem. 2002 Mar;13(3):175–187.

Rajnarayana, K., et al. Influence of rice bran oil on serum lipid peroxides and lipids in human subjects. Indian J Physiol Pharmacol. 2001 Oct;45(4):442–4.

Thompson, L.U. Antioxidants and hormone-mediated health benefits of whole grains. Crit Rev Food Sci Nutr 1994;34(5-6):473–97.

Tomotake, H., et al. A buckwheat protein product suppresses gallstone formation and plasma cholesterol more strongly than soy protein isolate in hamsters. J Nutr. 2000 Jul;130(7):1670–4.

Woldemichael, G.M., Wink, M. Identification and biological activities of triterpenoid saponins from Chenopodium quinoa. J Agric Food Chem. 2001 May;49(5):2327–32.

legumes

Anderson, J.W., et al. 1990. Serum lipid responses of hypercholesterolemic men to single and divided doses of canned beans. Am J Clin Nutr; 51: 1013–1019.

Awad AB, et al. In vitro and in vivo (SCID mice) effects of phytosterols on the growth and dissemination of human prostate cancer PC-3 cells. Eur J Cancer Prev 2001 Dec;10(6):507–13.

Bazzano, L. A., et al. 2001. Legume consumption and risk of coronary heart disease in US men and women. Arch. Intern. Med. 161:2573–8.

Bell, L.P., et al. 1990. Cholesterol-lowering effects of soluble-fiber cereals as part of a prudent diet for patients with mild to moderate hypercholesterolemia. Am J Clin Nutr; 52: 1020–1026.

Bourdon, I., et al. 2001. Beans, as a source of dietary fiber, increase cholecystokinin and apolipoprotein B48 response to test meals in men. J. Nutr. 131:1485–90.

Cobiac, L., et al. 1990. Can eating baked beans lower plasma cholesterol? Eur. J. Clin. Nutr. 44:819–22.

Dabai, F.D., et al. 1995. Comparative effects on blood lipids and faecal steroids of five legume species incorporated into a semi-purified, hypercholestrolaemic rat diet. Brit J Nutr; 75: 557–571.

Frühbeck, G., et al 1997. Hormonal implications of the hypocholesterolemic effect of intake of field beans (Vicia faba L.) by young men with hypercholesterolemia. Am. J. Clin. Nutr. 66:1452–60.

Jenkens, D.J.A., et al. 1983. Legumious seeds in the dietary management of hyperlipidemia. Am J Clin Nutr; 38: 567–573.

Kestin, M., et al. 1990. Comparative effects of three cereal brans on plasma lipids, blood pressure, and glucose metabolism in mildly hypercholesterolemic men. Am J Clin Nutr; 52: 661–666.

Kingman, S. M., et al. 1993. Comparative effects of four legume species on plasma lipids and fecal steroid excretion in hypercholesterolaemic pigs. Brit. J. Nutr. 69:409–21.

Macarulla, M.T., et al. 2001. Effects of the whole seed and a protein isolate of faba bean on the cholesterol metabolism of hypercholeserolaemic rats. Brit. J. Nutr. 85:607–14.

Mackay, S., and Ball, M. J. 1992. Do beans and oat bran add to the effectiveness of a low-fat diet? Eur. J Clin. Nutr. 46:641–8.

Mekki, N., et al. 1997. Effects of lowering fat and increasing dietary fiber on fasting and postprandial plasma lipids in hypercholesterolemic subjects consuming a mixed Mediterranean-Western diet. Am. J. Clin. Nutr. 66:1443–51.

Mengheri, E., et al. 1985. Modifications in plasma cholesterol and apolipoproteins of hypercholes-terolaemic rats induced by ethanol-soluble Factors of Vicia faba. Brit. J. Nutr. 53:223–32.

Messina, M.J. 1999. Legumes and soybeans: overview of their nutritional profiles and health effects. Am J Clin Nutr; 70(Suppl): 439S–450S.

Messina, M., et al. Gaining insight into the health effects of soy but a long way still to go: commentary on the Fourth International Symposium on the Role of Soy in Preventing and Treating Chronic Disease. J Nutr 2002 Mar;132(3):547S–551S.

Oakenfull, D., and Sidhu, G. S. 1990. Could saponins be a useful treatment for hypercholes-terolemia? Eur. J. Clin. Nutr. 44:79–88.

Shutler, S. M., et al. 1989. The effect of daily baked bean (Phaseolus vulgaris) consumption on the plasma lipid levels of young, normo-cholesterolaemic men. Brit. J. Nutr. 61:257–65.

Sidhu, G. S., and Oakenfull, D. G. 1986. A mechanism for the hypocholesterolaemic activity of saponins. Brit. J. Nutr. 55:643–649.

Southon, S., et al. 1988. The effect of Gypsophila saponins in the diet on mineral status and plasma cholesterol concentration in the rat. Brit. J. Nutr. 59:49–55.

Uberoi, S.K., et al. 1992. Role of dietary fibre from pulses and cereals as hypocholesterolemic and hypolipidemic agent. J. Fd. Sci. Tech. 29:281–83.

Zulet, M.A, and Martínez, J.A. 1995. Corrective role of chickpea intake on a dietary-induced model of hypercholesterolemia. Pl. Fd. Hu. Nutr. 48:269–77.

soy

Adlercruetz, H. and Mazur, W. 1997. Phytoestrogens and Western diseases. Ann. Med. 29: 95–120.

Baum, JA, et al. Long-term intake of soy protein improves blood lipid profiles and increases mononuclear cell low-density lipoprotein receptor messenger RNA in hypercholesterolemic, postmenopausal women. Am J Clin Nutr 1998 68: 545–551.

Brynin R. Soy and its isoflavones: a review of their effects on bone density. Altern Med Rev 2002 Aug;7(4):317–27.

Chiechi L.M., et al. Efficacy of a soy rich diet in preventing postmenopausal osteoporosis: the Menfis randomized trial. Maturitas 2002 Aug 30;42(4):295–300.

Hsieh CY, et al. Estrogenic effects of genistein on the growth of estrogen receptor-positive human breast cancer (MCF-7) cells in vitro and in vivo. Cancer Res 1998 Sep 1;58(17):3833–8.

Jenkins D.J., et al. Effects of high- and low-isoflavone (phytoestrogen) soy foods on inflammatory biomarkers and proinflammatory cytokines in middle-aged men and women. Metabolism 2002 Jul;51(7):919–24.

—. Effects of high- and low-isoflavone soyfoods on blood lipids, oxidized LDL, homocysteine, and blood pressure in hyperlipidemic men and women. Am J Clin Nutr 2002 Aug;76(2):365–72.

Kerckhoffs D.A., et al. Effects on the Human Serum Lipoprotein Profile of beta-Glucan, Soy Protein and Isoflavones, Plant Sterols and Stanols, Garlic and Tocotrienols. J Nutr 2002 Sep;132(9):2494–505.

Krauss R.M., et al. Soy protein and serum lipids. N Engl J Med 1995 Dec 21;333(25):1715–6.

Maddox D.A., et al. Protective effects of a soy diet in preventing obesity-linked renal disease. Kidney Int 2002 Jan;61(1):96–104.

Nicholls J., et al. Effects of soy consumption on gonadotropin secretion and acute pituitary responses to gonadotropin-releasing hormone in women. J Nutr 2002 Apr;132(4):708–14.

Sayegh R.A., Stubblefield P.G. Bone metabolism and the perimenopause overview, risk factors, screening, and osteoporosis preventive measures. Obstet Gynecol Clin North Am 2002 Sep;29(3):495–510.

Shamir R., Rozen G. Consumption of soy and phytoestrogens—is there a place for dietary guidelines? Harefuah 2002 Jan;141(1):44–5, 126.

Suzuki K., et al. Genistein, a soy isoflavone, induces glutathione peroxidase in the human prostate cancer cell lines LNCaP and PC-3. Int J Cancer 2002 Jun 20;99(6):846–52.

Wu A.H., et al. Adolescent and adult soy intake and risk of breast cancer in Asian-Americans. Carcinogenesis 2002 Sep;23(9):1491–6.

nuts and seeds

Albert, C.M., et al. Nut consumption and decreased risk of sudden cardiac death in the Physicians' Health Study. Arch Intern Med 2002 Jun 24;162(12):1382–7.

Alper, C.M., and R. D. Mattes. Effects of chronic peanut consumption on energy balance and hedonics. Int J Obes Relat Metab Disord. 2002 Aug;26(8):1129–37 2002.

Anderson, K.J, et al. Walnut polyphenolics inhibit in vitro human plasma and LDL oxidation. J Nutr 2001 Nov;131(11):2837–42.

Bracher, F. Phytotherapy of benign prostatic hyperplasia Urologe A 1997 Jan;36(1):10–7.

Brooks, J.D., et al. Plasma selenium level before diagnosis and the risk of prostate cancer development. J Urol 2001 Dec;166(6):2034–8.

Brown, A.A., F.B. Hu. Dietary modulation of endothelial function: implications for cardiovascular disease. Am J Clin Nutr 2001 Apr;73(4):673–86.

Chun, J. Lee, J. Ye L., R.R. Eitenmiller. Effects of Variety and Crop Year on Tocopherols in Pecans J. of Food Sci., Vol. 67, No. 4, 2002.

Clark, W.F., et al. Flaxseed: a potential treatment for lupus nephritis. Kidney Int 1995 Aug;48(2):475–80.

Cooney, R.V., Custer, LJ, Okinaka, L, Franke, AA. Effects of dietary sesame seeds on plasma tocopherol levels. Nutr Cancer 2001;39(1):66–71.

Cunnane S.C., et al. High alpha-linolenic acid flaxseed (Linum usitatissimum): some nutritional properties in humans. Br J Nutr 1993 Mar;69(2):443–53.

—. Nutritional attributes of traditional flaxseed in healthy young adults. Am J Clin Nutr 1995 Jan;61(1):62–8.

Curb J.D., et al. Serum lipid effects of a high-monounsaturated fat diet based on macadamia nuts. Arch Intern Med 2000 Apr 24;160(8):1154–8.

Duffield-Lillico, A.J., et al. Baseline characteristics and the effect of selenium supplementation on cancer incidence in a randomized clinical trial: a summary report of the Nutritional Prevention of Cancer Trial. Cancer Epidemiol Biomarkers Prev 2002 Jul;11(7):630–9.

Dabrosin, C., et al. Flaxseed inhibits metastasis and decreases extracellular vascular endothelial growth factor in human breast cancer xenografts. Cancer Lett 2002 Nov 8;185(1):31–7.

Edwards, K, et al. Effect of pistachio nuts on serum lipid levels in patients with moderate hypercholesterolemia. J Am Coll Nutr 1999 Jun;18(3):229–32.

Engelhart, M.J., et al. Dietary intake of antioxidants and risk of Alzheimer disease. JAMA 2002 Jun 26;287(24):3223–9.

Feldman, E.B. The scientific evidence for a beneficial health relationship between walnuts and coronary heart disease. J Nutr 2002 May;132(5):1062S–1101S.

Frank, L, et al. Exposure to peanuts in utero and in infancy and the development of sensitization to peanut allergens in young children. Pediatr Allergy Immunol 1999 Feb;10(1):27–32.

Fraser, G.E. Nut consumption, lipids, and risk of a coronary event. Clin Cardiol 1999 Jul;22(7 Suppl):III11–5.

Fulgoni, V. Almonds Lower Blood Cholesterol and LDL-Cholesterol But Not HDL Cholesterol or Triglycerides in Human Subjects: Results of a Meta-Analysis. Experimental Biology Presentations New Orleans, 2002.

Gonsalves, J. L. et al. Effects of Almonds and Almond Skins on Antioxidant Status in Sprague Dawley Rats Experimental Biology Presentations New Orleans, 2002.

Hu F.B. and M.J. Stampfer. Nut consumption and risk of coronary heart disease: a review of epidemiologic evidence. Curr Atheroscler Rep 1999 Nov;1(3):204–9.

Ikeda S, et al. Dietary sesame seed and its lignans inhibit 2,7,8-trimethyl-2(2'-carboxyethyl)-6-hydroxychroman excretion into urine of rats fed gamma-tocopherol. J Nutr 2002 May;132(5):961–6.

Iwamoto. M, et al. Serum lipid profiles in Japanese women and men during consumption of walnuts. Eur J Clin Nutr 2002 Jul;56(7):629–37.

Jenkins. DJ, et al. Dose response of almonds on coronary heart disease risk factors: blood lipids, oxidized low-density lipoproteins, lipoprotein(a), homocysteine, and pulmonary nitric oxide: a randomized, controlled, crossover trial. Circulation 2002 Sep 10;106(11):1327–32.

Kapadia G, et al. Chemopreventive effect of resveratrol, sesamol, sesame oil and sunflower oil in the epstein-barr virus early antigen activation assay and the mouse skin two-stage carcinogenesis. Pharmacol Res 2002 Jun;45(6):499.

Kirkmeyer SV, Mattes RD. Effects of food attributes on hunger and food intake. Int J Obes Relat Metab Disord 2000 Sep;24(9):1167–75.

Kris-Etherton PM, et al. High-monounsaturated fatty acid diets lower both plasma cholesterol and triacylglycerol concentrations. Am J Clin Nutr 1999 Dec;70(6):1009–15.

Matus Z, et al. Carotenoids in pressed seeds (Cucurbitae semen) of oil pumpkin (Cucurbita pepo convar. pepo var. styriaca). Acta Pharm Hung 1993 Sep;63(5):247–56.

McManus K, Antinoro L, Sacks F. A randomized controlled trial of a moderate-fat, low-energy diet compared with a low fat, low-energy diet for weight loss in overweight adults. Int J Obes Relat Metab Disord 2001 Oct;25(10):1503–11.

Milbury, Paul, et al. Polyphenolics (PP) from Almond Skins with A-tocopherol (aT) Synergistically Increase the Resistance of LDL to Oxidation. Experimental Biology Presentations, New Orleans, 2002.

Morris M.C., et al. Dietary intake of antioxidant nutrients and the risk of incident Alzheimer disease in a biracial community study. JAMA 2002 Jun 26;287(24):3230–7.

National Academy of Science, Institute of Medicine. Dietary Reference Intakes for Energy, Carbohydrates, Fiber, Fat, Protein and Amino Acids (Macronutrients) 2002 National Academies Press.

Noguchi T., et al. Effects of vitamin E and sesamin on hypertension and cerebral thrombogenesis in stroke-prone spontaneously hypertensive rats. Hypertens Res 2001 Nov;24(6):735–42.

Ren, Y. K.W. Waldron, C. W.C. Kendall, J.F. Pacy, D.J.A. Jenkins, P.R. Ellis. Bioavailability of Lipids in Almond Seeds: The Role of Plant Cell Walls ("Dietary Fiber") Biology Presentations New Orleans, 2002.

Sabate J, et al. Effects of walnuts on serum lipid levels and blood pressure in normal men. N Engl J Med 1993 Mar 4;328(9):603–7

Sujatha Rajaram, et al. The Effect of Almonds on Factors of Inflammation and Hemostasis in Healthy Adults. Experimental Biology Presentations, New Orleans, 2002.

Thompson L.U., Li T., Chen J., Goss P.E. Nutritional Sciences, University of Toronto, Toronto, ON, "Biological Effects of Dietary Flaxseed in Patients with Breast Cancer." Abstract from the San Antonio Breast Cancer Symposium – December 2000.

Young R. Seo, et al. Selenomethionine regulation of p53 by a ref1-dependent redox mechanism Proc. Natl. Acad. Sci. USA, 10.1073/pnas.212319799.

Zambon D, et al. Substituting walnuts for monounsaturated fat improves the serum lipid profile of hypercholesterolemic men and women. A randomized crossover trial. Ann Intern Med 2000 Apr 4;132(7):538–46.

herbs, spices and oils

Aratanechemuge, Y., et al. Selective induction of apoptosis by ar-turmerone isolated from turmeric (Curcuma longa L) in two human leukemia cell lines, but not in human stomach cancer cell line. Int J Mol Med 2002 May;9(5):481–4.

Braga, C., et al. Olive oil, other seasoning fats, and the risk of colorectal carcinoma. Cancer. 1998 Feb 1;82(3):448–53.

Clark, R.M., et al. A comparison of lycopene and astaxanthin absorption from corn oil and olive oil emulsions. Lipids 2000 Jul;35(7):803–6.

De M, Krishna, De A, Banerjee A.B. Antimicrobial screening of some Indian spices. Phytother Res 1999 Nov;13(7):616-8.

Friedman, M., et al. Cinnamaldehyde content in foods determined by gas chromatography-mass spectrometry. J Agric Food Chem 2000 Nov;48(11):5702–9.

Gururaj, A.E., et al. Molecular mechanisms of anti-angiogenic effect of curcumin. Biochem Biophys Res Commun 2002 Oct 4;297(4):934–42.

He, L., et al. Isoprenoids suppress the growth of murine B16 melanomas in vitro and in vivo. J Nutr 1997 May;127(5):668–74.

Heck, A.M., et al. Potential interactions between alternative therapies and warfarin. Am J Health Syst Pharm 2000 Jul 1;57(13):1221-7; quiz 1228–30.

Imai T, et al. Inhibitory effects of cinnamaldehyde on 4-(methylnitrosamino)-1-(3-pyridyl)-1-butanone-induced lung carcinogenesis in rasH2 mice. Cancer Lett 2002 Jan 10;175(1):9–16.

Lee A, et al. Consumption of tomato products with olive oil but not sunflower oil increases the antioxidant activity of plasma. Free Radic Biol Med 2000 Nov 15;29(10):1051–5.

Mo, H., Elson, C.E. Apoptosis and cell-cycle arrest in human and murine tumor cells are initiated by isoprenoids. J Nutr 1999 Apr;129(4):804–13.

Murakami, A, et al. Zerumbone, a Southeast Asian ginger sesquiterpene, markedly suppresses free radical generation, proinflammatory protein production, and cancer cell proliferation accompanied by apoptosis: the alpha,beta-unsaturated carbonyl group is a prerequisite. Carcinogenesis 2002 May;23(5):795–802.

Nalini, N., et al. Influence of spices on the bacterial (enzyme) activity in experimental colon cancer. J Ethnopharmacol 1998 Aug;62(1):15–24.

Owen, R.W., et al. Olive-oil consumption and health: the possible role of antioxidants. Lancet Oncol 2000 Oct;1:107–12.

—. The antioxidant/anticancer potential of phenolic compounds isolated from olive oil. Eur J Cancer. 2000 Jun;36(10):1235–47.

—. Identification of lignans as major components in the phenolic fraction of olive oil. Clin Chem 2000 Jul;46(7):976–88.

—. Phenolic compounds and squalene in olive oils: the concentration and antioxidant potential of total phenols, simple phenols, secoiridoids, lignans and squalene. Food Chem Toxicol 2000 Aug;38(8):647–59.

Suja Pandian, R, et al. Gastroprotective effect of fenugreek seeds (Trigonella foenum graecum) on experimental gastric ulcer in rats. J Ethnopharmacol 2002 Aug;81(3):393–7.

Surh, Y.J. More than spice: capsaicin in hot chili peppers makes tumor cells commit suicide. J Natl Cancer Inst 2002 Sep 4;94(17):1263–5.

Zava, D.T., Dollbaum CM, Blen M. Estrogen and progestin bioactivity of foods, herbs, and spices. Proc Soc Exp Biol Med 1998 Mar;217(3):369–78.

tea, red wine and chocolate

Arts I.C., et al. Catechin intake might explain the inverse relation between tea consumption and ischemic heart disease: the Zutphen Elderly Study. Am J Clin Nutr 2001 Aug;74(2):227–32.

Arts M.J., et al. Interactions between flavonoids and proteins: effect on the total antioxidant capacity. J Agric Food Chem 2002 Feb 27;50(5):1184–7.

Asou H., et al. Resveratrol, a natural product derived from grapes, is a new inducer of differentiation in human myeloid leukemias. Int J Hematol. 2002 Jun;75(5):528–33.

Chung, F.L. The prevention of lung cancer induced by a tobacco-specific carcinogen in rodents by green and black tea. Proceedings of the Society for Experimental Biology and Medicine, Vol 220, 244–248.

Connor W.E. Harbingers of coronary heart disease: dietary saturated fatty acids and cholesterol. Is chocolate benign because of its stearic acid content? Am J Clin Nutr 1999 Dec;70(6):951–2.

Dashwood R.H., et al. Cancer chemopreventive mechanisms of tea against heterocyclic amine mutagens from cooked meat. Proc Soc Exp Biol Med. 1999 Apr;220(4):239–43.

Ding X.Z., Adrian T.E. Resveratrol Inhibits Proliferation and Induces Apoptosis in Human Pancreatic Cancer Cells. Pancreas. 2002 Nov;25(4):E71–E76.

Duffy S.J., et al. Short- and long-term black tea consumption reverses endothelial dysfunction in patients with coronary artery disease. Circulation 2001 Jul 10;104(2):151–6.

Dulloo A.G., et al. Efficacy of a green tea extract rich in catechin polyphenols and caffeine in increasing 24-h energy expenditure and fat oxidation in humans. Am J Clin Nutr 1999 Dec;70(6):1040–5.

—. Green tea and thermogenesis: interactions between catechin-polyphenols, caffeine and sympathetic activity. Int J Obes Relat Metab Disord 2000 Feb;24(2):252–8.

Fujiki H., et al. Mechanistic findings of green tea as cancer preventive for humans. Proceedings of the Society for Experimental Biology and Medicine, Vol 220, 225–228.

Geleijnse J.M., et al. Inverse association of tea and flavonoid intakes with incident myocardialinfarction: the Rotterdam Study. Am J Clin Nutr 2002 May;75(5):880–6.

Hakim, I. Tea and Cancer: Epidemiology and Clinical Studies, Third International Scientific Symposium on Tea & Human Health: Role of Flavonoids in the Diet.

Hegarty V.M., et al. Tea drinking and bone mineral density in older women. Am J Clin Nutr 2000 Apr;71(4):1003–7.

Hirano R., et al. Antioxidant effects of polyphenols in chocolate on low-density lipoprotein both in vitro and ex vivo. J Nutr Sci Vitaminol (Tokyo) 2000 Aug;46(4):199–204.

Hollman P.C., et al. Addition of milk does not affect the absorption of flavonols from tea in man. Free Radic Res 2001 Mar;34(3):297–300.

Hurrell R.F., et al. Inhibition of non-haem iron absorption in man by polyphenolic-containing beverages. Br J Nutr 1999 Apr;81(4):289–95.

Itakura H., et al. Mood modulation by food: an exploration of affect and cravings in "chocolate addicts." Br J Clin Psychol 1995 Feb;34 (Pt 1):129–38.

Judd, J. Tea and Blood Lipids, Third International Scientific Symposium on Tea & Human Health: Role of Flavonoids in the Diet.

Keli S.O., et al. Dietary flavonoids, antioxidant vitamins, and incidence of stroke: the Zutphen study. Arch Intern Med 1996 Mar 25;156(6):637–42.

Kris-Etherton P.M., Keen C.L. Evidence that the antioxidant flavonoids in tea and cocoa are beneficial for cardiovascular health. Curr Opin Lipidol 2002 Feb;13(1):41–9.

Li N., Z. Sun, C. Han and J. Chen. The chemopreventive effects of tea on human oral precancerous mucosa lesions. Proceedings of the Society for Experimental Biology and Medicine, Vol 220, 218–224.

Lou Y.R., et al. Effects of oral administration of tea, decaffeinated tea, and caffeine on the formation and growth of tumors in high-risk SKH-1 mice previously treated with ultraviolet B light. Nutr Cancer 1999;33(2):146–53.

Mack W.J., Preston-Martin S., Bernstein L., Qian D. Lifestyle and other risk factors for thyroid cancer in Los Angeles County females. Ann Epidemiol 2002 Aug;12(6):395–401.

Mukamal K.J., et al. Tea consumption and mortality after acute myocardial infarction. Circulation 2002 May 28;105(21):2476–81.

Pearson D., et al. The effects of flavanol-rich cocoa and aspirin on ex vivo platelet function. Thromb Res 2002 May 15;106(4–5):191.

Prior R.L., Cao G. Antioxidant capacity and polyphenolic components of teas: implications for altering in vivo antioxidant status. Proc Soc Exp Biol Med 1999 Apr;220(4):255–61.

Rao D.N., Ganesh B., Dinshaw K.A., Mohandas K.M. A case-control study of stomach cancer in Mumbai, India. Int J Cancer 2002 Jun 10;99(5):727–31.

Rein D., et al. Cocoa inhibits platelet activation and function. Am J Clin Nutr 2000 Jul;72(1):30–5.

Samman S., Lai N.T., Sullivan D.R. The effect of a lipid-lowering diet on plasma lipids and lipoproteins in mildly hypercholesterolaemic subjects: a potential role for occasional treats. 0955-2863 2000 May 1;11(5):250-254.

Sayama K., et al. Effects of green tea on growth, food utilization and lipid metabolism in mice. In Vivo 2000 Jul-Aug;14(4):481–4.

Schramm D.D., et al. Chocolate procyanidins decrease the leukotriene-prostacyclin ratio in humans and human aortic endothelial cells. Am J Clin Nutr 2001 Jan;73(1):36–40.

Sun C.L., et al. Urinary tea polyphenols in relation to gastric and esophageal cancers: a prospective study of men in Shanghai, China. Carcinogenesis 2002 Sep;23(9):1497–503.

Wan Y., et al. Effects of cocoa powder and dark chocolate on LDL oxidative susceptibility and prostaglandin concentrations in humans. Am J Clin Nutr 2001 Nov;74(5):596–602.

Wargovich M.J. Colon cancer chemoprevention with ginseng and other botanicals. J Korean Med Sci 2001 Dec;16 Suppl:S81–6.

Weisburger J.H. Tea and health: the underlying mechanisms. Proc Soc Exp Biol Med 1999 Apr;220(4):271–5.

—. Chemopreventive effects of cocoa polyphenols on chronic diseases. Exp Biol Med (Maywood) 2001 Nov;226(10):891–7.

Zhang M., Binns C.W., Lee A.H. Tea consumption and ovarian cancer risk: a case-control study in China. Cancer Epidemiol Biomarkers Prev 2002 Aug;11(8):713–8.

index